Love Was There

Love Was There

A Testimony of Faith

SUSAN PATRICE GUARASCIO

RESOURCE *Publications* · Eugene, Oregon

LOVE WAS THERE
A Testimony of Faith

Copyright © 2022 Susan Patrice Guarascio. All rights reserved. Except for brief quotations in critical publications or reviews, no part of this book may be reproduced in any manner without prior written permission from the publisher. Write: Permissions, Wipf and Stock Publishers, 199 W. 8th Ave., Suite 3, Eugene, OR 97401.

Resource Publications
An Imprint of Wipf and Stock Publishers
199 W. 8th Ave., Suite 3
Eugene, OR 97401

www.wipfandstock.com

PAPERBACK ISBN: 978-1-6667-4265-7
HARDCOVER ISBN: 978-1-6667-4266-4
EBOOK ISBN: 978-1-6667-4267-1

JULY 12, 2022 8:05 AM

Scripture quotations are from The Catholic Edition of the *Revised Standard Version (RSV) of the Bible*, copyright 1965, 1966 by the Division of Christian Education of the National Council of the Churches of Christ in the United States of America. Used by permission. All Rights Reserved.

Scripture quotations are from *The New American Bible,* copyright 1991, 1986, 1970 Confraternity of Christian Doctrine, Inc., Washington, DC. Used by permission. All Rights Reserved.

Excerpts from *Discovering Christ* video series, copyright 2009 ChristLife, Inc., (www.christLife.org; info@christlife.org). Used by permission.

Excerpts from *Medjugorje Day by Day,* by Richard J. Beyer. Copyright 1993, 2004 by Ave Maria Press, Inc., P.O. Box 428, Notre Dame, IN 46556, www.avemariapress.com. Used with permission of the publisher.

Dedicated to the Blessed Trinity in gratitude to:

... God the Father, for creating me and this beautiful world, his countless blessings, and allowing me to share in the creative miracle of the birth of my three daughters.

... Jesus, for his unconditional love, example, and ultimate sacrifice for our sins.

... The Holy Spirit, for healing, comforting, guiding, helping, and inspiring me to write this book.

Also, dedicated to:

... The Blessed Mother Mary, through her loving intercession, she has never let me down.

... My Mother and Father, for loving me into existence, providing me with a loving and happy home, and teaching me the true meaning of love and commitment.

... My Inner Circle ... Eddy, my husband and hero, the love of my life; Bridget, Kaitlin, and Tierney, my devoted daughters; Sheila, and Denise, my sisters, my forever friends; for their love, prayers, sacrifices, and support during my illness. Thank you for getting me through it.

Contents

Prologue | ix

CHAPTER 1
Growing Up | 1

CHAPTER 2
Fairhaven Heights | 10

CHAPTER 3
St. Robert Bellarmine Elementary School | 14

CHAPTER 4
Serra Catholic High School | 30

CHAPTER 5
We Are!! Penn State | 40

CHAPTER 6
Newlyweds | 44

CHAPTER 7
Motherhood | 51

CHAPTER 8
Middle Years | 68

CHAPTER 9
The New Millennium | 77

CHAPTER 10
Sad Times | 100

CHAPTER 11
My Miracle & Transformation | 124

CHAPTER 12
Normalcy | 138

CHAPTER 13
Suffering and Death | 143

CHAPTER 14
Faith | 159

CHAPTER 15
Changes, Gains, and Losses | 167

CHAPTER 16
Reflections | 179

CHAPTER 17
Adversity, Courage, & Resilience | 185

CHAPTER 18
Wedding Bells | 190

CHAPTER 19
Senior Care Compassion | 192

CHAPTER 20
Living the Message | 194

CHAPTER 21
Pools and Beaches | 197

CHAPTER 22
Retirement | 199

CHAPTER 23
The Emerald Isle | 208

CHAPTER 24
Gratitude | 219

CHAPTER 25
Grace and True Grit | 223

CHAPTER 26
COVID | 230

CHAPTER 27
Perseverance | 240

Epilogue | 243

Prologue

MISTER Rogers, beloved children's television icon, once asked an audience of celebrities as he was accepting the Emmy's Lifetime Achievement Award, who loved them into being. As he spoke into the microphone to accept his honor, he said, "All of us have special ones who have loved us into being. Would you take, along with me, *ten seconds*, to think of the people who have helped you become who you are . . . Ten seconds of silence." After a few seconds of uncomfortable laughter, the people realized he wasn't kidding, and so they began to think, and the tears began to flow. Then, Mister Rogers looked up from his watch, and asked God to bless all those adult celebrities, who were once upon a time children.

When I gave myself ten seconds to think of all the people who helped me become me, there were too many names to fit into that time allotment. I was created by a loving God, born out of love into the embrace of two loving parents, welcomed into a loving and large extended family, and have been supported by loving friends, neighbors, teachers, and acquaintances throughout my life. To top it off, God sent me a loving husband, and blessed me with three loving daughters. Sounds like a charmed life. I've been so lucky, but you know what people say about luck . . .

My luck abruptly changed on Valentine's Day, February 14, 2009, when I was rushed to the UPMC (University of Pittsburgh Medical Center) McKeesport Hospital emergency room. The following Thursday, I was diagnosed with *non-Hodgkin's lymphoma*, a blood cancer that had spread into my duodenum, liver, intestines, and areas around my heart. Wasn't that the cancer that killed Jackie Kennedy?! It felt so surreal, like it wasn't really happening to me. Several weeks later, as I was lying in bed fighting for my life, trying to process it all, I felt anything but lucky. As I prayed and struggled to make sense of what was happening to me, I soon realized that God was in control. Consequently, I truly believed with an expectant faith that he would help me get through it. Love had always been there, from the beginning. And it was love that would sustain me throughout the fight of my life. One thing, I knew for sure, I needed a miracle!

CHAPTER 1

Growing Up

Looking back, I realize my life has been abundantly blessed from the moment of birth. I was born on September 21, 1956, the first born daughter of three girls to John Soltis and Mary Pat O'Grady Soltis. I was also the firstborn grandchild on both sides of the family. My Grandfather and Grandmother O'Grady lived down the street from us in a cozy development called Fairhaven Heights in a small eastern suburb outside Pittsburgh, Pennsylvania. We moved there from Swissvale when I was five years old, and my little sister Sheila was one. My baby sister, Denise, was born when I was nine. My grandparents, being good Irish Catholics, had eight children. My mother was the oldest of the three sisters and five brothers. They were: Mary Pat, Jeanne, Sheila, Harry, Denny, Timmy, Johnny, and Kippy, in that order. So I came along after my five O'Grady uncles. The three youngest were more like my brothers growing up since they were only two, three, and seven years older than me, and lived at the other end of our street. Even though we lived in two different houses, it was like one big family. All I know is that I was surrounded by love.

My dad came from a broken home. His father never married his biological mother. His mother left when he was three weeks old, and nobody ever told me the real story, except that her absence and lack of love left a hole in my dad's heart that would never heal. Consequently, Daddy was raised by his Grandmother Susan Soltis, my Bubba and namesake, until his dad married his stepmother, who gave birth to his only half-brother, named Charles, AKA Chickie, when my dad was twelve. Sadly enough, that situation became what some might call a *Cinderfella* story.

Daddy was often left out and not included when his dad, stepmother, and Chickie went to her parents for Sunday dinners, Christmas, Thanksgiving, and Easter. He probably felt double rejection, first by his biological mother, and then by his stepmother. Daddy was always treated like an outsider, while Chickie was showered with love, attention, and material gifts. Therefore, my dad was always grateful and more than happy to embrace all the new brothers and sisters that came along with marrying my mother. Marrying my mother gave my father the large, loving family he had always wanted. Then together, they created our own little family of five.

Our home became a refuge and a fun place for all, especially after my dad installed a pool in our backyard. My dad took great pride in keeping our pool immaculately clean. He was always running up to Valley Pools or Pool City on Route 30 to make sure we had just the right amount of chlorine. He loved to check the chemicals and announce that our pool water was perfectly clean and crystal clear. Our summer long pool parties and volleyball games often lasted until late in the evening. Fortunately, our nice neighbors never complained. Well, at least not to us. Besides, they knew they were always invited to join us. Everybody was welcome at 999 Diane Drive, thanks to my wonderful parents. My mother was always a loving hostess, cooking and feeding whoever walked through our front door. Both of my parents possessed hearts of gold. Many years later, I hired an artist to paint a watercolor of my parents' house as their Christmas gift. I wrote the following poem to accompany it, which I think summarizes our *House of Love*.

House of Love

A thank you poem to my parents

We moved here in August of 1961,
From Swissvale to Fairhaven, our transition had begun,
Our extended family had already moved on our street,
Having them close by brought us memories so sweet,
A new L-shaped ranch was the style of our house,
To the suburbs we'd settle, once farmland with more than one mouse,
Pine trees surrounded 999 Diane Drive,
A cozy place to begin our lives,
School buses stopped right at our place,
As children we played in woods and lots of open space,

Growing Up

> Birthdays, parties, holidays, and events,
> As long as we were together, our time was well spent,
> You opened our home to family and friends,
> Your gracious hospitality yielded warm dividends,
> We played monopoly, canasta, and pinochle, too,
> We laughed and we fought until quarter to two,
> In the hot summer, when we didn't have school,
> Everyone came to swim in our pool,
> In the 70s, Steeler parties were always a treat,
> We cheered them to victory with plenty to eat,
> Delicious Sunday dinners were open to all,
> You fed whomever happened to stop by or call,
> You gave to us all when you didn't have money,
> The atmosphere here was always quite sunny,
> This cozy little house with the rotating door,
> Always had enough room to welcome one more,
> You've made our house a loving home where
> God has blessed us from above,
> Thank you both for making it our family's House of Love.

Summer has always been my favorite time of year ever since I've been a child. My dad always made sure he took us on family vacations no matter how much we struggled financially. Our first family vacations took us to Tionesta, Pennsylvania, where my Grandfather Soltis and his brother, our Uncle Tony, had hunting cabins up in the mountains of Cook Forest. Even though we didn't have running water or indoor plumbing in the cabins, and had to use the outhouse, it was always a great adventure. Daddy had taught my sisters and me how to swim in Tionesta Creek when we were babies, and since then, we've always loved the water. We loved swimming in the ice cold water in Tionesta Creek, pumping our drinking water out of sparkling mountain springs, buying our fresh eggs, milk, and butter from the local farmers, fishing in the Allegheny River, bathing and washing our hair in the clear-flowing mountain streams, visiting Rosie the Bear in her cage behind the local general store, spotting deer frolicking in the fields at night, looking for the Big Dipper in the bright night stars, and just appreciating the beauty of nature. My dad loved taking us to Tionesta every summer. He was the consummate outdoorsman and sportsman. Daddy was an excellent swimmer, skilled hunter, and fisherman. He was an all-around natural athlete.

Years later when I was an adult, Daddy was inducted into the Swissvale High School Sports Hall of Fame along with his friend, the legendary

Pittsburgh Pirate Dick Groat, for being an outstanding athlete in both basketball and baseball. After that event, I found out my dad had been drafted by the St. Louis Cardinals to play professional baseball. When the Cardinal's scout came to their farmhouse to talk about my dad playing professional baseball, my Grandfather Soltis chased him off his property with a shotgun and declared that playing baseball was no future for his son. So my dad went to work in the Pittsburgh steel mills, and then ended up serving our country in the army during the Korean War. Somehow, my dad forgave his father for squashing his dreams, and he would never talk about it. I learned all of this from my dad's paternal aunts, Aunt Marie and Aunt Helen, and my mother. Even though my dad never played professional sports, he continued to be a superior athlete. No matter what sport my dad played, he excelled at it. He took up golf when I was in high school, and soon became an avid and accomplished golfer. Before Daddy retired from the Port Authority Transit in 1993, his passion for golf resulted in his winning the 1975, 1988, and 1990 PAT Golf Championships.

Daddy also won numerous Carradam Golf Club Championships. Carradam Golf Course sat on top of the rolling hills of North Huntingdon, Pennsylvania. It was affectionately referred to as *Goat Hill* by my uncles who had also played there with Daddy and Grandpap O'Grady. Years later, after my dad's last championship game, my husband Eddy and I drove up to the club house to find out who won. We poked inside the packed place and asked the bartender if the game was over and who won. I told him that my dad had played, and I was curious if he placed. So, the bartender asked me over the noisy room who my father was. I didn't think anyone else heard us, because everyone was so loud drinking, celebrating, and talking. As soon as I said, "John Soltis," the entire room erupted into a resounding, simultaneous chorus, and exclaimed, "He won!" I was so surprised, not because Daddy won, but because I didn't think anyone else even heard my conversation with the bartender. Everyone raised their glasses and cheered, "Congratulations!" Daddy wasn't even there. He had already gone home, so we drove back to my parents' house to congratulate him. We were all so excited. It was such a nice surprise and happy memory. Dad also won the Champion Lakes 1994 Invitational Championship, (Champion Lakes is the golf course owned by Dick Groat). Daddy also scored numerous holes in one there. He loved being outdoors on the beautiful golf courses where he said he always felt connected to God through nature.

I know it bothered Mummy that Daddy didn't take us to weekly Mass, and he didn't seem to have the gift of faith that my mother had, but he was a loving father, hard worker, good provider, and had great mechanical skills. He could fix any appliances that broke in our house. When I was a little girl, I adored him. He was movie star handsome, (people would tell me that about my father throughout my life), had a humble charisma, and most important, he always made me feel loved and cherished. When I was a child, I remember intently watching Daddy shave. I would sit on the closed toilet seat, and marvel at how he'd glide the razor up and down his face. Mummy reminded me of one occasion when I was two years old, where I tried to shave my face *like Daddy*, and ended up snipping off the tip of my toddler nose. In my childhood mind, I was just trying to be like Daddy.

After Denise was born, I remember Daddy taking Sheila and me ice skating at Alpine Ice Chalet Rink in Braddock Hills, literally down the hill from our Soltis Grandparents' house. He would skate backward with such ease as he tried to teach us how to ice skate. It is such a happy memory. I have no doubt that God brought my parents together, and that my mom was instrumental in helping my Dad develop a relationship with Jesus during his later years. Sometimes I think we were much too hard on my Dad, and I have guilt for judging him for not going to church. As an adult, I now realize how very wrong that was. My dad was a kind and good man, who always felt close to God the Father in nature, and was in awe of him and his Creation. I can recall how proud Daddy was when he recited the Our Father prayer in Slavic remembering how his grandmother, my Bubba, had taught him to pray as a young boy.

Daddy always taught us to respect the earth, and to appreciate the beauty of nature. When he took our family to Tionesta, he was sharing his love of nature with us. My parents also took most of my O'Grady aunts and uncles with us to Tionesta over the early years. When we grew older, after my Grandfather Soltis passed away, my Step-Grandmother, Margaret Soltis, sold the cabin, and that ended our yearly visits to Tionesta.

Soon after that, my dad and mom started taking my sisters and me to the ocean for beach vacations. At first, we started going to Myrtle Beach, South Carolina with my mom's sister, my Aunt Sheila and her husband, Uncle Bob Riberich, and their three kids, Cousins Diane, Robert, and Mariane. We loved going there to relax on the beautiful white beaches and swim in the warm gulfstream waters. It wasn't as nearly built up with condominiums, shopping, restaurants, and commercial attractions as it is today. After several summers at Myrtle Beach, we ventured further south and vacationed in Florida. We traveled to places like Clearwater, Tampa, and St. Petersburg. I loved the Gulf Coast. Two restaurants there stand out as my favorites. The Kapok Tree Restaurant actually featured a massive, real live kapok tree that stood in the center of the eatery. The other restaurant was on the top floor of the Hilton Hotel, where it rotated in a complete circle ever so slowly while you dined and enjoyed an ever changing panoramic view of the city and ocean. It was quite a unique experience.

Mostly, we just enjoyed swimming in the warm, calm clear water in the Gulf. Uncle Bob always got us the best accommodations at the Hilton Hotels through Delta Airlines, his place of employment. After all of us kids were grown and married, my parents, aunt and uncle finally settled on Naples, Florida as their favorite bi-annual vacation spot. They vacationed there together every May and September for another 25 years.

During my childhood, Sunday dinners and holidays were celebrated together at my O'Grady Grandparents' house. Grandma's eye of round roasts, breaded pork chops, and scalloped potatoes were legendary. She would cook for a small army. I loved going to their house, because it was always bustling with loving relatives. Grandma had nine siblings who often came to visit. Her two youngest sisters, my Great-Aunts Elsie Friend and Theresa Paul, would bring their kids, so the house would be rocking and rolling with fun and excitement with my five young uncles and all my cousins.

Grandma O'Grady was an attractive woman who still had an amazing figure even after giving birth to eight children. She was real character who wasn't afraid to speak her mind. She loved to play poker, card games, and dance. Music was always playing on her large wooden stereo. Grandma helped instill in me a love of music. I think I know the words to every Nat King Cole song ever recorded. Grandma would dance around the living room by herself whenever she played the stereo. And on special occasions when Grandpap would dance with her, you could just feel their chemistry. As the kids today would say, "They were a hot couple." No wonder they had eight children.

Lawrence Welk was on the television Saturday nights. When we would have sleepovers, Grandma made us watch him whether we wanted to or not. I have to admit, that I really did like the Lennon Sisters, but my favorite television shows during my childhood were Bewitched, Father Knows Best, Ozzie and Harriet, The Brady Bunch, Leave It to Beaver,

Petticoat Junction, Green Acres, Gilligan's Island, and That Girl. Marlo Thomas was one of my idols. Years later, after I grew up, many people would tell me that I reminded them of her with my big eyes, dark hair with bangs and a flip. Growing up, I couldn't decide who my favorite television role-model was: Samantha Stevens, who played the perfectly supportive magical wife on Bewitched, or Ann Marie, who played the wide-eyed would-be actress pursuing her dreams as a young single woman in New York City. Looking back, I realize there were times in my life that I tried to be both.

Anyway, back to Grandma. She made me feel like a princess. She frequently told me she thought I was gorgeous all the way up to the time she passed away when I was married and pregnant with my firstborn daughter, Bridget. Of course, she was a bit biased, and it didn't hurt that I was the first born grandchild, a baby girl, after her five sons. Funny thing, I used to think I was her favorite grandchild until one Mother's Day brunch when my sisters Sheila and Denise each told me they thought they were her favorite! Hmm . . . guess we'll never know. But one thing's for sure, we all knew we were loved.

I remember going shopping to the small local grocery store, the Clover Farm, with Grandma and Kippy, when we were little children. My mom didn't drive yet. Kippy and I were close in age, about the same size, and had that thick, curly, Black-Irish hair. Grandma would pretend we were twins, so people wouldn't think she was old enough to be a grandmother. Consequently, Kippy and I would play along with her wishes, or else. You didn't want to cross *Mare*, as my three youngest uncles would call Grandma in later years.

Kippy and I grew up together. He was the youngest of my grandparents' children, and my mother was their eldest with a 20 year age difference. They affectionately called themselves the *engine* and the *caboose*. My dad and Uncle Bob both told me at different times when we were older, that Kippy was the *apple of everyone's eye*. He was intelligent, athletic, competitive to a fault, quick-witted, loud, loyal, had a kind, loving heart, a photographic memory, and a strong enduring faith. These qualities helped sustain him much later on in his life.

Since Kippy was only two years older than me, I never called him uncle. We had a special and unique relationship. We were raised like brother and sister. We were always together during our childhood. Kippy taught me so much when we were kids. He taught me how to play pinochle, canasta, chess, and Monopoly. We were playmates. It wasn't just

Sundays for dinner at Grandma's house, or the wonderful holidays our family celebrated, it was the everyday memories. It was riding the same school bus to St. Robert Bellarmine Grade School, and when we got there, knowing Kippy was only down the hall. It was summers in our pool playing volleyball, or him organizing the backyard carnivals we'd have for the neighborhood kids to raise money for muscular dystrophy. Kippy was always the ringleader, the organizer, whether it was carnivals, or summertime neighborhood games like release, hide and seek, and whiffle ball.

Summers were a magical time back then and seemed to go on forever. In our extended family, it was a *Cousins Summer* every year for a very long time. Aunt Sheila and her kids, Diane, Robert, and Mariane, came *home*, and stayed at our grandparents from June until September. Uncle Bob would fly back and forth on weekends. Aunt Jeanne and her kids, Cathy and Christopher, would come and stay for a week, but we always wished they could stay with us much longer. When all the cousins were home, we'd sleep over at our grandparents and put the mattresses on the floor, because there were so many of us, and not enough beds. We loved it! We always had so much fun being together. Years later, after our grandparents were both gone, my parents stepped in and assumed the traditions of family Sunday dinners, sleepovers, and holidays, opening their hearts and home to everyone. My Dad never complained as he tripped over all of us kids laying on the floors in our tiny ranch house. The happy memories we cherish from those summers together are priceless.

My uncles, cousins, sisters and I grew up as siblings playing games like Monopoly, Stratego, chess, canasta, and double-pinochle. Our family was extremely competitive when it came to board games, card games, and sports. I never won at board games with Kippy, because anytime I even came close to winning, he would flip over the board, and the game pieces would fly. No wonder I don't have much of an ego. I can laugh about it now, but back then I would get so mad at him, until the next time we played. It was something like Lucy and Charlie Brown in reverse. Kippy would ask me to play a game and I would say, "No, you always win, or flip over the board if I come close to winning!" Then he would convince me to play, and he would either win, or upset the board if I came close to beating him. That scenario played out over and over during my childhood, and like Charlie Brown and Lucy with the football, I always went back for more!

Playing cards was our favorite O'Grady family past-time. You had to earn your way to the card table after years of waiting, watching silently, and learning how to be a good card player. We were the *Children should be seen and not heard generation*. I grew up in an adult-centered society, so it was a privilege to finally be invited to join the adults' card tables. My Grandfather O'Grady set the high standards, and followed the card game rules according to Hoyle. And you better not make a mistake when you were finally allowed to join the table. Again, I can laugh about it now, but we took our card games way too seriously.

CHAPTER 2

Fairhaven Heights

*K*IDS played outdoor games a lot back then, usually from morning until night, or at least *until the street lights come on,* per the orders of many of our young mothers. We rode bikes and played neighborhood games like Indian ball, dodgeball, spud, hide and seek, and release with the multitude of neighborhood kids in Fairhaven Heights. We would ride our bikes up into the woods where the older boys in the neighborhood had made bike trails that all us Fairhaven kids called *The Alamo.* In addition to riding up and down the bike trails, we would swing on tree *monkey vines* scattered throughout the woods. The fears and precautions that guided me in school didn't apply to playing outside in Fairhaven where we played with abandon, sometimes performing dangerous dare-devil stunts. I loved the free feeling flying down the hills of Fairhaven Heights on my blue Schwinn bicycle with no hands while the wind blew through my hair flipping my pony tails up like Pippy Longstocking. Building treehouses and shacks in the woods was another favorite summer pastime. We would carve out areas in the trees and pretend they were our houses. We'd section off rooms with branches, while tree stumps became tables and chairs. We were the baby boom generation, and we always found ways to use our imaginations and entertain ourselves. There were so many of us, that I remember standing in line on Halloween nights to get to our neighbors' doors to receive our candy.

Neighbors and suburban neighborhoods were different back in the 1960s. Everybody knew everyone else's business back in those days in Fairhaven Heights. I can probably still recite the names of every family who lived in every house on Diane Drive, and I can almost remember the names of each family who once lived in every house on Angeline, Joanne, and DiChicco Drive. As background, Mr. DiChicco was the developer who bought a farm, cleared the land, built a housing plan, and called it Fairhaven Heights. The four streets in New Fairhaven, as it was called, were named after his wife, daughters, and himself: Diane, Joanne, Angeline, and DiChicco. The two roads in Old Fair Haven were named Arlene and Mary Ellen Drive after the daughters of the original builder, Jim Tucci. Also, interesting to note, is that Joanne Drive somehow evolved into, and is currently called Joan Drive. Sometime over the years, the names were changed on the street signs, and none of the locals know why. Another interesting fact is that before Fairhaven Heights became a housing development, it was the weekend farm for the Clark Family, the manufacturers and founders of the famous Clark Bar Candy Company in Pittsburgh. The Clark mansion and carriage house are still standing atop the hills of Fairhaven Heights.

Most Fairhaven wives back then were stay-at-home mothers, and most dads were the sole bread winners, many who worked in the booming Steel Mills, or for Westinghouse Airbrake in East Pittsburgh. Most of the Fairhaven moms knew all us neighborhood kids, watched out for us, and kept us in line. My mom started playing cards one Friday evening each month with seven other young mothers in our neighborhood and called themselves the *Crazy Eights*, even though they were playing *500 Bid*. The week before it was my mom's turn to host the club, my mother would clean the house like a crazy lady, and we were all expected to help. My dad jokingly referred to that week as *Hell Week*. We weren't allowed to mess things up, touch certain serving bowls, or eat the delicious foods mom would prepare in advance. She even broke out her fancy white milk glass dishes for the occasion. Mummy wasn't typically like this, consequently, we all dreaded when it was her turn to have *club*. The perk for us though, if we could stay up late enough, was waiting until the end of the night, usually around midnight, to eat the leftover goodies Mummy made the times she was hostess. By the way, the *Crazy Eights* were all nice ladies, and none of them were too crazy.

Many of the original families of Fairhaven, primarily my parents' generation, still live there, but sadly, many of them are dying and in their eighties and nineties. In some cases, several of the adult baby boomers of my generation have moved back there with families of their own. Fairhaven remains a nice neighborhood, where my mother, her first cousin Anna Marie, who still lives next door, and several of her adult children, my Barbarino cousins, currently live.

In any case, mine was a happy childhood filled with lots of family, friends, security, and love. My best friend was my cousin, Kathy, who lived next door. Our mothers were first cousins, and our grandmothers were sisters, so that made us part of the Jessell family from Swissvale. We were both born in September, ten days apart. Growing up together, we started out playing with our Chatty Cathy dolls. As we got older, we played with our Barbies. After that, we played canasta, Monopoly, jacks, and listened to the Beatles. Kathy liked Paul and I liked George. We collected Beatles trading cards which came in bubble gum packets. We couldn't wait to watch them perform on the *Ed Sullivan Show*, Sunday night, February 9, 1964, after they had taken America by storm. Our other girlfriends from the neighborhood were Linda, Dawn Ellen, and Judy. When we weren't outside playing or riding our bikes, the four of us would play canasta on our porches in the summertime for hours. When we were in grade school, another neighborhood girl named Polly, who was a few years older than us, would let us play four squares on her front patio. When we got older, we were socially backward with boys, and Polly quickly outgrew us. Our parents were relieved, because sometimes the police would have to come and break up her wild high school parties she would throw when her parents weren't home. Polly, and her mischievous younger brother, Philip, who was always wreaking havoc in the neighborhood, lived a few houses down the street from us on Diane Drive. There was always something exciting going on at their house, and their parents seemed oblivious.

Philip was my age, but I grew up feeling afraid of him since he was always getting into some kind of dangerous trouble. I used to think he would grow up to be a mad scientist someday, because he liked building underground shacks, treehouses, playing with fire, and conducting dangerous chemistry experiments like making pipe bombs and exploding them in his back yard! Philip was famous in Fairhaven for making a haunted house in his parents' basement. All us kids in the neighborhood were charged a quarter before we were allowed to go through it, and it was very scary. For example, it was pitch black, and he would guide us through the cellar telling us to touch olives that were really the eyes of a dead monster, or cooked spaghetti noodles that were his intestines or brains. Philip was quite a unique character. When we were kids I thought he hated me. Once he swore at me, and I ran home crying and told Kippy.

Kippy was always very protective of me. Kippy ran out the door to find Philip, and proceeded to chase him around the circular streets of Fairhaven Heights until he caught him and punched him in the nose for me. That ended the name calling. Many years later, as an adult, when my sister Sheila and I ran into Philip at Ken and Jean's Dance studio, while we were all dropping off our daughters and nieces, Philip admitted to me that he had a crush on me our whole childhood! What a surprise that was to hear. I laughed and joked, "Well, you sure had a funny way of showing it!"

Kippy turned out to be my other best friend growing up. We were together at every family function. I idolized him for much of my childhood. I thought he was the last word on everything. He taught me every childhood game I ever played. And more importantly, he gave me big brotherly advice about boys when we were teens. He would tell me what guys really liked and didn't like about girls, and I believed him. He encouraged me to be a *good girl* with boys when I got older, as did my parents and the nuns. I was triple-teamed into being *good* growing up! Kippy's approval meant the world to me. I thought if he said something, it must be gospel. And more often than not, he was right. He always had a quick wit, or hilarious joke which I appreciated, since I always took life so seriously. He had such a great influence on my personality. He was loud, funny, and the center of attention, and I remained quiet, serious, and reserved, because he did all the talking for us, and provided all the excitement. I was proud to be his niece. I was proud of all my uncles, and proud to be half O'Grady.

Half of the kids in Fairhaven Heights went to Sunset Elementary Public School, then Park Terrace Junior High, and after that, it was Westinghouse Memorial High School in Wilmerding, until it became East Allegheny High School in North Versailles. The other half of the kids in our neighborhood, including me, went to Catholic school at St. Robert Bellarmine Elementary for grades one through eight.

CHAPTER 3

St. Robert Bellarmine Elementary School

*T*HE Vincentian Sisters of Charity taught us at St. Robert's, and had a big impact on our lives. Our Catholic faith was so ingrained in us, and integrated into every part of our lives. For example, my cousin Kathy and I would conduct May Crowning Ceremonies for our Blessed Mother every month of May in our front yard around our lawn statue of the Virgin Mary. We would recruit other neighborhood friends and their mothers to join us in our celebration ceremonies to honor Mary. Sometimes, we would have our front yard full of kids and a few moms singing hymns and/or saying the Hail Mary to honor Our Lady. We would process down our sidewalk to the statue of Mary where we would then crown her with a homemade wreath of fresh flowers. Then we would finish our little tribute to Mary with our rendition of "Salve Regina," which is still one of my favorite Marian church hymns. Looking back, I'll bet it was pleasing to Jesus that we would honor his mother. No wonder he is partial to children. We were so sweet and innocent.

May has always been, and still is, my favorite month, not just because all the spring flowers are in bloom, but because the nuns taught us that it was the month to honor our Blessed Mother. In the early grades at St. Robert's, during the month of May, we students would each be assigned a day to be the Child of Mary. This was a special honor. When you were the Child of Mary, you were allowed to dress up in your Sunday best, and not wear your school uniform that day. The Sister/Nun would pin a powder blue ribbon tied to the miraculous medal on you. You would bring in fresh flowers from your mother's or grandmother's garden, and place them in the vases in front of the Blessed Mother statue that was standing on the shelf in every classroom. I always wore a pretty dress, and brought in fresh cut pink peonies, roses, or white snowball flowers from my parents' yard. I felt so special when it was my turn to be the Child of Mary, because you were granted special privileges that day. You were expected to lead the daily prayers and hymns, recite the Pledge of Allegiance, were allowed to be first in line to leave the classroom, and did classroom jobs as the teacher's helper. The Child of Mary program obviously left an important impression on my cousin and me. Kathy and I both have a devotion to Mary to this day. Whenever I pray to our Blessed Mother for her help and intercession with her son, I can honestly say that she has never let me down. In addition to our teachings of Jesus, the Blessed Mother, and the saints, *Baltimore Catechism* was drilled into our heads every day during Religion class. We had a litany of prayers and responses to memorize. "Why did God make me? God made me to know him, love him, and serve him in this world." These words have been the guiding force that has helped me discern my life's purpose.

Even though many of my peers had lots of negative memories of the nuns in grade school, I have mostly positive ones. I even felt like teacher's pet for a few of my elementary school years, probably because I was quiet, obedient, docile, and tried so hard to please. For example, the nuns drilled into our heads the importance of keeping our papers and supplies neat and clean. The name plates on our desks were inspected periodically, so I made sure mine was never wrinkled, dirty, ripped, or had stray pencil marks on it. This was one way to gain praise, and not get your hands slapped with a ruler. It seemed easy enough for me to gain favor and stay out of trouble. So, I spent the better part of my youth and early adulthood trying to be neat, clean, well-behaved, and perfect. I was a real Goody Two Shoes. Ugh! It wasn't fun! It was well into my adulthood that I finally figured out it was a futile endeavor to strive for perfection. But as a child I kept trying. Back then, fear was a great motivator to be good, but I secretly admired the *troublemakers* for having the courage to assert and express themselves, despite their consequences. It took me many years as an adult to find my voice, and assert it.

The nuns were very strict. No talking meant no talking. I once had my mouth taped shut in school for talking, when I was simply turning around to give Daryl Mitchell, a fellow classmate, a sharpened pencil after he tapped me on my shoulder asking if I had one. That experience traumatized me enough to barely speak the rest of the year. I remember very vividly the big tears that dropped onto my printing paper after Sister Julia taped my six year old mouth. It was just another reason why it took me years to find my voice. Poor Daryl apologized to me later, but it wasn't his fault. We were both good kids who were used to set an example for the rest of the class. Daryl was one of the nicest boys all through grade school. As far as I can remember, he belonged to the only African American family in our school. He was one of the first friends I met in first grade, and I couldn't wait to come home from school that day to tell my parents about my new friend who was *chocolate*. I must have realized his skin color was different than mine, but I didn't assign a negative value to it. In my childhood innocence, it just made him special to me. Fortunately, I was never taught racial discrimination, and it broke my heart whenever I witnessed it later on in the world. In my eyes, we were all God's children, and he loved us all the same.

Just watching many of the boys in school get paddled was enough incentive to keep me on my best behavior for the rest of my school years. Corporal punishment wasn't just a Catholic school form of discipline during my childhood. The boys in the public schools were getting paddled back then just the same. Things certainly were different. And one thing was for sure, if you got in trouble with the teachers, then you got disciplined again from your parents when you came home from school. Parents typically supported the nuns' and teachers' disciplinary methods back then, unlike today, where they typically question them, and make excuses for their children. Anyway, back to St. Robert Bellarmine School.

In first grade, Sister Julia redeemed herself and selected me to play Saint Anne, the Blessed Mother's mother, in our school's annual May Crowning ceremony. Johnny Bison, a fellow classmate, was chosen to play Saint Joaquim, Mary's father. During our last minute preparations before the ceremony, I recall Sister Julia sprinkling baby powder on our hair to make it look white. As I held a baby doll representing Mary wrapped in a blue blanket, I felt my first connection to Our Lady. I think it was from that moment that she decided to keep me under her mantle of protection.

In second grade, I made my First Holy Communion. My mother and Grandmother O'Grady took me shopping to buy a beautiful white communion dress and veil. We also bought a little white purse which included a white rosary and Holy Mass prayer book. We had a huge party at our house to celebrate me receiving the body and blood of Jesus Christ for the first time. There were buffet tables set up in our dining area to serve all the delicious food. On a separate card table, there was a huge white First Holy Communion cake. All of our Jessell relatives, (my Grandma O'Grady's maiden name), who made up half the population of Swissvale, (kidding, not kidding), came to celebrate my big day. I felt and looked like a baby bride. Even though I was happy and excited to receive my First Holy Communion, I was just too young and immature to really understand the significance of the celebration, that I would be receiving the Body and Blood of Christ for the first time. After all, my journey of faith was just beginning. My First Holy Communion was my happiest memory that year.

My saddest memory of second grade happened on November 22, 1963. We were in the middle of Reading class, when Sister Gabriel, our school principal, burst through our classroom door, announcing that President Kennedy had been shot in Dallas, Texas. We were immediately ordered by Sister Julia, (who was my teacher two years in a row), to get down on our knees and pray the rosary for him. Both nuns were crying, so I knew it must be bad. When I got home from school that afternoon, my mom was also crying, and immediately told me that President Kennedy was dead. Our nation went into shock and mourning for a very long time. President Kennedy was such a beloved young and charismatic president. Our O'Grady family particularly loved him because he was Irish and Catholic, one of our own. Our country was enamored with him and his beautiful wife, Jackie. They had brought youth and glamour to the White House. The *Camelot Era* was abruptly ended with his assassination. We watched his funeral on television, cried for his children, Caroline, who was a year younger than me, and John-John, my sister Sheila's age. We wondered how this could have possibly happened in our civilized country.

It was a scary time growing up in the 1960s. First, President Kennedy was shot, then, Martin Luther King, and Bobby Kennedy was also assassinated in that volatile decade. In between those killings, there were massive violent civil rights race riots in Detroit, Chicago, Newark, and Los Angeles, along with the frequent announcements of our neighbors' sons killed in the ongoing and controversial Vietnam War. It was frightening for me to watch the news when I was a child, and so my mother and the nuns would tell me to pray frequently for world peace. In addition to those fears, the nuns had me terrified that the Communists in Russia were going to drop the nuclear bomb on us. Our school used to conduct air raid drills where we would have to hide under our desks. As young as

I was back then, it never made any sense to me. How in the world would hiding under a desk keep me safe in a nuclear war? But, we children did what we were told to do, because obedience was a virtue, next to cleanliness, and Godliness.

The Vincentian Sisters of Charity, (who are now the Sisters of Charity of Nazareth), who taught us students at St. Robert Bellarmine School back in the 1960s, worked hard to instill in us a great devotion to our Blessed Mother and her son. Even as we headed our paper assignments, we were required to write a capital JMJ, for Jesus, Mary, and Joseph, in the space above our name. Aside from daily prayers and Religion classes, every Friday morning during the school year, we would begin our school day by walking down Fifth Avenue in East McKeesport to attend 9:00 a.m. Mass at St. Robert Bellarmine Church, which was on the corner of Fifth Avenue and Route 30 at that time. It was only a ten minute walk, but we walked, regardless of the weather; in snow, sleet, rain, or hail. We girls always had to wear our *chapel veils* to cover our heads in respect before entering God's house. Chapel veils were either long white lace mantillas, which hung down over our hair, or short round pieces of lace that looked like old-fashioned doilies. If you forgot your chapel veil, then the nuns would place a Kleenex tissue on top of your head and secure it with bobby pins. No matter what, your head had to be covered, and your navy blue jumper had to be long enough to touch the floor when you were told to kneel down for checking purposes. The boys always needed to wear a shirt and tie. So, we wore our school uniforms and were instructed to behave respectfully and fully participate in Mass, or else. I never misbehaved enough to find out what the *or else* was.

Something I never understood, that always bothered me as a child, was why *altar boys* were only allowed to help serve Mass. Why couldn't we have *altar girls* at Mass? Why couldn't we just have *altar servers*? Why weren't girls good enough, especially since we were generally better behaved than the boys, according to the nuns. It felt so unfair. There were many instances during my childhood where I felt left out on the sidelines because I was a girl. Don't forget I grew up when women were just starting to advocate for women's rights in the 1960s, and before Title IX of the Education Amendment was signed into law by our president in 1972, prohibiting discrimination on the basis of sex in any education program or activity that is federally funded. Eventually, girls were permitted to be altar servers in the 1980s, but were not officially allowed until 1994. Fortunately, later on in life, my own daughters all served as altar servers.

Unfortunately, it breaks my heart that our Catholic Church still doesn't permit women to be ordained as priests. So, I ask myself, if Jesus were walking here on earth, what would Jesus do? And I truly believe beyond a shadow of a doubt, that Jesus would welcome women into the priesthood as he was all-loving, all-welcoming, and all-inclusive during his 33 years living on this planet. As the Founder of Christianity, I wonder if Jesus would be disappointed with some of the exclusionary laws and practices of our current patriarchal Catholic Church. In the meantime, all I can do is pray for my church to evolve. As an adult writing this book, I am filled with hope and gratitude for our current pontiff, the unprecedented, progressive, inclusive, and beloved Pope Francis, who remains in my prayers for God's grace and guidance. Speaking of prayer, back to St. Robert's.

Even after the long Mass was over, we students were expected to stay put, kneel down, and pray a litany of prayers and devotions that the nuns trained us to recite. By the time we got back to school each Friday morning, it was almost time for lunch.

It's interesting to note that our enrollment in St. Robert Bellarmine School in the 1960s for grades one through eight was well over one thousand students. We averaged three classes per grade with approximately 50 students per class. We students were packed in those rooms like sardines. In fact, we were so crowded, that the year I was in fifth grade, our parish had to rent out classrooms from Sacred Heart School in McKeesport. We were picked up at our regular bus stop, traveled to St. Robert's, and then transferred to the other buses waiting to drive us south down Fifth Avenue to Sacred Heart School. What I didn't know was that my future husband went to that very school, and was also in fifth grade the same time as me. I might have even run into him on the playground, except for the fact that the nuns didn't allow us to mingle with the McKeesport kids. They kept us separated during outdoor recess which took place on the wide sidewalk and blocked off street in front of the school. There was a little pizza shop across the street from the school that kept its doors open during recess, so all we could smell was that delicious aroma, and all we could hear was the popular jukebox song, "Winchester Cathedral," playing loudly over and over all during recess. No wonder the nuns had a hard time getting us to concentrate back in class.

Fifth grade was my favorite year in grade school. Sister Michaelette Pavlik was a young and modern nun who taught us, and seemed to love kids and teaching. This was back in the mid-60s, where she *engaged her students in the learning process* before it was a popular method of teaching.

It was during this year I first knew I would be a teacher someday, because she was an exemplary role model who inspired me. My sisters Sheila and Denise, and my first cousins, Diane, Robert, and Mariane, remember pretending to be my students as we played *school* at our grandparents' house during those middle childhood years. Sister Michaelette eventually became friends with my mother, and attended many of our family events. Both of her parents were deceased, and she didn't have much family in Pittsburgh. So, she would join us for Sunday dinners and a few holidays. We still keep in touch and exchange Christmas cards to this day.

Four notable events stand out to make my fifth grade year memorable. First, my fifth grade classmates elected me to be *Miss Smile* in our school dental health contest. The new principal, Sister Angela, called me into her office and took a Polaroid picture of me and hung it on the school entrance bulletin board. Not having an abundance of self-confidence, and typically not wanting to be noticed, this did wonders for my self-esteem. Boy, did I feel special. My mom had always told me that I was one of *God's own*, and I truly believed it then, and still do, even to this day.

Mom also told me she had dedicated my sisters and me upon our births to the Blessed Mother. Growing up, I never wanted to disappoint either of them, my earthly mother, or my heavenly Mother. Sometimes I think that my mother would have been a nun if she hadn't married my father. Some people might say that she bleeds holy water. Being a devout Irish-Catholic defined the way my mother lived. Consequently, it also defined the rest of us. Maybe this helps explain the second memorable experience I had when I was 10 years old.

I remember having a beautiful dream about the Blessed Mother that year. I was playing in a park with friends. We were running around through the trees when I came upon a huge evergreen tree. When I ran behind it, I saw a vivid vision of Mary, our Blessed Mother. She was standing tall with outstretched arms, dazzling white with a warm sweet smile, and bright stars encircled her head. I felt her love and presence as if she were real. When she smiled at me, I knew then that we would always have a close relationship. I'm much older now, and I have never forgotten that dream. Since then, I have always prayed to Mary for her grace, help, and intercession with her Son. She has never let me down.

The third significant event that happened that year occurred in February 1967. We had a huge snowfall and many of the neighborhood kids decided to go sled riding on our neighbor's, the O'Brien's, backyard hill that evening. My parents didn't let me go because it was too cold, late, and dangerous. The steep hill ended on a back road. Well, many kids did go that night including my two youngest uncles, Johnny and Kippy. What started out as a night of fun, ended in a terrible disaster. Johnny slid down the hill like everyone else, except that when his sled wouldn't stop and crossed the road, a car came down at precisely that exact moment, and accidentally ran over him and fractured his skull. I remember someone pounding on my parents' front door to tell us what happened. My dad stayed with us girls, and my mom ran out to be with my grandparents and go to McKeesport Hospital where they had rushed Johnny by ambulance.

Dr. Michael V. Miklos, his neurosurgeon, didn't expect Johnny to live. Dr. Miklos used to do full-scale brain surgery at McKeesport Hospital. Johnny was a month shy of his 14th birthday. His only hope was to have his skull operated on to relieve the pressure on his brain. After surgery, Johnny lay unconscious, packed in ice, for two long weeks. We all took turns visiting him in the hospital, even though he never knew we were there. His siblings took turns cleaning out the tube in his throat. It was all so scary. Johnny didn't even look like himself anymore. He looked like he was dying. Dr. Miklos said that he did all he could do for him, and that Johnny was in God's hands. Then he told us to pray. Up until that point in my life, I had never prayed so hard for a miracle.

Our family specifically prayed novenas to St. Jude Thaddeus, patron saint of hopeless cases. My mom placed a statue of him in our house on our living room windowsill, and promised that a shrine would be built in his honor if our prayers were answered. We prayed at home, and then the nuns prayed with us at school. John Richard O'Grady, *Johnny*, was an eighth grade student at St. Robert's at the time. I remember praying for him in our school auditorium and singing a song that went something like this: "It's me, it's me, it's me O Lord, standing in the need of prayer, of prayer. It's me, it's me, it's me O Lord, standing in the need of prayer. Not my brother, not my sister, but it's me O Lord, standing in the need of prayer." Since then, I've been able to identify that song as the church hymn "Standin' in the Need of Prayer." I closed my eyes and sang with all my heart. I prayed to St. Jude that he would ask Jesus to help Johnny.

That same day after praying in the auditorium, when I went home from school, my mother was crying with joy, and told me that Johnny had woken up from his coma and that he would live. The nuns had taught us that God always answers children's prayers, so I wondered if all the prayers of our student body that day in the auditorium had reached heaven and helped Johnny wake up from his coma. Johnny had to learn how to walk and talk again. He couldn't even feed himself. He was like a baby. Johnny bravely endured years of physical therapy. The doctors at McKeesport Hospital told our family that it was a true miracle as they never expected Johnny to wake from his coma. As promised by my mother Mary Pat, their brother Timmy built a spectacular shrine to St. Jude, waterfall and all, in my grandparents' backyard. Today John Richard O'Grady is a retired special education teacher and grandfather, with a lovely wife, Claudia, and two adult married sons, Ryan and Danny, who each have two beautiful healthy children. Johnny is also coincidentally a non-Hodgkin's lymphoma cancer survivor! But it was his complete recovery from that car/sledding accident when we were kids that I knew for the first time that God answers our prayers, and miracles do happen, because I had been witness to one.

The Vietnam War was raging during the time of John Richard's accident. Millions of young boys had been drafted there. My Uncle Denny O'Grady, his older brother, was stationed in Saigon. He was an Army MP, (Military Police). One day in fifth grade, Sister Michaelette asked us students if anyone had a relative or friend stationed in Vietnam. She wanted to teach us how to write *friendly letters* in English class to cheer up our poor soldiers. I excitedly raised my hand and told the class about my young uncle. Denny O'Grady, with his curly blond hair and baby blue eyes, was one good looking Irishman, as cool as James Dean, with a great Irish wit. Many of the older girls in our neighborhood had crushes on him. Needless to say, I felt honored to submit his name for this assignment.

My entire fifth grade class wrote Uncle Denny and his platoon *friendly letters*. As an adult many years later, I recall him telling how hilarious these letters actually were at a family gathering. Many of the boys in my class apparently wanted to learn about the bloody details of war and were anything but cheerful. In any case, these letters gave the soldiers a good hardy laugh as they shared and read them aloud from their bunks. Shortly after our letters arrived in Saigon, Johnny's accident occurred back here in the states. Since John Richard was not expected to live, my grandparents were advised that the Red Cross could make arrangements to bring Denny home from Vietnam to finish out his year of duty. Denny did come home six weeks early from his deployment and was able to see Johnny recuperate. Had he stayed in Saigon that last month and a half and not come home, he would have been killed by enemy fire. The soldier who took over Denny's post was called out on maneuvers and shot to death. I often wonder if God allowed the accident to happen to Johnny in order to save the life of his brother, Denny O'Grady. If he hadn't come home when he did, he wouldn't have met and married Aunt Lynne, his sweet little daughter, Jane, wouldn't have had a daddy, and his mini-me son, Patrick, my Godson, would never have been born. Sometimes it seems God has plans and allows things to happen that we may never understand.

Uncle Harry was the eldest of my O'Grady uncles. He was married and had moved out of the house when I was growing up. He married Mary Ellen Nardozzi, and they went on to have six great kids, five boys and a girl. One of their sons, Brian, is also my Godson. He is now a nuclear engineer in the U. S. Navy, happily married with two children of his own. I was 14 years old when Uncle Harry and Aunt Mary Ellen asked me to be Brian's Godmother. Timmy, the middle son of my grandparents' five boys, was chosen to be his Godfather. We were both very honored to be Godparents at such young ages.

Before Uncle Harry and Aunt Mary Ellen had their own children, Aunt Mary Ellen had more time to make memories with my sisters and me. The winter of that same year, she took my sister Sheila and me to downtown Pittsburgh, where she had worked at that time, and treated us to a shopping spree at Kaufmann's Department Store, and to see Santa Claus. It was a big deal to go into the city, especially during the Christmas holiday season. That was actually the first time I remember going downtown. Sheila and I were dressed up for the big occasion, and both wore our *Bunny Hats*, which were white fur hats that were in fashion that year. We loved looking at the beautiful holiday decorations in Kaufmann's Department Store windows, and riding the monorail train that ran along the ceiling in magical Santa Land! Aunt Mary Ellen made us feel like we were little princesses. She would have four sons before she would birth a princess of her own. Her daughter Erin would be the flower girl in my future wedding. Aunt Mary Ellen has been a blessing to our family since the day she married Uncle Harry back in 1964.

The summer of 1966, after fifth grade, was a happy time. Our neighborhood sponsored a girls' softball league that played all their games in the local Sunset Elementary baseball field right behind the school. My cousin Kathy and I decided to try out for the teams. Our mothers allowed us to play since we could walk to the field which was located at the bottom of Old Fair Haven Heights.

Our teams were named after cars. Kathy played for the Firebirds, and I ended up on the Camaro's team. I was a pitcher, and also played shortstop. High school boys were our coaches. We had a blast. I remember I had my first crush on a boy named Gary DeFalco. Don't even know if that's how to spell his last name, or what happened to him after that summer. He was just a nice older boy who encouraged us to play our hearts out, and taught us young girls a lot about the game of baseball. Those were the days when Roberto Clemente, my favorite player, who wore my favorite number, 21, played for the Pittsburgh Pirates. They were also the days of hot summer nights when my family would sit outside on the front porch listening to Bob Prince announce our Pirate baseball games over the transistor radio. It felt like a magical time. Even today, as a veteran teacher, I still believe that fifth grade is the last magical age of childhood.

Besides being allowed to play girls' softball that summer, I was also permitted to walk to our local convenience store, named Blanchard's that was located at the top of Foster Road directly above Fairhaven Heights. Kathy and I would walk to the store to get our mothers milk or bread, along with some yummy penny candy and Bazooka bubble gum as our reward. That was also the summer when we walked to the local greenhouse to get our moms lilies for Easter, or geraniums for their Mother's Day presents. The greenhouse was also located at the bottom of Old Fair Haven across from Sunset School on the other side of the road. I felt so grown up and gained a new sense of independence that summer after fifth grade.

Another favorite summer activity from my childhood was the Backyard MD (Muscular Dystrophy) Carnivals we used to conduct in Fairhaven for all the neighborhood kids. The first time we conducted a backyard carnival I was in third grade, but we continued hosting them for a few additional summers. Kippy, Kathy, Karen, Dawn Ellen, Vesta, Sheila, (Denise wasn't born yet.), and I made backyard games, collected prizes like stuffed animals and penny candy, and manned the game and refreshment stations. My mom and Anna Marie would pop popcorn, and bake homemade cookies for us to sell. We would make gallons and gallons of Kool Aid for the refreshments stand. All the proceeds from our backyard carnivals were sent to Paul Shannon's *Adventure Time Show* at our local WTAE ABC affiliate in Wilkinsburg, where he then sent the money to the Muscular Dystrophy Association. Since our house was the first house in the development and on a large corner lot, we would have the carnivals there in our yard. We drew up advertisement posters and tacked them on telephone poles around Fairhaven days in advance. All the neighborhood kids would come, but I don't think we ever made anywhere close to a hundred dollars. Back then, we never made much money, but we had fun. Our games included a mini-golf putt-putt station, penny pitch, Chuck-a-luck, drop the clothespins in the glass milk bottles, knock down the plastic bowling pins, guess how many marbles in the jar, and a slip 'n slide. The games were simple and homemade, but we had a blast making them. The best perk was that we thought we were making a difference in our own little way. It was such fun, and we felt like we were growing up. Flash forward many years later, when my own daughters hosted similar backyard carnivals on our corner lot and gave the money they earned to a needy family from our church.

As much as I loved fifth grade in elementary school, that's how much I disliked sixth grade. It all started when my teacher, Sister Patrice, refused to call me by my baptismal name. Before I share this part of my story, it's important to note that I went through all eight grades of elementary school with another girl in my class who had the same name as me. There were two of us with the name, Susan Soltis. I was Susan Patrice Soltis, and her name was Susan Marie Soltis. We were known as Susan P. and Susan M. She was a blond girl, and I was a brunette. Teachers always had ways to differentiate us, so it wasn't a problem until sixth grade.

On the first day of school in sixth grade, our teacher, Sister Patrice was taking roll call. She excitedly announced to the class that she was happy to see that someone in our class had her name. Hoping she didn't mean me, I sank down lower in my seat. She called out loudly, "Patrice Soltis." I didn't say *here*, or raise my hand to acknowledge that name. She persisted and repeated even louder, "Patrice Soltis, where are you?" Knowing she wouldn't quit, I raised my hand and said, "Sister, my name is Susan Soltis, and Patrice is only my middle name." Seeming to ignore what I just said, she then announced to the class that from that day forward, I would be known as Patrice in her honor. I wanted to die. I was furious. I held back the tears until I got home from school that day. I ran into my bedroom and threw myself on my bed and cried. My mother came into my room to see what was wrong, and when I told her what happened in class that day, she thought it wasn't a big deal. She said that at least the nun seemed to like me, and that I shouldn't put up a fuss. In those days, parents didn't argue with the nuns. And so it was decreed, for one year of my life, in my sixth grade classroom, I would be known as Patrice Soltis, like it or not. Fortunately, for me, my family and friends still called me Susie.

My best friend in sixth grade was Geralyn Matvya. Geralyn had long straight brown hair to her waist. She, like my father, was raised as a motherless child. She lived with her father, three brothers, and her grandma. Geralyn was cooking and cleaning like an adult at this tender age. She was a hard worker who never complained. On occasion, we would have sleepovers at each other's house. Once, I remember sleeping over her house and helping her paint her bedroom walls in pretty pink and white stripes. We had lots of fun together, and we also shared a devotion to the Blessed Mother. Those Vincentian Nuns taught us well. We both had Slovak fathers and grandmas that we called *Bubba*. Geralyn was a bright spot in my life the year of Sister Patrice and the name fiasco.

Many years later, Geralyn and I would reconnect as adults when she and her husband moved into the same development in North Huntingdon as my sister Sheila, and joined our parish church. Geralyn and her husband, Mike, both give of their time, talent, and treasure to St. Agnes Church. When I was sick with cancer, Geralyn was one of the first people to send over food for my family. One of the nicest perks of getting older is when you can sometimes see your life come full circle. Geralyn invited me to join the Christian Mothers in our parish as she is a board member. We also completed a spiritually enlightening *Discovering Christ* Lenten renewal conference sponsored by our pastor, Monsignor Paul Fitzmaurice. Geralyn remains very active in our parish. She still makes delicious Slovak foods (haluski, perogies) like she made as a child for her father and brothers, but now she makes it for our parish Lenten Friday Fish Fries, and our annual church bazaar. It's been a long time since we were in sixth grade back at St. Robert Bellarmine School, but some things never change. Geralyn is still the same sweet giving person that I met when we were 11 years old, and you can still find her cooking Slovak foods in a kitchen.

Another highlight in sixth grade, besides my friendship with Geralyn, was making my Confirmation that year. All of us students had to choose a saint for our Confirmation name. We were told to pick a saint we wanted to emulate; someone to help us become better *soldiers for Christ*. I chose Catherine, in honor of Saint Catherine Laboure. Our Lady manifested the Miraculous Medal to Sister, now Saint Catherine Laboure, in the motherhouse of the Sisters of Charity of St. Vincent de Paul in Paris, France on November 27, 1830. Saint Catherine had a dazzling vision of the Blessed Mother where Mary spoke to her giving her instructions on the design of the medal. Mary promised that many graces and blessings would shower down upon those who wear her medal. I have worn this Miraculous Medal most of my adult life and believe her promise to be true. I have clutched this medal during childbirth, before mammograms and sonograms, on airplane flights, during chemotherapy, MRIs, CT scans, and in my hospital bed as I battled non-Hodgkin's lymphoma during the fight for my life. Looking back to sixth grade, I can now see that it was providential that I took the Confirmation name of Catherine, because of our devotion and connection to our Blessed Mother Mary. Little did I know at the time, that I would have a daughter someday named Kaitlin, whose patron saint was Saint Catherine, who was also devoted to the Blessed Mother.

When I was in seventh grade, my Grandfather O'Grady passed away of a sudden heart attack while working at his desk for Westinghouse in East Pittsburgh. His secretary heard a thump through his office door, and when she went inside to see if he was ok, he was slumped over dead at his desk, phone still in hand. It was January 14th, and when I walked into our house after school that afternoon, my dad was home from work, and he was crying. I had never seen my dad cry before. When I asked him what was wrong, he told me my grandfather had died. My first question was, "Which one?" He said my mom was with my grandmother and her siblings. My mother was devastated, as were my Grandmother O'Grady, and the rest of the clan. My mom had a special bond with her father whom she idolized, and she mourned her great loss for a very long time. His death was such a shock, since he seemed in perfect health, and was only 56 years old. Kippy and Johnny were only in their freshman and sophomore years at Serra Catholic High School when they were called into the office to find out the life changing news. For many years after, my grandmother, mother, uncles, and sisters went to Mass on the anniversary of Grandpap O'Grady's death to pray for the repose of his soul.

Our family dynamic changed drastically after Grandpap's death. My grandmother was grief stricken. My dad stepped up and took Kippy and Johnny golfing and fishing, and tried to be a father figure, but nobody could replace the great loss of their dad. The boys would miss his daily presence and guidance, especially as they tried to navigate their way through their teen years and into young adulthood.

Grandpap O'Grady was the O'Grady family patriarch, and our rock. He was a man of integrity and great faith who lived his life as an example to others. Every Sunday, he would drive up the street to pick us up at 11:40 a.m., and take us to noon Mass. Church was only five minutes away. My mom didn't have her driving license then, and my dad unfortunately didn't go to church. My mom would tell us girls that Daddy wasn't blessed with the *gift of faith*, because he never was taught religion, or had a mother's love, and that we should pray for him. And so, I grew up praying really hard that he would *get it* someday.

Sometimes, Grandpap would babysit us if my parents went out, or when my mom and grandma went to Friday evening card club until my dad returned home from work. What were we going to do without Grandpap O'Grady? He was the moral compass for everyone in the family. He not only talked the talk, he walked the walk. I'll always remember the image of him wearing his white shirt, sitting in his chair, reading books, reading newspapers, or doing the Pittsburgh Press crossword puzzles. My mother would tell me how he was such an intellect, but he also liked to play chess, cards, go fishing, and golf. He loved his Church, my grandmother, and our whole family. What were my young uncles going to do without their great role model? Grandpap's influence would certainly be missed. I remember when my young uncles would have to drive me to evening Mass if we were allowed to sleep in Sunday mornings, and they would suggest sitting in the car parking lot for an hour instead of going inside the church. I would threaten to tell Grandma on them, and so we ended up going inside for Mass. What they didn't realize is that I wouldn't have tattled on them, because according to my uncles, there wasn't anything worse than being a squeal! That would never have gained me their approval!

Unfortunately, Grandpap's passing left an emotional void on Kippy that nothing could ever fill. He was his baby boy, his Kipper. Between that great loss, and the traumatic effect of Johnny's accident, Kippy was scarred in ways we wouldn't see until many years later. The loss of Grandpap O'Grady affected our family deeply and permanently. This was only the second time in my young life that I lost someone I loved. Two years earlier, my Bubba died.

When I was in fifth grade, my Great Grandmother Susie Soltis, died after a short illness at the age of 86. She was also a person of great faith, who had a great devotion to the Blessed Mother. Bubba, her Slovak nickname for Grandma, as we called her, was the matriarch of the Soltis family, and a very holy woman. She had birthed and raised eleven children, and then raised my father. She would walk many miles from the farmlands in Braddock Hills to Rankin, to go to Sunday Mass. Bubba was a fabulous cook, and gardener. Her vegetable and flower gardens were magnificent. I credit her with my dad's and my inherited green thumb.

Bubba lived with my Aunt Marie and Uncle Al, my Grandpap Soltis's sister and husband, when I was a child. When we would visit them on Sunday afternoons, there was always a big pot of homemade soup brewing on the stove along with haluski, stuffed cabbage, and some other delicious Slovak foods. We always felt more welcome and comfortable visiting them, than when we visited my Grandpap and Grandma Soltis, because we were told to sit quietly there, and not ask for anything except maybe a glass of water. Aunt Marie, affectionately referred to as Aunt MiMi, and Uncle Al lived up the hill from my Soltis Grandparents. Aunt MiMi was like the surrogate grandmother on the Soltis side of the family. She was loving, kind, and dear to us. Bubba and Aunt MiMi would always invite us to eat there, and Uncle Al would always surprise us kids with a Fudgesicle and a quarter. Having and saving that quarter for some penny candy from Blanchard's Convenience Store was a big deal in those days. Another plus when visiting Aunt Marie and Uncle Al's was when our Andolina cousins, Bobby, Stevie, Becky, and Beth would be visiting as well. They were always lots of fun, and I completely idolized Becky, who was two years older than me.

During my childhood, Bubba and my Uncle Bob Andolina, her grandson, my dad's first cousin, Best Man, and my Godfather, would take me on annual pilgrimages to Mount St. Macrina Byzantine Catholic Monastery in Uniontown, every Labor Day weekend. Bubba was a Greek Orthodox Catholic, and I was raised Roman Catholic. So I was always excited to go receive Communion there, because it was given differently, on a spoon under both species, a cube of bread on a teaspoon of wine. Back then, Roman Catholics received the bread, a small round wafer host, but not the wine. I appreciated that Bubba was sharing her faith with me. Both of my grandparents, Grandfather Henry O'Grady, and Great-Grandmother Susan Soltis, who had passed away when I was in grade school, were devout Catholics, heads of large families, who had lived their lives as Christ-like examples in service to others. They both had set me quite extraordinary examples of how to live a faith-filled life. I had been blessed that they were in my life for the formative years of my childhood.

CHAPTER 4

Serra Catholic High School

My first two years in secondary school were spent at an all girls' Catholic high school in downtown McKeesport called Mon Yough Catholic, formerly known as St. Peter's High School. Most of my friends from St. Robert Bellarmine attended the newly built East Allegheny High School only a few miles from home. They were all getting new clothes and were just delighted to have no more uniforms. The day my cousin Kathy called me next door to show me her new school wardrobe, I ran home and threw myself on my bed and burst into tears. My Catholic high school meant more ugly navy blue uniforms with white blouses. What can I say, other than my mother, a devout Catholic, thought it was her obligation to provide my sisters and me with a twelve year Catholic education. Lucky for me, my dad seemed to agree. Looking back, I'm grateful for my parents' financial sacrifice to send me to Catholic school, especially when my dear dad didn't yet grasp the importance of his sacrifice, but did it anyway.

Instead of taking a regular school bus to school with my neighborhood friends, I would have to take a Port Authority Transit bus to downtown McKeesport, and then walk several blocks through the city to my school building. McKeesport was a very busy place back in the 1970s. The National Tube Works steel mills were still in production, and business was booming. The stores along Fifth Avenue such as Jaison's Department Store, Cox's Department Store, Immels, Reisenstein Shoes, G.C. Murphys, and Goodman Jewelers were still doing a good business, since it was before the closing of the steel mills changed everything. How

I dreaded walking through those busy city streets and enduring the *cat calls* every day on my way to and from high school.

Just when I thought I couldn't take it anymore, my Uncle Tim O'Grady came to my rescue. He worked for Bell Telephone just a few blocks away from my high school. When he offered to pick me up every morning and drive me to school, I was so grateful. He has always been so good to me. Once in high school, when I mentioned to him how much I liked the music group Crosby, Stills, Nash, and Young, he offered to drive my best friend Ellen and me to their concert in Cleveland. That was the first time I'd been to a rock concert, and the music was magnificent. I was surprised to see so many people at the concert smoking marijuana, but that was fairly common at rock concerts back then. On our way home from the late night concert, we stayed overnight in a local motel. The next day, Timmy drove us back home to Pittsburgh. The CSN&Y concert was such a thrill, and yet another happy memory during my early teen years.

Of all my five O'Grady uncles, Timmy has been the closest to me throughout my adult life. He has been a true friend through thick and thin. He has helped me move into new houses twice, fixed our electrical and plumbing problems over the years, generously bought Christmas presents for all his great nieces and nephews, hosts annual St. Patrick's Day and O'Grady family Christmas parties, and has been there when needed during the sad times of my life. He is one of the first people I remember, and I don't remember much of that infamous February, who came to the hospital to visit me the week I was diagnosed and very sick fighting for my life with stage four non-Hodgkin's lymphoma.

Timmy has helped so many people in our family aside from me over the years. He has extraordinary mechanical, electrical, and carpentry skills. He actually finished the construction of my parents' house addition after Chickie, who had been hired to do the job, took their money and skipped town. In addition, Timmy has provided room and shelter in his home for his two younger brothers at different times in their lives when they needed a place to stay. He invites his out of state sisters and their families to stay in his house when they're home for the holidays. He's designed and built an incredible train display the length of his basement that has provided entertainment and fun for many generations of our family. His talents are amazing. He was flipping houses, designing new kitchens, and building basement bathrooms long before HGTV made it cool! But his greatest talent just might be the fun St. Patrick's Day parties he throws every year. They are epic!

In many ways, Tim O'Grady became the patriarch of the O'Grady family after my grandfather's death. Even though he wasn't the eldest son in the family, he has assumed the role of the *rock* for many of his brothers and sisters and their children. Even though Timmy never married, I don't think he ever felt like he missed out not having his own kids. He had plenty of adoring nieces and nephews who seemed to fill that role. My daughter Kaitlin recently reminded me of how her Great-Uncle Timmy helped with her Pennsylvania Junior Academy of Science projects. She won two First Place awards for building a Doppler ball and a seismograph thanks to his guidance! Timmy has been a blessing to all of us in the O'Grady family, and I credit him and my mother in keeping all the clan together. For as long as I can remember, all the way back to my two year old birthday party, he has always been there. Back to high school!

Fortunately, the summer before my junior year in high school, Mon Yough Catholic all girls' high school merged with Serra Catholic all boys' high school. Even though I had to ride two yellow school buses to get there, and still wear ugly uniforms, at least there were boys!

Serra High School was famous for hosting wonderful weekend dances in the early 1970s. Those Serra dances sometimes featured rock 'n roll pop groups such as the Jaggerz or Eddie Holman. Over a-thousand high school kids would be in attendance. The dances were held Saturday nights in Serra's huge and crowded gymnasium. We paid $3.00 to get into the gym. All teenagers were welcome, and many would come from the other local public high schools in our area. Starting in our freshman year at Mon Yough Catholic, I would attend these dances with my best friends, Ellen and Maureen. They both had brothers who were in Kippy's junior class at Serra, and so usually one of those boys would drive us there. It was such a thrill when a Serra boy asked you to slow dance. If you weren't dancing, then you were socializing with your friends, meeting new friends, or watching to see who was *making out* on or under the bleachers in the darkened gymnasium. Boys and girls were always flirting and scouting out who they wanted to date next. We listened and danced to great music! I can close my eyes and see us girls spinning around the Serra gym to the beat of "Dance to the Music." We just had lots of fun!

Kippy and Johnny would also drive me to high school play practices after school, in addition to the Serra Dances Saturday nights with my friends. They never seemed to resent me, or treat me like a tag-along. My three youngest uncles always took care of me like they were my big brothers. Kippy, Johnny, and I enjoyed having small roles in the Serra

High School spring productions of *The Crucible* and *Masterplan 237*, an original play written by Mr. Bob Shank, the Serra High School drama teacher. We made lots of new friends and had tons of fun at the play practices. The year prior, Kippy was in the chorus of *Bye Bye Birdie*, and Grandma and my mom took me to see the show. That was the first time I fell in love with live theater. Theater shows also remind me of the earlier times in 1964–65 when my dad took my sister Sheila, (Denise wasn't born yet), and me to the local Eastland Mall Theater to see the premier of *The Sound of Music*, starring Julie Andrews and Christopher Plummer, and *My Fair Lady* with Audrey Hepburn. I guess I fell in love with theater long before high school!

My last two years of high school were very happy years. I was elected to Student Government, a member of National Honor Society, French Club, and Cheerleading Co-captain. The highlight of my high school memories was when our school guidance counselor, Mr. Richard Andreko, asked me to represent Serra Catholic High School in the local Junior Miss Pageant which was being sponsored by the Greater McKeesport Jaycees, a group of local business leaders. Junior Miss was a national scholarship/beauty pageant which awarded many financial college scholarships to high school senior girls. You were judged on the following criteria: poise & appearance, grades, fitness, personality, and talent. There were awards for each of these categories and for the runners-up. The winner would be crowned Junior Miss and flown by Allegheny Airlines to Reading, Pennsylvania to compete in the state pageant. The state winner would then go on to compete in Mobile, Alabama for the national crown. Much to my surprise, I won the local contest and was crowned Greater McKeesport's 1974 Junior Miss. My family, friends, fellow students, and teachers (who were mostly nuns and priests) all came to the local public high school, West Mifflin North, auditorium to cheer for me. I will never forget their love and support. Right before the emcee announced the winner and called out my name, the audience became stone silent, a drum rolled, and a voice screamed out amid the silence, "It's in the bag, Suz!" I'd recognize that loud mouth anywhere . . . as Kippy, who'd turned out to be my biggest fan and supporter! Like I said before, his approval meant the world to me. It meant so much to know my young uncles were all there and, hopefully, proud of me.

The Saturday night that I won, Father Joe Avella, (who would officiate years later at my wedding), came to my parents' house teeming with family and friends and conducted a Midnight Mass right there in our home. I'll always remember what an honor it was to celebrate the holy sacrifice of the Mass in our humble home. It was such a sight to see so many of my high school friends receive Holy Communion right there in our living room.

My high school drama teacher, Mr. Bob Shank, had helped me write and prepare my pageant talent presentation, which was an oral comedic interpretation of the Wicked Witch of the West from the classic *Wizard of Oz*. During my three minute talent presentation, dressed in a black witch's costume, pointed hat and broom to boot, I retold the story of the *Wizard of Oz* from the Witch's point of view, a fractured fairytale, so to speak. Mind you, this was a good thirty years before the Broadway hit show, *Wicked*, appeared on the scene giving a *voice* to the Wicked Witch of the West. Anyway, it was such a happy time for my family and me. I remember being so relieved and grateful for the scholarship money which would enable me to go to Penn State University where I would get my bachelor's degree in Elementary Education.

There were many other Junior Miss perks aside from the scholarship money. The first one, which I really appreciated after wearing Catholic school uniforms my whole life, was a new wardrobe to wear the week when I was in Reading for the state competition. Mrs. Elaine Swartz, my chaperone, who was married to Mr. Robert Swartz, one of the sponsoring Jaycees, took me to the upscale, local, Cox's Department Store in downtown McKeesport to pick out my new clothes. After that, there were speaking engagements at local venues such as the Lemon Tree Restaurant, the Youghiogheny Country Club, and parade appearances. It was such an exciting year.

That November, I flew on an airplane for the first time without my family to Reading for the Pennsylvania state pageant. I stayed for a whole week with a local host family, the Zerbes, who were sponsoring Reading Jaycees. My assigned roommate was Charmaine Kowalski, a nice girl from Centre County, whom I would reconnect with three years later at Penn State University Main Campus. There were twenty some contestants from counties all over the state of Pennsylvania competing for the state title. I felt very fortunate to be there. The outpouring of support from my high school back home was overwhelming. The priests at Serra Catholic had chartered buses to take my fellow students, friends, teachers, and chaperones to travel across the state to Reading to support me. Students' escapades at their hotel, and tales of teenage lost virginity that November weekend in Reading, have become legendary topics at class reunions. Enough said! Nevertheless, I had the loudest cheering section of all the contestants.

Even my dear Aunt Sheila Riberich, flew up from her home in Atlanta with her three young kids to support me. Traveling with three children in the cold, and making those close call connecting flights into Reading couldn't have been easy. My three youngest O'Grady uncles and my Grandmother O'Grady were also there. The outpouring of love and support was overwhelming. One of the most magical moments of my life was when I received a standing ovation from the thousands of people in the audience, who came from all over the state, for my talent presentation after I melted onstage as the Wicked Witch of the West. The feeling was euphoric as I held the audience in the palm of my hand. I had prayed to the Holy Spirit right before I went onstage to help me do my best, and I had never performed better. My original comedic interpretation of the Wicked Witch earned me the Junior Miss PA State Talent Award, and runner up, and more college scholarship money. Even though I didn't win the state title, my Junior Miss scholarships and achievements helped pay my college tuition at Penn State University, and opened many more doors, particularly broadcasting opportunities, for me later in life in my twenties.

My Junior Miss experience also had a positive impact on my dear mother's life. Mummy had been a stay-at-home mom until my senior year in high school. Parenting my sisters and I was her life. Every evening, mom would cook us a delicious, nutritious, homemade dinner, which always included a dessert. My mother was a fabulous cook, who took great pride and joy in feeding our family, and her extended family of seven brothers and sisters. After my Grandma O'Grady stopped cooking Sunday dinners for the clan, my mother picked up right where her mother left off. My mother cooked Sunday dinner for everyone for the next thirty years! When I was a little girl, she had *Spaghetti Tuesday* dinners in Swissvale for Timmy, and cousin, Marilyn Jessell, who would occasionally babysit me. When I was older, on the Friday nights that Mummy didn't have card club, she would make my three youngest uncles and my sisters and me, popcorn and homemade fudge. We would play pinochle, canasta, hearts, or Monopoly, sometimes well past midnight. Mummy was always trying to create special memories for her family, and she did.

Mummy made our holidays magical! Christmas presents would cover the floor of our game room, and you barely could walk from one side of the room to the other. Daddy would just shake his head in disbelief. How she hosted a Christmas Eve open house for our family and friends, and then get-up in the morning and cook dinner for Christmas Day was beyond me! We always had more than enough food for the people who would pop in knowing they were always welcome. And she made sure we never forgot the reason for the season. Christmas Eve Mass was the most important part of the evening. Thanksgiving turkey dinners were also magnificent, and she always invited a few unfortunate souls who didn't have family in town, to join us. Sister Michaelette, Dad's friend Emil from Germany, Annie and Chuck from the bank, were all visitors who come to mind. Fourth of July picnics included volleyball games in our front yard or swimming pool. And on Easter, we always had a new dress and bonnet, and mom and dad would hide Easter eggs in all our pine trees that surrounded our little house. Years later, my parents would continue to conduct Easter egg hunts for their grandchildren. It would become a special memory for the next generation. Mom also started having St. Patrick's Day parties at our St. Robert Bellarmine school auditorium when we were young, and then continued hosting annual St. Paddy's Day Parties years later when she worked at McKeesport National Bank. .Those parties were legendary, where local politicians, dignitaries, and common folk would attend *wearing of the green* whether they were Irish or not.

Anyway, back to my young Mummy. She volunteered at our church and school, was a Girl Scout leader, a CCD teacher, and was active in bettering our local community. She was the best mother and role model any girl could have. Mummy was a beautiful woman inside and out. She taught my sisters and me how to love, and that love was a choice. She used to say, "Love is an action verb!" She taught us how to give, and to do it lovingly. She never complained. My mom is one of the best human beings I know, and I feel privileged that God chose her to be my mother. Being a leader, my mother set quite an example. I can't say it was always easy living up to her standards, but I tried. Being the oldest and being told repeatedly it was my duty to set a good example for my little sisters, I really tried.

Now to get back to how my Junior Miss experience impacted my mother's life . . . My mom had been a stay-at-home mother until my Senior Year in high school. During my year as Junior Miss, my mother met Mr. Bob Swartz, one of the sponsoring Jaycees, who was also a Vice President at McKeesport National Bank. He needed a part-time teller to fill in for a worker on leave. My mom was offered that position which started her career in banking that lasted for another twenty-six years. When my mother retired from banking in 2000, she had risen to the position of Senior Vice President of Sky Financial. She has served on the Board of Directors for Huntingdon Bank, (formerly Sky Bank, formerly Three Rivers Bank, previously McKeesport National Bank), Allegheny County Pittsburgh International Airport Board of Directors, Allegheny County Regional Asset District (RAD) Board, UPMC McKeesport Hospital Board, served as First Woman President of the Mon Yough Chamber of Commerce, Penn State University McKeesport Campus Advisory Board, McKeesport YMCA Board, and last, but not least, the Auberle Foundation Board.

Incidentally, while mom was extremely busy working full time building her career and volunteering on all her boards, she never stopped cooking Sunday dinners and huge feasts, or hosting all the holidays for our family and extended family. As the matriarch of the O'Grady clan, after her parents passed away, she felt it was her loving responsibility to carry on the family traditions. And never once did she utter a word of exhaustion or complaint. When my mother sacrifices and gives of herself, she does it lovingly. She has been our rock, a woman of faith and wisdom, who always reminds us that anything is possible with faith and trust in God. She always likes to say that if you put God first in your life, everything else will fall into place.

On a side note, for those of you who might not know about the work of the Allegheny County Regional Asset District (RAD), I'd like to explain it. In 1993, Pittsburgh city leaders were looking for a long-term solution to sustain the arts. So the legislature created RAD, and authorized the additional 1percent county sales tax. Half of the 1percent of those funds were earmarked to support the region's parks, libraries, sports and civic facilities/programs, and arts/cultural organizations, while the other half was allocated to municipal governments. The RAD Board was charged with allocating these funds to the various cultural organizations and recreational amenities that needed financial assistance. As one of the board members, my mom told me one of her greatest accomplishments was casting the deciding vote to build the city of Pittsburgh's new football stadium, now known as Heinz Field. At the time of the vote, there were many people in Pittsburgh who did not want Three Rivers Stadium to be demolished, and were vehemently opposed to funding and building a new sports arena. My mom felt that you shouldn't stand in the way of progress, and so courageously cast the final deciding vote to implement Plan A, *Heinz Field*, and then Plan B, *PNC Park*. I tell my adult children they can thank their Grandma Mary Pat that the city of Pittsburgh has two of the best sports facilities in our country. Heinz Field, home for the Pittsburgh Steelers, and PNC Park, home of the Pittsburgh Pirates, are among the most beautiful sports venues in America. And my dear mother, a humble, once upon a time, stay-at-home mom, had a hand in bringing those dreams to fruition. Today, people from all over the country can come to our fair city and enjoy the fruits of her labor. I want to publically thank her for having the courage to vote *yes* in the midst of much criticism and dissention.

The Auberle Foundation Board is probably the board membership that means the most to my mom. Auberle is a faith-based Catholic agency that helps troubled children and familics to heal themselves. The agency serves more than 3,250 children and families each year through residential care, foster care, emergency shelter, in-home intervention, education, and rehabilitation programs. My mother's commitment to Auberle was evident to me when the leadership named the reception room of their facility after her. It was quite an honor for Mummy. The bishop himself came to the dedication of the room, and a plaque was hung on the wall in my mother's honor. My husband Eddy and I have chosen to donate our United Way Contribution Funds to Auberle to help carry on the legacy of Auberle in our own little way.

As I look back on all of this, I can see the hand of God guiding and directing us according to his plan. My mother took her leadership skills, intelligence, and talents to the highest levels, and has truly made a difference in so many people's lives through her life of service to others. And it all started when my humble stay-at-home mom went back to work when I was a senior in high school.

The summer before my junior year in high school, I was invited to a picnic at a fellow classmate, Sandy Katchur's, house. It was supposed to be a get-acquainted party for the cheerleaders, jocks, and friends at the newly merged Serra Catholic High School. This was the first time I met my future husband, Eddy Guarascio. We had gathered to play a game of badminton, girls verse the boys. He had a broken wrist, and was playing left-handed. He was sweet and shy. He was a real mop top. He had such a nice head of long, thick, dark hair, and sort of looked like he could be one the Beatles. I remember he wore a hooded white sweatshirt. I can't remember who won the game, but I remember having fun and liking him and his friends. I ended up dating his best friend, Mike, for the next two years in high school. We went to both proms together, and had lots of fun dating our junior and senior years.

Anyway, a few weeks after Sandy's party, my friends and I could barely contain our excitement as we started our junior year at the newly co-ed Serra Catholic High. No more walking through polluted dirty downtown McKeesport to get to the dilapidated Mon Yough Catholic High School building by the noisy railroad tracks and blazing Steel Mills. Our old building would shake every time a train rolled by. We were onto bigger and better things.

Serra Catholic High School was situated on the outskirts of the city of McKeesport in an upscale neighborhood called Haler Heights where many doctors, lawyers, and other professionals lived. The area was nicknamed *Pill Hill* in reference to the many doctors who lived there in their lovely homes. Serra Catholic High School was a modern building with lots of amenities that we didn't have at our all girls' city school. There was a fabulous football field that overlooked the suburban campus, and of course, there were now boys on our campus. The boys were eagerly welcoming and obviously instructed by the priests to continue to be "Serra Gentlemen" to us newcomers. The first couple of weeks of school were spent getting to know our new surroundings, our fellow classmates, and our teachers, who were mostly Franciscan friars and nuns.

Tragically, our back to school excitement turned out to be short lived, and soon turned to horror as we were informed by our teachers that Eddy's older brother, Bruce, had been killed in a car accident the day after Labor Day on his way to begin his freshman year at West Virginia University. Bruce had been a star athlete at Serra where he lettered in football, basketball, and baseball. He was popular, good looking, and just a really great kid. I met him the previous spring when we were both selected by our administrators to appear in a photo in the McKeesport Daily News newspaper featuring an article concerning the two local Catholic high schools merger. Bruce was friendly and kind to me as I nervously waited to be photographed and even teased with his buddy, Don Socrates, they should fix me up with his younger brother Eddy who I hadn't met yet. Years later when we actually did get married, I thought that Bruce would have given us his blessing. It was shortly after Eddy's return to school after that tragedy that I spotted him walking alone in our high school parking lot one day after school. He was obviously heartbroken and had the saddest eyes I'd ever seen. He was picking up stones and throwing them across the parking lot lost in his thoughts. I'm sure he didn't realize anyone was watching him, but it was at that moment that I had a *knowing* that someday I would make him happy.

CHAPTER 5

We Are!! Penn State

DURING my first two years in college, I attended the Penn State University McKeesport Campus, which is now known as the Penn State Greater Allegheny Campus. It was December of our freshman year that Eddy and I started dating. He played on the Penn State McKeesport basketball team, and I was a Penn State cheerleader. Soon enough, we became college sweethearts. We had lots of fun traveling to all of our away games at the other Penn State Commonwealth Campuses across the state. On the nights we didn't have basketball games, Eddy and I would have date nights usually going out for pizza at Nigro's Restaurant and a movie. Our first date was a Christmas party on December 28 hosted by a friend we knew who worked with me weekends at the Cox's Department Store in the Monroeville Mall. I found out years later that Eddy's friend George Grimball was actually the one to dial my phone number for Eddy to ask me out as he was too shy to call me. I remember slow dancing with Eddy at that Christmas party, and then taking a walk outside in the snow and not caring that my hair would get wet and frizzy. Our second date was pizza and then to the movies to see *The Godfather*. Eddy would pick me up in this old little green Fiat Spyder convertible. I was so excited the first time riding in it until I saw the ground through the hole in the floorboard and had to straddle the seat! During this time living at our homes our freshman and sophomore years in college, we spent a lot of time getting to know each other's families. We would watch television shows at each other's house and go out on fun dates with Eddy's parents. We became very close during that time, and realized that our families and our mothers' Irish Catholic backgrounds were similar in many ways. Our both sets of parents welcomed lots of company with their warm hospitality and open door policy. As I grew to love Eddy's family, it felt natural that we belonged together.

The local two year campus, proved to be a nice transition for us from our small high school to the huge Main Campus at University Park. Another perk attending the PSU McKeesport Campus was that my cheerleading membership counted as a physical education elective. After I found that out, I decided to take the remainder of my physical education electives at the McKeesport Campus, and take advantage of their smaller class sizes.

My first gym elective was a beginners' tennis class. I had played tennis for fun with my family and friends, so I thought this class would help me refine and sharpen my tennis skills. Plus, I thought it would be an easy A. The first day of class, we students were instructed to sign-in on an attendance sheet before taking our seats. I wrote my name, Susan Soltis, in cursive, and then went to sit on the bleachers. Our young, and obviously newly hired tennis instructor, apparently used this sign-in sheet for roll call in subsequent classes. She called out our names, and we would respond *here*, if we were present. As she pronounced the names on the class roster, I waited to hear my name called. When she asked if "Swan Soltis" was present, I cringed and hoped she didn't mean me. Unfortunately, she did. I raised my hand after a bit, thinking this couldn't be happening again . . . a teacher who refused to call me by my right name. I explained that my name was Susan Soltis, and I had apparently written in cursive, so that the S-u- s- a- n looked like it spelled S-w- a- n. Believe it or not, our tennis instructor spent the rest of the trimester calling me "Swan." So for three months of my life, I was known as Swan, not Susan, not Susie, not Sue, not Susan P, not Patrice, but Swan. My friends in class couldn't believe it. At first, it was funny, and then later, it actually became hilarious. I still crack up when I think of it to this day, and consequently, I have an unusual affection for swans! Swans have since become my Spirit Animal as they glide serenely, elegantly, and effortlessly along the waters, while they're paddling like heck underneath the ripples.

It was during this time that I met my best friend in college, a beautiful blond, named Noelle. She was from North Huntingdon Township, (where I've lived most of my adult married life), and was also a cheerleader. We ended up being dorm roommates in Hoyt Hall when we went to the Main Campus our junior year at Penn State. Noelle and I are still very close friends, and Eddy and I are Godparents to her son Brett. Penn

State University Main Campus in University Park in the late seventies was quite a culture shock for a girl as sheltered and protected as me after going through twelve years of Catholic School and two years at the small local Commonwealth Campus.

Noelle was dating a boy who was already a student at Main Campus when we arrived for our junior year first trimester at University Park. He was a member of the Phi Psi Fraternity and invited us to our first fraternity party that autumn. Fraternity houses at Penn State are stately magnificent mansions on beautiful tree-lined streets. I was so thrilled to be going to my first frat party. Freshmen fall initiation rites were going on at that time. I'll never forget my first impression of a frat party as we walked toward the frat house, and saw the image of that young pledge hanging upside-down, naked, dangling from a flag pole! Fraternity brothers would periodically stagger over to taunt him, or slap his naked butt with sticks. It was a rather shocking sight! That night was the first time I realized that I *wasn't in Kansas anymore.*

Not long into our junior year in college, Noelle and her boyfriend broke up, so that ended our Phi Psi frat parties. After that, Noelle and I were able to spend more time together. She even joined Eddy and me at Mass Sunday mornings at the Eisenhower Auditorium. Noelle hadn't attended Catholic schools and wasn't raised strict Catholic like I was, but was intrigued and interested in strengthening her faith during that time, so we started going to church together. We would meet Eddy at the 11:00 a.m. Mass in Eisenhower Auditorium, or at 4:30 p.m. Mass in the Forum Building, and then go out to eat, usually sticky buns with coffee or tea from the Penn State Diner. It was nice that my college friends also became friends with Eddy. Soon enough, there were plenty of other cute college boys calling and coming around to date beautiful Noelle.

Another perk for attending Sunday morning Mass at the Eisenhower Auditorium was spotting Joe Paterno, our beloved football coach, his wife Sue, and their five children, usually seated in the fifth row. We would try to sit as close to them as possible. Joe and his wife were weekly communicants, and just good people who lived out their faith by doing lots of philanthropic work for our university. We were always thrilled to run into Joe at the Penn State Creamery or anywhere on campus, and delighted years later when they renamed Pattee Library, the Paterno Library, in his and Sue's honor. Football games at Beaver Stadium and tailgate parties in *Paternoville* are happy lifelong memories. *Joe Pa* was a father figure to most of us Penn Staters, in addition to being our legendary coach. His death in January 2012, and the circumstances surrounding it, broke the hearts of those of us alumni who loved and respected him.

It was during our junior and senior years at Main Campus that I knew Eddy really loved me. Neither of us ever had any extra spending money, but when he had even a few extra dollars, he'd take me on a date to the Train Station Restaurant, and order us their famous French onion soup and salad combo, and give most of it to me. It was the, *you get the last potato chip or spoon of ice cream level of love*. He always took care of me, and wanted to make me happy. Other times I knew he really loved me was when he'd walk across the freezing tundra on campus in the dead of winter to see me, or walk back to his dorm in a 2:00 a.m. blizzard. I remember watching him leave my apartment in Penn Towers my senior year in the dead of winter, and calling Noelle out of bed to come to our balcony window to witness him writing *I love you* with his boots in two feet of snow. That just melted my heart, and I knew that Eddy was a keeper. There was never any pressure to change me, or guilt me into doing something I wasn't ready to do. I've said it before, and I'll say it again, "He's the most patient person I've ever known in my life."

The last trimester of my senior year at Penn State, I was assigned a 5th grade student teaching position back home at Regency Park Elementary School in Plum Boro. That was the grade I had requested and was grateful for the local suburban assignment. Eddy had graduated earlier, so we were both back home that spring. That May, Eddy asked me to fly with him, his brother Danny, and his dad, Rick, to New York City to meet his dad's extended family in Brooklyn. My parents gave me permission, so off we flew to The Big Apple!

CHAPTER 6

Newlyweds

*O*N Saturday afternoon, May 11, we decided to visit Central Park during our site seeing spree. Rick and Danny went off on their own as Eddy and I hopped on a horse drawn carriage. I started to feel a little nervous wondering if he was going to propose. We had been looking at engagement rings those past few months, so I was sort of hoping he would. I can't remember much of the scenery at Central Park, as it was such a blur, but it was a beautiful and warm spring day. People were everywhere in the park, roller skating, playing catch with baseballs and footballs, sitting and laying on picnic blankets, making out, walking hand in hand, and riding in carriages. Half way through our ride through Central Park, Eddy asked me to marry him. He must have been as nervous as me, because he was shaking as he pulled the ring box from his jacket pocket. It was all so romantic, a horse-drawn carriage ride through scenic Central Park on a sunny spring afternoon in New York. Of course, I said, "Yes!" After our carriage ride, we met up with Eddy's dad and brother. As we were walking down Fifth Avenue, who do we spot but two celebrities, Dustin Hoffman and Kate Jackson! Rick ran right up to them and introduced himself, as he was so star struck. "Dustin Hoffman! Rick Guarascio here. Nice to meet you!" Then, he told them we just got engaged. They were the first to congratulate us. We smiled shyly, walked away, and couldn't wait to tell our family and friends back home about our celebrity sighting.

Later that night, Eddy's Aunt Terri, Rick's sister, threw us an engagement party at their home in Forest Hills. I got to meet many of my future husband's extended Italian family, and show off my new diamond solitaire. When I called my parents that afternoon to announce my engagement, my parents were thrilled, because they loved Eddy almost as much as I did. Good things come in threes. I had graduated from Penn State with a Bachelor of Science degree in Elementary Education in May of 1978, got engaged, and was hired to teach first grade at St. Robert Bellarmine School in August. My life as an adult was just beginning, and my journey of faith would continue.

My first teaching position took me back to where it all started, St. Robert Bellarmine. My first class consisted of 42 first graders, and my starting salary was just $6,000 for the year. It's hard to believe that this is what a first year Catholic school teacher was paid back in 1978. Fortunately, I still lived at home that year and didn't have many bills. I was hired to teach all subjects, except Religion. The nun who taught 2nd grade, Sr. Erhard, would teach my class about our Catholic faith, since I wasn't certified. The better part of my day was spent teaching Reading and Math to three homogeneous groups of students . . . the Redbirds, Bluebirds, and Yellowbirds. Those were the days of the ditto machine which was always a hot commodity as teachers stood in line to use the only copy machine in the building. Dismissal was extremely challenging in the winter months as I helped 42 six years olds put on boots, scarves, mittens, gloves, coats, and hats. There were no teachers' aides or learning support teachers in the classrooms back then. It's a good thing I was an energetic 22 year old woman. Another advantage was having my baby sister Denise, and her best friend Chris Eckert, who were in eighth grade at St. Robert's at that time, come upstairs to help me decorate my classroom, hang up the students' papers on the bulletin boards, or help put on coats and boots at dismissal. Even still, it was physically exhausting. Weekends were spent doing lesson plans on my parents' dining room table. I worked lots and lots of overtime. I was just grateful to have a job my first year out of college and felt blessed that I was hired to teach in a Catholic School. Teaching wouldn't be just a job, it would become my vocation. Besides teaching the three r's, I would be teaching children about God along with good Christian values. When I asked my principal, Sister Janice, how I could get certified to teach religion, she directed me to a diocesan class available to Catholic school lay teachers. It was held over the summer months at Synod Hall on the Oakland Campus of the University of Pittsburgh. Since I was engaged to be married the summer of 1979, I decided to wait until the summer of 1980 to take the class.

Eddy and I were married on June 16, 1979 at St. Robert Bellarmine Church. It was a hot and humid summer day. It was so hot, and we were so hungry after not eating prior to the wedding that Eddy's brother, Danny, our best man, and my sister Sheila, our maid of honor, talked us into driving through the North Versailles Dairy Queen for chocolate milkshakes in route to the reception. Oddly enough, I was wearing a white high neck, long sleeve wedding gown. The nuns would have approved. In fairness, that's what most of the bridal salons were showing back then. Styles weren't nearly as sophisticated or as sexy as they are today. We had invited over 350 friends and family to our wedding, and most of them had attended. Our reception was held at Lakeview, a popular wedding venue in Greensburg, about a half an hour away from home located right on Route 30. Most of Eddy's New York relatives came down for the big event. Aunt Terri and Uncle Frank often commented that it was one of the most fun weddings they had ever attended. One of the comedic highlights of the night was when Rick's handsome cousin, Mario, danced with my widowed Grandmother Mary O'Grady. He threw her back over his arm at the end of the dance, and laid a big fat kiss on her lips. Everyone held their breath waiting for her reaction until she smiled, and we realized that Grandma actually liked it!

In attendance at our Marriage Mass were my 42 first graders and their families. The church was packed, and we had three priests, who taught us at Serra Catholic High School, concelebrate on the altar. Father Joseph Avella, a dear family friend and our Serra High School English teacher was the main celebrant. After seeing all those priests on the altar, Uncle Denny commented to his wife, Aunt Lynne, "Holy hell, Lynne, I think we're in for a High Mass." Translated . . . a High Mass meant a very long Mass. In any case, it was a beautiful ceremony. 1979 turned out to be a really great year, not just for us, but for the whole city of Pittsburgh. That year the Pittsburgh Steelers won the Super Bowl, the Pittsburgh Pirates won the World Series, Pittsburgh Pennsylvania was proclaimed *The City of Champions*, and Eddy and I were pronounced husband and wife.

We honeymooned in St. Thomas of the Virgin Islands, which seemed appropriate for obvious reasons. Pun intended. Eddy was extremely patient with me as I had to make the overnight mental adjustment from thinking that sex was a *mortal sin* to thinking sex is ok. The nuns and my mother did a real good job convincing me not to have sex before marriage. Poor Eddy. All I can say is . . . my young husband just might hold the world's record for sustaining the longest erection!

Newlyweds

We moved into a little apartment in East McKeesport not far from my school. Eddy got a job at Fisher Body, a General Motors Plant. We lived upstairs from an older Italian widow named Mary Jane. She was childless, a little nebby, and loved having us live upstairs. I think we brought some much needed excitement and diversion to her life. We loved coming home from work on Fridays, because she always had a homemade pizza cooking in her oven. We loved it even more when she made extra for us. It was delicious!

The next summer I enrolled in the diocesan class, *Communicating the Christian Message*, (CCM) in order to teach Religion at St. Robert's the following year. The class was filled with Catholic School lay teachers from all over the diocese of Pittsburgh who needed this certification to teach religion. Father Larry DiNardo was our instructor. He was a brilliant young priest in the Pittsburgh Diocese who was also a Canon Lawyer, specializing in Catholic Church Law. At that time, he was also secretary to Bishop Leonard of Pittsburgh. Father Larry was the first person to teach me about our Catholic Faith at an adult level. It was a wonderful and spiritual awakening as he clarified so many of our questions regarding our faith. At this writing, Father Larry's official title is Vicar for Canonical Services and Director of the Department of Canon and Civil Law Services for the Diocese of Pittsburgh. On July 4, 2014, it was announced in the Pittsburgh Catholic Newspaper by Bishop David Zubik that Father Larry DiNardo had been promoted to vicar general and general secretary of the diocese of Pittsburgh. The general secretary is similar to a chief operating officer, responsible for administrative matters for which the bishop has the ultimate authority. Little did we know back then how far our dear Father Larry would rise in the church hierarchy!

After graduating from CCM class, I invited Father Larry to dinner at our little apartment. I was so excited to make him and Eddy chicken marsala and fettuccini alfredo. I must have done something wrong though, because Father Larry spent the rest of the evening sick in our bathroom. He's never let me forget it. However, he must have forgiven me, because that same summer, he invited Eddy and me to the bishop's mansion on Fifth Avenue in Shadyside for dinner. The bishop wasn't there at the time, so we were treated to a tour of the thirty-nine room house. They had a five-car garage, breakfast nook, butler's pantry, wine cellar, and lots of fireplaces. It was filled with fine art and beautiful antiques. Their cook made us a filet mignon feast, and we ate in the elegant dining room. I wondered about all the important people who had ever dined in that room. We felt so honored to be eating there. Since then, the Pittsburgh diocese has sold that building, and the bishop no longer lives there.

That wasn't the only time Father Larry treated us like royalty. Father Larry has been a dear friend for the past thirty-some years. We were delighted to attend his sixtieth birthday party at his home parish of Holy Wisdom on the North Side of Pittsburgh. We were deeply touched when he sat with Eddy and me at dinner, virtual nobodies on the social registry, instead of sitting with the many church, university, and business dignitaries, such as the Donahues of Federated Investors, of Pittsburgh, who were also in attendance. Father Larry baptized our youngest daughter Tierney thirty-three years ago, officiated at our daughter Kaitlin's wedding at St. Paul Cathedral in Oakland, in June 2013, and married our daughter Bridget in May 2017 also at St. Paul Cathedral.

In May 2014, Father Larry DiNardo celebrated his 40th Anniversary of the Priesthood. Our family attended the Mass and reception at Holy Wisdom Church in his honor. It was such a momentous occasion for this dear, beloved priest who devoted his life's work in the service of God. We look forward to having him involved in our lives throughout our spiritual journey.

After three years of teaching first grade at St. Robert Bellarmine School from 1978–1981, I decided to spread my wings and teach in the public school system. Why did I decide to leave? I was only making $6,800 a year, and that isn't much when you're a newlywed trying to help your young husband save up for a down payment on a house in hopes of raising a family. When Father Scanlon refused my request for more money, I knew it was time to try to get a job at one of the local public school districts which were paying their teachers much more. I applied and went on interviews at East Allegheny School District, my home school district, and McKeesport Area School District. Neither district was hiring at the time, so I proceeded to substitute teach for both districts the next two years. Teaching different grades, K through 8, at two entirely different school districts, one suburban, and one urban proved to be quite challenging. The grass isn't always greener on the other side as the saying goes.

During this time, I was asked to serve on the Penn State McKeesport Campus Alumni Board. One of the members of the board, Mrs. Kathleen Easler, was well-connected to many important people in the Pittsburgh television and radio community. When I told her my substitute teaching tales of woe, she eagerly offered to help me find a job in the local entertainment and communications industry. When I expressed concern that I might not be qualified with a degree in education for that type of employment, she persisted in trying to help me anyway. Soon after, she told me that Mr. Eddie Edwards, news director at WPTT, Channel 22 in Monroeville, Pennsylvania, was looking to hire a weekend news anchor. She forwarded him my name, and then I immediately took my resume in person to drop it off at the station in Monroeville. A week later, I was called in for my first interview. After a series of interviews, which lasted approximately four months, I was hired to be the weekend and part-time news anchor at WPTT, Channel 22 in Pittsburgh. This was certainly something I never dreamed of whenever I thought about my future. This job had been an unexpected gift granted to me by a gracious God of surprises.

It was a wonderful and magical time in my life, and it came out of the blue. This was back in the early eighties, a time for padded shoulder fashions and big hair. I succumbed to both fashion trends. Eddy was almost as excited as me when I got the job. The first thing he did after I was hired was to buy me a few nice new outfits to wear on camera. My favorite piece was an electric blue blouse that tied into a bow at the neck. Patti Burns, a local Pittsburgh KDKA news anchor icon, had been my idol. She was Irish, had piecing blue eyes, and wore the color blue well on camera. Eddy gave me the new blue blouse with a note attached that said, "If you're going to work like Patti Burns, you might as well look as good as her. Good luck with your new job." Yikes, talk about pressure. I knew I'd never be as good as Patti Burns, but I sure tried. I worked the weekend shift from 4:00 p.m. until midnight, and a couple mornings during the week from 5:00 a.m. until 1:00 p.m. What a rude awakening it was when the alarm went off at 3:30 a.m. Typically, I reported five minute hourly news briefs highlighting international, national, state, and local news including sports and weather. We used the UPI and the AP machines, and an old fashioned typewriter. We also used a single camera in the studio, equipped with the much appreciated teleprompter. Technology wasn't nearly as sophisticated as it is today. This was the early 1980s, long before cell phones, laptops, or home computers.

Soon enough, I started being recognized out in public. It was such a kick when we would go shopping at Monroeville Mall and people would walk up and ask me for my autograph. I even started getting fan mail. One such fan letter alarmed our station manager, because the man who wrote it sounded like somewhat of a stalker. He had mailed the letter to my home address and expressed his admiration in a creepy sort of way. Shortly after that, Eddie Edwards, our news director, suggested that I not use my real name so people couldn't just look up my home address or phone number in the telephone book. Here we go again with another name issue in my story. First, Mr. Edwards said asked me what my maiden name was. When I told him Susan Soltis, he said, "Too much use of the letter s." Then he asked me if I had a middle name, and when I told him it was Patrice, he said, "That's it then, if it's ok with you, you'll be known on camera as Susan Patrice." So for the next three years, that was my professional news anchor name. In the meantime, I was still a substitute teacher, known as Mrs. Guarascio, for East Allegheny and McKeesport School Districts most weekdays.

In May of 1982, my Grandmother O'Grady passed away at age 66 after a seven month battle with lung cancer. Grandma had been a smoker for most of her adult life. She suffered terribly, and had to endure radiation and chemotherapy for months. She lost her beautiful thick head of hair. Grandma lived with my parents the last year of her life. My parents moved her into my old bedroom, so she would have home health care during her last days. My mother enlisted the aid of visiting nurses, and became Grandma's primary caregiver. Aunt Sheila flew up from Atlanta often to help with Grandma's care and support my mother. And Uncle Tim came to help daily. It was the three of them who shouldered most of the burden. The last week of her life, I went to visit Grandma after work as I usually did. She was barely conscious, but managed to talk to me. It was getting late in the evening, when out of the blue, she told me to go home to my husband and take care of my *little family*. In retrospect, I soon realized that she knew I was pregnant with my first child before I even knew. I hadn't even gone to the doctor's yet to confirm it. With her death on May 29, 1982, and my new pregnancy, I could see the eternal cycle of life more clearly than I had ever seen it before. We mourned and missed Grandma, as she was such an important part of our lives, but took great comfort in the fact that her pain and year long suffering were over. She had lived a good full life, and was now in the arms of the angels, and back with Grandpap O'Grady, the only man she had ever loved.

CHAPTER 7

Motherhood

SPEAKING of angels, about eight months later, I gave birth to Bridget Rose Guarascio, my first born child. Bridget was born on January 28, 1983. She was so beautiful with her big bright eyes and pouty perfect lips. I thought she was the most beautiful baby in the world. She was tiny, weighing in at 6 lbs. 8 oz. and was 20 inches long. She fit nicely in the palm of Eddy's hand. I was 26 years old, and so ready to be a mother. Eddy and I had taken pre-natal parent classes and Lamaze classes at McKeesport Hospital. I had embraced and enjoyed my pregnancy. I loved feeling the new life growing inside of me. Every feathery flutter I felt was such a thrill. Eddy loved placing his hands on my stomach to feel our baby kick and move. I loved playing my part in the process of creation, and was grateful to God for the privilege to share in the miracle of life. I felt my first strong connection to God the Father, our Creator. Prior to my pregnancy, my strongest God relationship had always been with Jesus. During my pregnancy, my relationship with our Blessed Mother grew even stronger. I had prayed for her intercession throughout my pregnancy for a happy and healthy baby. I prayed while laboring to give birth to Bridget, and thought about Mary having labor pains and birthing Jesus in an animal stable, moments before I was about to deliver my first baby at Forbes Regional Hospital.

The birth of Bridget began a whole new chapter of my life. God had blessed me with the gift of motherhood. She was such a good baby. She never cried, slept for long periods of time, and loved to nurse. Bridget loved breastfeeding so much that I nursed her the first nine months of her life. When she was awake, breastfeeding Bridget was a beautiful baby mother bonding experience. It seemed so natural, just like Mother Nature and God intended. I was in love with my baby girl. Having a baby for me was like falling in love again. I loved teaching her how to do things, snuggling her, holding her, feeding her, singing to her, taking her for walks outside, and letting her smell flowers for the first time. She was such a bright and happy baby. Everything felt like a miracle. I often wondered how I could love another child as much as I loved her.

Eddy's mother, Beverly, who babysat Bridget while I worked part-time, put my concerns to rest when she told me, "When you have other children, your love doesn't divide, it multiplies." Beverly's words of wisdom proved to be true, my love did multiply. Three years later, I gave birth to my precious new daughter, Kaitlin, and I thought my heart would burst with so much love. Kaitlin Leigh Guarascio was born on April 9, 1986 in Forbes Regional Hospital. She weighed in at 7 lbs. and 11 oz. and was 21 inches long. As Dr. Dan Natali, my obstetrician, delivered her, he proudly proclaimed, "How about a little lady?" She was and has always been a little lady indeed. Kaitlin popped out of me bright eyed and serious. She seemed to be looking around the delivery room taking it all in, and assessing the situation. My mother was the first person to tell me that she had been blessed with the gift of beauty. She had such delicately defined feminine features. Kaitlin's birth was especially miraculous as she was born full term and healthy after I'd had unexpected bleeding with her six months into the pregnancy. Once again, I prayed to our Blessed Mother for a healthy baby, and followed doctor's orders for complete bed rest until my ninth month. With the exception of a crooked little foot which was fixed with an orthopedic baby boot for the first six weeks of her life, Kaitlin was born perfectly healthy. Much to my chagrin, Kaitlin didn't take to nursing as easily or as happily as Bridget. As much as I wanted to continue, Kaitlin decided to wean herself from breast feeding around three months of age. Maybe she wasn't getting enough milk. She stubbornly seemed to prefer the ease of the bottle, and so I acquiesced to her wishes. The defining differences of my first two children were already beginning to become apparent.

Shortly before Kaitlin's birth, Eddy and I moved from our second apartment to our first house in North Huntingdon, in a development called Camelot. We lived in the last phase, on top of a hill, on a short street called Guinevere Drive, which ended in a cul-de-sac. It seemed like a nice, safe place to raise our children. From our backyard, we could look over the horizon, beyond Kerber's Dairy Farm, and see St. Agnes Church, our new parish, and the St. Agnes Elementary School parking lot where the students would play during outdoor recess. We knew then that was where we would send our children to school someday.

Another important event occurred shortly before Kaitlin's birth. The FCC, (Federal Communications Commission), came out with a ruling that independent television stations, such as WPGH, Channel 53, and WPTT, Channel 22, were no longer required by law to air so many minutes/hours of news each day. Soon after that ruling, our station manager called all of us reporters into his office to inform us that WPTT, Channel 22 would soon be phasing out our entire news department. Those full-time news reporters/anchors were set on making a career in broadcast journalism, and were very upset by these developments, because they would soon be out of a job. I, on the other hand, felt a sense of relief, as I was hoping to take some time off anyway to be a stay-at-home mother. It wasn't so glamorous getting up at 3:30 a.m., or working until midnight when I had a two year old and a baby on the way.

Eddie Edwards helped us network, and provided us with the names of the news directors at the three network stations in Pittsburgh. At that time, the network stations were KDKA, Channel 2, WTAE, Channel 4, and WIIC, Channel 11. He also recommended the Donna Belajac Agency if we were interested in doing commercials, modeling, or print work. I went on several interviews soon after we shut down. On February 16, 1987, I auditioned at KDKA for a new Saturday morning children's show, tentatively titled *Let's Read A Story*, but didn't get hired. That job went to Frank Cappelli. I did end up getting a few nice commercial jobs. My favorite was a *You've Got a Friend in Pennsylvania* tourism promo which we filmed in West Park on the North Side of Pittsburgh. The crew set up a merry-go-round and carnival booths as our background. I walked around the park with an actor husband and pretend six year old son on a beautiful summer day. At the end of the commercial, the camera pulled back and there appeared the words *You've Got a Friend in Pennsylvania* which was our state motto at the time. It was something I'd never done before, so I got a real kick out of it. If you blinked during the commercial, you probably missed me. My Uncle Tim drove me there and spent the whole day waiting and watching while we shot the commercial from morning until night. As I've said before, he has always been there to support me.

Shortly after our news department shut down ending my stint as a newscaster, I stopped substitute teaching as well, and devoted myself to being a full time, stay-at-home mother. Lucky for me, Eddy was able to support us financially.

When Bridget was three years old, I enrolled her in the Creative Adventures Preschool Program a couple afternoons a week. The pressure was already on us young mothers to give our children a head start. It was here that I met my dearest friends, Maggie Balmert and Ginny Merchant, who I've remained close to the past 35 years. We met as we were dropping off our daughters, Bridget, Ana, and Jessica, for their preschool class. We started talking and found comfort and friendship in our harried young mothers' lives. We were all former teachers who were taking time off from our careers to raise our young children. Fortunately, our husbands all had jobs that allowed us that privilege. On Sundays, we would even meet in our church's cry room with our babies in tow. All three of us belonged to St. Agnes Parish. Ginny's sister, Sally Caric, joined our group soon after, and so the four of us became known as the *Ya-Ya Sisters*, as our friendship mirrored the closeness of the characters in the now famous book, *The Divine Secrets of the Ya-Ya Sisterhood*. Later, we just shortened our nickname to the *Ya-Yas*. We've had so much fun over the years. We have partied together, did birthdays together, pregnancies together, First Holy Communions together, Confirmations together, high school graduations together, weddings together, funerals together, health scares together, picnicked together, educated our children together, went to church together, shopped together, played cards together, traveled together, vacationed together, and spent over 30 New Year's Eves together. We have such a beautiful bond that has lasted through the years. My friends have been one of my greatest blessings. When I was fighting non-Hodgkin's lymphoma, Sally drove me to a couple of my doctor's appointments at the UPMC McKeesport Cancer Center, Maggie came and planted my spring flowers, (I called her my Gardening Angel), and all three *Ya-Yas* sent dinners and prayed. They showered me with lots of love and moral support. Their husbands have been dear friends to Eddy and me as well. The eight of us share so many happy memories as we were raising our children and celebrating their milestones together. Our husbands seemed to get a kick out of our *Ya-Ya* friendship, starting back in the 1980s, as we shopped at the same stores, wore Liz Claiborne clothing with padded shoulders, watched television shows like *Thirtysomething* and *Knots Landing*, attended our favorite rock and roll concerts together, had big hair, and gave birth to all our babies.

Speaking of babies, my sweet baby daughter, Tierney Anne Guarascio, was born on May 3, 1989 at Forbes Regional Hospital. Tierney weighed in at 7 lbs. and 10 oz. and was 20 inches long. She was such a beauty with her big luminous blue eyes, and light brownish blond hair. Her Grandpap Ricky Guarascio was the first person to comment on what beautiful skin coloring she had. Tierney had so much hair that the nurses asked me if they could use her as a baby bath model to demonstrate how to bathe and wash a newborn's hair for the other new mothers on the floor. We were so proud of her when she cooed and smiled during the bath demonstration. She loved it. Tierney's birth made our circle of love complete. Tierney's big sisters, who were 6 and 3 years old at the time, were hoping and praying for a baby girl. They were thrilled with her birth and remember jumping up and down on their bed in celebration. Tierney too stubbornly preferred the bottle to breast feeding, so I reluctantly weaned her after 6 weeks of nursing her. Even after that, Tierney always preferred being held and cuddled. She would cry until you picked her up. Not thinking you could spoil a baby that young, I spent the first three years of her life with her in my arms or on my hip. Tierney was our littlest angel, all the way down to the crooked halo. I always used to say that she should have sprouted angel wings, because we spent the better part of her early years flying around taking her big sisters to all of their extracurricular activities. Looking back, I realize all that running around wasn't fair to Tierney. I should have eliminated some of those unnecessary activities, and spent more one-on-one time at home playing with my beautiful baby girl.

The first year after Tierney was born was happy and hectic. Eddy and I were finally outnumbered by our children. Eddy was in his second year of evening Law School at Duquesne University in Pittsburgh while working full time as a Purchasing Manager for Westinghouse at the Bettis Atomic Laboratory in West Mifflin, Pennsylvania. He had already earned his MBA degree at the University of Pittsburgh several years before starting law school. I tried to support him in every way. I missed him coming home after work at a decent time, but understood he was doing this to ensure a better financial future for our little family. We fell into living out very traditional gender roles during this time in our lives.

This might be a good place to interject how supportive both of our extended families were. For example, both Danny and Uncle Timmy were such good uncles to our children. Danny would take the girls out occasionally on fun dates, or come visit us just to play with them. He eventually married a pretty flight attendant and future teacher, named Marie Tomei, and they went on to have three wonderful children of their own, Michael, Danielle, and Anthony. Timmy never married, but continued to be an important and supportive presence in our daughters' lives while celebrating every holiday with us their entire childhood and into their adulthood.

Anyway, back to our early parenthood years. Money was tight back then. We were literally living paycheck to paycheck. There were lots of financial sacrifices we had to make on one income, and many nights I served pancakes or eggs for dinner. Usually, the girls would try and stay awake to see their daddy before they went to bed. Sometimes I felt like a single parent, but I never resented Eddy for it. I was extremely proud of my intelligent and hardworking husband. Everywhere we ventured, it was our three little girls and me, like the mother duck with her three little ducklings in tow. Grocery shopping was always a challenge with Tierney in the front seat, and Bridget and Kaitlin in the back of the shopping cart. Somebody was always trying to climb out and grab goodies. Even though we were on our own during the week days, Eddy was always there for us on the weekends. Saturday night was often date night for Eddy and me, and usually Beverly and Rick would offer to babysit. On Sundays, we took our three children to noon Mass, and then visited both of our extended families every Sunday afternoon and evening. We would go to Beverly and Rick's every Sunday after Mass for a 2:00 spaghetti dinner, and then join my parents, siblings, and extended family for a roast dinner at 5:00. This went on for many years, and became a bit hectic, as we were trying to make both sets of grandparents happy.

One evening during the summer of 1990, Eddy, our three young daughters, and I stopped to visit my Aunt Sheila and Uncle Bob who were back in Pittsburgh staying with my parents. We always enjoy seeing them when they are in town. When we left that particular night, it was dark and raining, so we made extra sure Bridget had on her seatbelt, and Kaitlin and Tierney were secured in their car seats. We only had a 15 minute drive to get back home to Camelot. As we drove down Route 30, in route to our home, another car in oncoming traffic, crossed over two lanes, and hit us head on! The driver had been drinking. He proceeded to throw his empty beer cans out his window. The first thing we did was check the back seat to make sure our daughters were ok. They were all still in their seats, except that Tierney's car seat was pushed out toward the edge of the back seat. All the girls were crying. It was such a loud, scary, sudden, and shocking impact. Eddy's foot was jammed up by the engine that jammed up under the dashboard. He knew instantly that his foot or ankle was broken. My ribs were hurting from the seatbelt, and I was having difficulty breathing. Before we could even get out of the car, the police and ambulance were there. This was before everyone had cell phones in their cars, so we didn't even know who called for help. Eddy and I were taken in two separate ambulances to Forbes Regional Hospital in Monroeville. I was worried about our young daughters, and kept asking where they were. Apparently, a sweet elderly couple, both with snow white hair, brought them in their car to the hospital. They stayed until my parents and aunt and uncle arrived at the hospital to care for our children. The elderly couple never gave the paramedics or us their names, and disappeared as quickly as they had arrived on the scene of the accident. Nobody in the emergency room got their names either. I've always wanted to thank them for helping us. Since then, I've often wondered whether they were heavenly angels sent down to help us in our time of need.

Eddy ended up needing an operation to put screws in his ankle to repair the damage from the accident. He was scheduled for surgery on Friday, September 14th at Forbes Regional Hospital. He was in so much bone pain after the surgery that his doctor decided to keep him overnight. Eddy's dad, Rick, called me around 9:00 Friday night to tell me not to worry, that he would bring Eddy home from the hospital the next day. He said that I had my hands full with the girls and that he'd be happy to help. I thanked him, told him I loved him, and hung up the phone. After getting the girls bathed and in bed, I went to bed early for a change, exhausted from worrying about Eddy, but relieved that Rick would get him in the morning.

The telephone rang at 9:00 a.m. Saturday morning. I had just woken up, and was surprised to hear my sister-in-law, Julie, on the other line. Julie was crying and saying, "My dad is dead, Rick is dead!" I couldn't believe my ears! I had just talked to him twelve hours earlier, and he seemed fine. This couldn't be true! I hung up the phone with Julie, and immediately called her back to make sure I wasn't dreaming. She confirmed the worst, and said she knew Rick was supposed to get Eddy, but that I'd have to make other arrangements. My sister Sheila, who lived down the street from us at the time, came up to my house to watch our kids, so I could drive to the hospital, pick up Eddy, and tell him about his beloved father. It felt like such a nightmare. I drove to the hospital in a trance, wondering how I was going to tell Eddy that his beloved father was dead. When I arrived on his hospital floor, a nun came by the nurses' desk and told me that she would help me go in and relay the horrible news. When I refused her offer, she said she would stand outside his room and pray for us.

It seemed so unfair. Rick Guarascio was only 57 years old, never was sick, and always seemed healthy. He had been blessed with one of those happy dispositions and was always easy going. Everyone enjoyed being around him, because he was so much fun. He adored our children, babysat them often, and was a wonderful family man. Sometimes when he and Beverly would come to babysit on a Saturday night, he would slip Eddy a $20.00 bill to help us out. The weekend before he passed away, he came over to our house with his brother Frank, and was trying to fix our broken down car. Every Sunday, he cooked delicious spaghetti and meatballs dinners for anyone who stopped by their home. What were we going to do without Rick? I loved him like a second father. We had spent so much time with Rick and Beverly ever since we started dating. The four of us used to go out on dates together before we had our children, and then they would babysit for us so that we could still go out on dates after we had our children. So many happy memories: the four of us dancing at the Sheraton Hotel when Beverly worked the front desk, trying to ride the bull at the Foggy Bottom Inn in West Mifflin while listening to the country music, and vacationing together in Ocean City, Maryland. Those were the good old days, and they were gone.

Rick used to drive Eddy and I back to Penn State Main Campus after trimester breaks when we were in college. At that time in the late 1970s, CB radios were popular, and so we gave each other CB names so we could talk to the truckers during our three hour drive to Penn State. He named me *Green Eyes*. His name was *Rico*. It was fun to choose a *handle*. I think he loved me like another daughter. He even helped me pick out furniture for our first apartment when Eddy was working second shift at the Fisher Body General Motors Plant. Rick was just always there for us. There would be such a void in our lives. Life would never be the same.

The next year Eddy threw himself into his job and law school. I kept busy with raising our three little girls and doing lots of volunteer work. Eddy graduated from Duquesne University School of Law on June 14, 1992 with his Juris Doctor degree in spite of working full time at Westinghouse, supporting a wife and three daughters, surviving a terrible car accident, mourning the death of his father, and doctoring with a newly diagnosed eye disease.

Eddy had been having trouble with his eyes for several years. He had been experiencing severe eye pain and his contact lenses would frequently either pop out or stay suctioned to his eyeballs. These symptoms were happening so often that they were interfering with the quality of his life. There were many visits to ophthalmologists, and later to Eye and Ear Hospital in Oakland, Pennsylvania. He was eventually diagnosed with keratoconus eye disease and was fit with special contact lenses. The symptoms worsened and made reading and studying for his law classes and upcoming bar exam almost unbearable. We even made trips to Eye and Ear Hospital Emergency Room in the middle of the night because he was in so much pain and literally was unable to remove the contact lenses suctioned to his eyeballs. He was becoming extremely discouraged about getting relief from the pain. He couldn't see without his contacts, as his vision was that bad. He wasn't a candidate for regular eyeglasses, because they don't help patients with keratoconus. Specially designed contact lenses actually adhere to the cornea, and press it in to round out the abnormal cone shaped corneas, which is what distorts the vision, and why it's called keratoconus. Eddy actually ended up taking the dreaded bar exam with one contact in and one contact out. Thank God he passed the exam and only had to take the test once.

Since keratoconus is a degenerative eye disease, we were afraid if we didn't get help soon, that he might eventually become blind. Eddy's eye problems actually got so bad that I started praying novenas to the Blessed Mother and St. Jude Thaddeus for their intercession and guidance. Help finally came from an unlikely place. One day, shortly after his graduation, I was talking on the phone to Noelle, and updating her on how everyone was doing. I told her about Eddy's eye disease, and our frustration in not finding a physician in Pittsburgh who could help alleviate his pain and correct his vision. Noelle lives in a suburb outside Philadelphia, and had recently heard about a specialist in Lancaster who had miraculous results in treating keratoconus patients. Eddy was skeptical and didn't even want to make the appointment, but eventually I talked him into going. As we were driving through the beautiful bucolic Pennsylvania countryside to Lancaster for the first time, Eddy turned to me in the car and said, "Let's be realistic. I'm hardly going to get the help I need out here in the boondocks. I should be going to a specialist or research hospital in New York City, not a small doctor's office in Lancaster, Pennsylvania." I immediately responded without thinking and said, "Eddy, God sent his Son to be born in a tiny manger in Bethlehem, not a castle in Rome. He sends help in the most unlikely of places." He managed a small smile, and we continued the four hour drive. That was the first of many yearly drives that Eddy and I would make to Dr. Nick Siviglia's office in Lancaster, Pennsylvania. Dr. Nick invented and patented specialized contact lenses specifically to treat keratoconus patients. He was able to fit Eddy with these special lenses, alleviate most of his pain, and give him the vision correction that he so desperately needed. The results were nothing short of miraculous, and again I credit the Blessed Mother and St. Jude for their intercession. Eddy was able to resume living his life mostly eye-pain free. Life was good.

The happiest years of my motherhood life were probably those years we lived in Camelot. Those were the simple days of bedtime stories, goodnight prayers, baby dolls, backyard picnics, swing sets, catching lightning bugs, running through the sprinkler, Brownies, chocolate chip cookies and milk. My favorite times were when we would all snuggle safely in our queen size bed and I would read to our daughters. I loved having all my little birdies in my love nest where they were safe and secure. From infants, to babies, to toddlers, to young children, the years quickly flew by. Soon enough, we became very busy little bees. Before long, we were leaving to go to preschool, kindergarten, Ken and Jean's Dance Studio for tap, ballet, and jazz, elementary school, Girl Scout meetings, parent-teacher conferences, piano lessons, recitals, basketball, softball, and soccer practice. Our mother-daughter bonding moments at our little house in the cul-de-sac, and all those extracurricular activities occupied most of our time. In retrospect, I wish we didn't run around as much, but that's what my generation of young mothers did back then.

Aside from parenting our three daughters, I also became very involved doing volunteer work at St. Agnes Church and in our Norwin Community. It started with me teaching C.C.D. religion classes, Vacation Bible School, working at the annual parish bazaar, later co-chairing the Children's Corner at the bazaar, serving as one of the church Girl Scout leaders, teaching the Children's Liturgy of the Word during Sunday Masses, and finally with Eddy and me being a Marriage Preparation Pre-Cana Sponsor Couple for engaged couples planning on getting married in the Catholic Church. I also joined, and later became president of, a local service organization called the North Huntingdon Woman's Club that conducted fundraisers to help the needy of our community. I had been abundantly blessed and felt compelled to help those in need. Most importantly, I felt obligated to share and live out my faith. My mother's words echoed in my ears, an often repeated quote by Rose Kennedy, "To whom much is given, much is expected." Years later, the Catholic Church would frequently remind us to share our time, talent, and treasure, and that's what I was trying to do in my own simple way.

During these early volunteer years, we had a warm and wonderful pastor at St. Agnes Church, named Father Tom Bertolina. He was a gentle and kindhearted grandfather figure with white hair and mustache. I once teased him when he came to a Christmas party at our home that he looked like Santa Claus without the beard. He loved the children, delighted in all our young families, and connected with just about every one of his parishioners. He administered to a very welcoming family-oriented parish. Two dear nuns, Sister Francis de Sales, and Sister Grace Herle, who were Sisters of the Saint Joseph Order, helped Father Tom minister to us, and taught us how to better minister to each other. We enjoyed our volunteer work under their supervision, and their wise counsel and company. Their guidance helped us deepen our faith. Father Tom invited some of us parishioners over the years to participate in the Greensburg diocesan Alpha classes. Alpha was an educational, adult spiritual enrichment, and evangelization program. After graduating from Alpha, we were commissioned to educate, evangelize, and spread the Christian faith. It was an honor to be an Alpha graduate. Several years after completing the classes, I was invited, along with my sister Sheila, to attend an Alpha reunion at St. Joseph Center in Greensburg. Bishop Anthony Bosco was the guest of honor, and my sister and I were especially honored when he sat at our table. Sheila, and her husband Dominick, had also been Alpha graduates, and were very active parishioners at St. Agnes Church. Dom was also one of the leaders in our parish Bible studies faith sharing groups. Members took turns going to different neighborhood houses to share ideas on faith, pray, snack, and socialize.

It was such a blessing having Sheila and Dom live down the street from Eddy and me when we lived in Camelot. My little sister Sheila and I grew up together, shared the same childhood memories, loved the same parents, adored our baby sister Denise, went to the same schools, and both married nice Italian boys from McKeesport. During the Camelot years, we raised our daughters together. Maura, their eldest daughter, was a blue eyed strawberry blond who looked like Dom, but had a lot of my personality traits. She was a year younger than Kaitlin. Meghan, the youngest of the *Original Five*, as the girls like to call themselves, looked like Sheila when she was born. Meghan was nonstop action, and five months younger than Tierney. Together, they were mischievous and referred to as *Double Trouble*. The first five cousins played together and loved to put on shows with lots of singing and dancing at their grandparents' house. Tierney and Meghan even formed a little singing duo and called themselves *Ishcabibal*. Their performances were strictly limited to loving relatives attending family functions. Mostly, their audiences consisted of their parents, grandparents, Aunt Denise, Uncle Eric, and their Great-uncle Timmy. Anyway, it was wonderful having cousins and friends live only a block away. We sent our daughters to the same school, belonged to the same church, socialized with some of the same people, and most important, we were family.

For several of these middle years, Sheila, who is an excellent registered nurse, conducted aerobics classes for our parishioners. (In later years, Sheila earned her Master Degree in Nursing and went on to work in nursing management and education ending up as a Nurse Navigator for Breast Cancer Patients at Excela Health System.) Exercise sessions were held in the entrance area of St. Agnes School. In her heyday, Sheila was a gorgeous green eyed blond bombshell, and was always preaching and teaching us how to stay healthy and physically fit. At that time, she was a cardiac nurse who practiced what she preached. Many nights after our husbands were home and we put our young daughters to bed, we would power walk for exercise up and down the many hills of Camelot. It was hard keeping up with her, but I tried. We would walk and talk about everything and anything. We were extremely close in those days, and talked to each other every day on the phone. We were a support system for each other in the days when our mother was climbing the corporate ladder of success and unavailable for many of our trivial problems. Mostly, we had lots of fun together. At Sheila's prompting, Dom put in a swimming pool which led to lots of fun in the sun. They continued hosting the family pool parties in the tradition of our parents.

After many years of going on vacations with our parents, Sheila and I started going on vacation together with our husbands and children. We nicknamed Dom, *Clark Griswald*, after the Chevy Chase character in the popular *Vacation* movies back then. Eventually, we called ourselves *The Griswalds* due to our many mishaps traveling with two families and all those little girls. There were so many *potty stops* that we often wondered whether we would ever make it to our beach destinations. Our favorite vacation spots in those days were Ocean City, Maryland, Bethany Beach and Dewey Beach, Delaware, Nags Head, North Carolina, and eventually, Myrtle Beach, South Carolina. Our last beach vacation with the Farinas was in The Outer Banks, North Carolina. Aside from our husbands and daughters, our parents joined us along with a new little strawberry blond guest of honor. Sheila had recently given birth to a son, the first grandson, after five granddaughters. They named him Dominic John Farina. He was the spitting image of Dom with Sheila's features. And for being the first boy in our family, he was like the second coming. My parents were over the moon! You can imagine our surprise as we were all so used to little girls.

Speaking of little girls, you might be wondering where our baby sister Denise was when all this excitement was going on. Well, let me fill you in on her exciting life during these times. Denise graduated from Penn State University with a BS degree in Business Marketing. During her senior year at Penn State she met her future husband, Eric Reppermund, a fellow Business Major. Denise and Eric have always been a striking couple. Denise is an aqua-eyed, Black Irish beauty, and Eric is a handsome blue-eyed blond haired German American. After a whirlwind courtship, Denise and Eric married in October of 1988, and began their job relocation journey. As newlyweds, Denise and Eric lived in Pittsburgh. Shortly after, they moved to the Chicago suburbs for several years. We loved flying to the Windy City to visit them.

On a side note, actually, there was one flight to Chicago that gave my parents and me the scare of our life. We flew into a thunderstorm and lightning hit our wing which then started leaking fluid. Our 747 jet began rocking, rolling, dipping, and dropping precipitously. It was terrifying. People started crying and praying aloud. Ever since that flight to Chicago, I've been afraid of flying. During one point in the tumultuous flight, my mom turned to my dad and said, "John, I think this is it!" I knew what she meant. She then proceeded to pray the rosary. The whole airplane started praying after the captain's announcement confirmed the lightning strike. When we finally landed, the entire plane of passengers erupted into applause. We made it!

Chicago did not disappoint. We loved strolling and shopping on Chicago's Magnificent Mile, the northern part of Michigan Avenue, where you find luxury shops and upscale retailers such as Saks Fifth Avenue, Bloomingdales, F.A.O. Schwartz toy store, historic hotels, and fabulous restaurants. Lake Shore Drive was another great site with its parks, volleyball games, beaches, and view of Lake Michigan. The city's amphibious Ducky Bus and Boat Tour in and along the Chicago River was quite an enjoyable experience. Denise and Eric loved showing off their newly adopted city by land and by sea. They took us to the best restaurants, and to the top of the Sears Tower, which was the tallest skyscraper in the United States at that time. I felt so queasy when we ventured out onto the sky deck and stood on the glass balcony which afforded us a panoramic view of the city. Our only regret was that we never got into see a taping of the Oprah Winfrey Show during our city tours. We did get to see that Denise and Eric were happy in their newly adopted city. Chicago proved to be a very friendly city, just like our hometown of Pittsburgh.

After Chicago, Denise and Eric moved to Memphis, Tennessee for a few years. Now our family had another new city to adopt. Memphis was a city rich in Southern culture and charm. Memphis is also considered the *Home of the Blues* and the *Birthplace of Rock 'N Roll*. Eddy's and my favorite popular attractions of our Memphis trips include visits to *Graceland*, the home of Elvis Presley, and the historic Peabody Hotel where the famous Peabody Ducks make their daily promenade to and from the Grand Lobby at exactly 11:00 a.m. and 5:00 p.m. ever since 1933. We also enjoyed our visit to B.B. Kings Blues Club on world famous Beale Street where we ate the best barbeque ribs in the world. Beale Street is famous for its nightclubs, pubs, cafes, theaters, dancing, music, and the blues. Here we just sat back and enjoyed the best of Memphis music. On a more somber note, we drove to the historic Lorraine Hotel, now known as the National Civil Rights Museum, the site of the assassination of Dr. Martin Luther King Jr. A single wreath hung on the banister of the balcony in front of the place where he was killed. The atmosphere there was sad, eerie, and chilling.

Another happier memory was when we drove from Memphis to the Gambling Casinos in Tunica, Mississippi. None of us won any money, but we had a great day just the same. It was the first time I had ever been to a casino.

There were so many great places to visit in Memphis, but my favorite Memphis Memory was when we all drove down to Memphis to celebrate the Thanksgiving holiday at Denise and Eric's house. My parents, Sheila and Dom, Eddy, and I and all our children were welcomed with open arms. Denise and Eric and their beloved dog, Sydney, were the perfect hosts. They made us feel right at home. We women took turns making the side dishes in Denise's kitchen while our mother supervised the turkey and the rest of us. Eric said a beautiful grace before our Thanksgiving dinner, and we all felt blessed and just happy to be together. Denise had even bought all five nieces their own turkey stuffed animals and had them lined up on their living room mantle before her gift giving. Denise has always been a loving and generous aunt, great gift giver, and was ready and hoping to become a loving mother.

Denise and Eric were married over ten years and still childless. We all knew they wanted children, and so we started praying that they would be blessed with a baby. Six years of trying to get pregnant and still no baby. We put their names on various church prayers lists. Denise and Eric prayed at their nondenominational Christian Church, and we kept praying at our Catholic Churches, but still there was no baby. My mother started praying to St. Anne, the Blessed Mother's Mother, and St. Jude for their intercession. Sheila and I prayed to St. Gerard, the patron saint of pregnant women, and the Blessed Mother as well. We were all storming heaven with prayers. Denise thought that maybe the stress of her job and living away from family might be impeding her chances of getting pregnant, so she and Eric moved back home in 1998. Her company allowed her to work remotely, and Eric eventually got a new and better job with Snavely Forest Products. They bought a beautiful home in Murrysville, a wealthy rural and scenic suburb of Pittsburgh, where they were about a half an hour away from both their extended families. And lo and behold, Denise finally became pregnant after all of that prayer!

God had answered our many prayers all in his perfect timing. Rachel Lynn Reppermund was born September 20, 2000. She was a healthy, beautiful, black haired, blue eyed millennium miracle baby. Rachel's birth was such a joyous event in our family history. After the floodgates opened, Denise quickly became pregnant again, and gave birth to a healthy blond-haired blue-eyed baby boy, named Luke Eric Reppermund, on September 29, 2002. My parents always said that when they counted their many blessings, Rachel and Luke were their bonuses. Our circle of love was growing, and so was my faith in God for answering our prayers after six long years of praying. Patience is truly trusting in God's perfect timing as we continue on our journey of faith.

The best part of having Denise and Eric back in the Burgh was simply just having them back in our lives. Denise and Eric both ended up working in different capacities in the building manufacturing business. Denise is a manufacturer's representative and sells house wrap to the 84 Lumber stores and similar businesses. Eric represents manufacturers at the corporate level, and has become successful since going into the business for himself. Denise was fortunate to have been able to be a stay-at-home mother until 2009. That's when she started her own manufacturing representative business. The nicest perk of Denise's job is that it has allowed her to work remotely from home. This arrangement has been beneficial while raising their children, since Denise was home in the mornings to get Rachel and Luke off to school, and was there in the afternoons when they returned. It's been a joy to watch Rachel and Luke grow up. In later years, it's been fun cheering them on at Rachel's high school volleyball games, and Luke's high school football, baseball, and basketball games. Denise and Eric have created a happy home for their children. In 2013, they had an Olympic size swimming pool installed in their backyard along with adding a full size sand volleyball court in 2016. Their friends and family have enjoyed many fun-filled afternoons and evenings playing there. Denise and Eric are the Fun Family! They take their kids on tropical vacations over winter break, making Rachel and Luke more well-traveled than most adults. In the summers, the four of them frequently golf together at Greensburg Country Club. Denise told me that some of her favorite memories of our dad are those where they're playing golf together. Denise has turned out to be a great golfer herself who seems to have inherited some of our dad's driving skills, hitting those golf balls straight down the fairway!

Besides being great parents, Denise and Eric are good Christians who practice their faith. Both of them have taught the youth in their church at Cornerstone Ministries in Murrysville over the years. In addition, Denise leads a multi-denominational Bible study group in her home. Once every two weeks, Denise and her Bible study group travel to the *Sojourner House*, a women's shelter in Pittsburgh, to minister to the women there who are new mothers and recovering drug and alcohol addicts. Denise has relayed to me touching stories of how hungry these women are for the hope and inspiration brought to them in scripture, and how rewarding it is when the women express their gratitude asking when their group will return. But I'm getting ahead of myself here, so back to the 1990s.

After Eddy graduated from Duquesne Law School, we started looking for a larger house. We knew we were outgrowing the house in Camelot, and were hoping to find one with a bigger kitchen, more bedrooms, bathrooms, and a family room. We didn't think about building a new house until we met Bob Shuster, a local developer who was just beginning to build beautiful subdivisions on the vast amounts of farmland available in North Huntingdon Township. He and his wife Sally, were extremely helpful in enabling us to build our dream house, and for that

I'll always be grateful. After touring many of Bob's model homes with our three little daughters in tow, we eventually came up with an affordable plan. So, on April 30, 1994, our little family moved into our new home, a Shuster Home, a quality home built with only the best materials. It's been a wonderful home in which to raise our children, and hopefully, someday welcome grandchildren.

I learned another important faith lesson during those years of my young motherhood. God doesn't always answer our prayers just because we pray really hard for something. Case in point . . . Eddy and I had always dreamed of having a large family. I hoped we would have five children. I figured I'd have three girls first like my mother and grandmother before me. Then, I thought we'd have a couple boys. So when Tierney was three years old, we started trying to have another baby. Long story short, we tried to get pregnant for a couple years. I prayed that I'd have another baby, but it just wasn't meant to be. I learned a valuable life's lesson. I wasn't in control. God was, and he had other plans for me. We finally stopped trying to conceive after I woke up one morning and our bed was covered in blood and liver-like tissues, after I'd missed a couple periods. It was heartbreaking when I realized that chapter in the book of my life was being closed. I had been so excited thinking I was finally pregnant, and so sad when I miscarried. I wasn't that far along, so I didn't need a D & C. Since I was in my late thirties, I took it as a sign that it wasn't in God's plan for us. So, I stopped praying for another baby, and instead prayed in thanksgiving for the three little miracles we did have. I've learned that sometimes when God doesn't answer our prayers the way we want him to, his answer is just no. God knows and gives us what is best for us.

CHAPTER 8

Middle Years

THE years flew by and before I knew it, I was back to working outside the home and teaching again at Queen of Angels Regional Catholic School, formerly known as St. Agnes Elementary. As dictated by the bishop, our regional Catholic school was formed after several diocesan Catholic elementary school closures and consolidations. Tierney was in kindergarten the year I returned to teaching. Sister Grace Hertzog, our principal at Queen of Angels School needed a substitute for Sister Patty, whose parents were gravely ill. Sister Patty had to travel to Iowa to care for them, and would need a substitute for the remainder of the school year. Sister Grace called and asked me if I would help and that's how it all started. It felt good to be back in the classroom. I always feel like I'm in my element there. After finishing out that school year, I enjoyed the summer with my husband and young daughters.

In August of 1996, Sister Grace called me again to tell me that a principal friend of hers in the diocese of Greensburg needed a part time kindergarten teacher to teach half days at Holy Cross Elementary School in Youngwood, Pennsylvania. I wasn't interested in teaching kindergarten that school year, as Tierney would only be in first grade and I wanted to get her off to a good start. I wanted to be there to get my daughters off to school in the morning, and be there in the afternoon when they got off the bus. I didn't want to give up my volunteer work as a homeroom mother or Project Self-Esteem facilitator at Queen of Angels. I was still doing lots of volunteer work that I enjoyed for the church and our community, and I didn't want to spread myself too thin. Sister Grace just asked me to meet with the Holy Cross principal and see what she had to say.

Immediately after my conversation with Sister Grace, I received a phone call from Mrs. Sally Hurrianko, the Holy Cross Principal, who invited me to come to the school and discuss my possible employment. As soon as we met, we instantly clicked and took a liking to one another. Sally was a gracious and sweet lady who had three grown daughters of her own. She radiated goodness. She was dedicated to Catholic school education and seemed intent on hiring me. After explaining the teaching position, the job expectations, the pitiful salary, the culture at Holy Cross, the need for a good teacher to carry on the Catholic school legacy, and showing me the kindergarten classroom, I told Sally that I would think about it over the weekend and get back to her the next week. We were going out of town that weekend and not coming home until Monday. When we returned from our weekend getaway, and got our mail out of our mailbox, I noticed an envelope with Holy Cross School on the return address. After opening the envelope, I read the enclosed letter that was addressed to the entire faculty and staff of Holy Cross School. Basically, it was an announcement welcoming Mrs. Susie Guarascio as the new Holy Cross kindergarten teacher! I hadn't even said yes, or accepted the job! I was going to think about it. The envelope also included a welcome back to school letter to the entire school faculty and staff. After my initial shock and surprise, I finally laughed and said to Eddy, "Well, I guess I'm teaching kindergarten at Holy Cross School this year." Actually, I taught at Holy Cross School for the next several years. What's that old saying? *Man makes plans, and God laughs.* Or is it this one? *God puts us where we're meant to be.*

My years at Holy Cross School were very happy and fulfilling years. I grew both professionally and spiritually. After teaching kindergarten, I was assigned to teach Third Grade. I was finally allowed to teach religion after all those years, and I taught it with a passion. Several times when teaching my students about God and trying to explain to them how much he loves us, how much Jesus sacrificed for us, and how we should strive to give this love back to him and others, I think that I experienced the gift of the Holy Spirit. It felt like an adrenalin rush, a physical/spiritual tingling sensation throughout my body. That feeling only happened a few times that year while I was teaching religion in third grade. I'll always remember that wonderful physical feeling. Maybe it was the Spirit of God connecting with my spirit, or telling my soul that he was pleased with me. I don't know how else to explain it. I know it sounds strange, but it happened.

In any case, when I left Holy Cross School to take a teaching position for the Norwin School District my departure was bittersweet. I would miss daily school prayer, Friday and Holy Day Masses, teaching children about our Catholic faith, and obviously, the students and their families in general. I would also miss some of the dear friends I'd made at Holy Cross, especially my fellow dedicated teachers, and our beloved school secretary. I had thoroughly enjoyed teaching and working with the wonderful women who shared my Catholic faith, but I was looking forward to new challenges and opportunities teaching in the Norwin School District.

In the meantime, my daughters were growing up. They were excelling academically, in sports, and in the arts. Bridget and Kaitlin both were elected as Queen of Angels Student Council President when they were in the eighth grade. Tierney was developing a beautiful singing voice. They all danced for many years taking tap, jazz, and ballet at Ken and Jean's Dance Studio, and continued to play the piano. In addition, they all landed great acting parts in the Queen of Angels school plays. All three girls played soccer and basketball in the local Norwin community recreation league and in our diocesan church league. At different times, Eddy coached Bridget's, Kaitlin's, and Tierney's basketball team in the St. Agnes Church diocesan league. Basketball always was and still is his great sports passion. He still plays basketball three times a week to this day. Every time I ask him when he is going to grow up and put away his basketball, he says, "Never!"

Anyway, after Queen of Angels Regional Catholic School, Eddy and I sent our daughters to Greensburg Central Catholic High School, following in the Catholic school tradition of both of our families. The tuition costs of educating our children in the Catholic School System were quickly rising and becoming less and less affordable to many middle and working class families. Most parents who want to afford their children a faith filled education have to make substantial monetary sacrifices to do so. Unfortunately, many of our Catholic schools have morphed into private schools affordable for only the well to do. As the years have gone by, I've sadly witnessed our elementary schools shut down in city after city, town after town, due to lack of funds and enrollment. St. Robert Bellarmine School and Holy Cross School are sadly no longer in existence. I fear it's only a matter of time before they're all gone. It seems to me that many parish priests no longer want the financial burden of supporting elementary or secondary schools, and the diocesan bishops are relieved, to consolidate, and then close those schools, as well. Fortunately, we have many excellent public schools in our country. Little did we know of the jewel in our own backyard, known as the Norwin Public School District, until I was hired there.

Norwin School District hired me the summer of 1999 to teach Third Grade in Pennsylvania Avenue School in Irwin. Eddy also made a major career move that spring. After working for 20 years for Westinghouse at the Bettis Atomic Plant, Eddy took an exciting new job at Medrad, an up and coming medical device company, where he would be able to utilize both his MBA and Law Degree along with his purchasing experience at Westinghouse. Eddy's job afforded him the unique opportunity to travel to many of the most beautiful cities in Europe. He has also traveled to Japan, Brazil, and Australia for his work. We were both starting new chapters in our professional lives.

After years of teaching for both the Pittsburgh and Greensburg Diocese, I would be employed as a teacher in the Pennsylvania Public School System for the Norwin School District. My second assignment after Pennsylvania Avenue School was a fifth grade position at Stewartsville Elementary. I absolutely loved teaching fifth grade, and loved the fellow teachers I would be working with at that building. The students and parents at Stewartsville were wonderful as well. It was a joy to get up and go to work. I really felt like I was making a difference. Norwin has a great mentoring program for its new teachers to indoctrinate you into their culture. Norwin School District is ranked highly academically in Westmoreland County, Pennsylvania. Its administration promotes character education and good Christian values. After attending and teaching in Catholic schools, it was enlightening to discover the excellent education system in our Pennsylvania Public Schools. I have grown leaps and bounds in my career thanks to the professional development provided to me by the Norwin School District. Norwin also provides technological training for its teachers, and encourages us to earn additional graduate level degrees. I earned my Master of Education Degree in Curriculum and Instruction from Gannon University in 2007 while teaching at Hillcrest Intermediate School in Norwin. When people would ask me where I worked, I was always proud to say, "I'm a Norwin School District teacher." The Norwin teachers and staff have been like a second family to me, supporting me in good times and in bad.

The first time I had a family health crisis involving one of my daughters was when I was teaching at Stewartsville Elementary. It was January

2001, and I had just come home after an exhausting day at work, and had a bad headache. It was around 5:00 p.m. and I just started getting dinner ready when the telephone rang. The athletic trainer at Greensburg Central Catholic High School called to tell me that Kaitlin was having severe chest and back pains while practicing with the GCC girls' basketball team. He explained that it was so bad that they were going to take her to Westmoreland Hospital Emergency Room and that I should meet them there. I quickly called Eddy, and then drove directly to the hospital.

The emergency room doctors ran a series of chest x-rays and tests, and then informed us that Kaitlin had a spontaneous pneumothorax, meaning that 10 percent of her right lung had collapsed causing the severe pain. The doctor explained that this was more common in runners and tall, thin, male teenage athletes. Kaitlin certainly didn't fit that mold, however, she was tall, thin, and playing a strenuous sport when it happened. Anyway, they sent us home and told her to rest until the lung re-inflated itself which typically takes two to three days. We were also told that there was a 50 percent chance of a reoccurrence. That was a Monday, so I kept her home from school the rest of the week. Friday night, Kaitlin was invited to go to the boys' basketball game with her friend, Ashley. She had been housebound for four days and was anxious to get back out with her friends. She went to the game, against my wishes, and then out to eat at Eat'n Park Restaurant in Greensburg.

Eddy and I were home that evening when the phone rang. It was Yvonne, Ashley's mother, calling to tell us that she just rushed Kaitlin to the Westmoreland Hospital Emergency Room, because her lung apparently collapsed again while they were eating at Eat 'N Park. Again, Kaitlin had stabbing chest pain and difficulty breathing. This was the second time in one week. After another physical exam, chest x-rays, electrocardiogram, and more blood tests, the doctors told us this time 25 percent of her right lung collapsed and she was in intense pain. It hurt her to breathe. They admitted Kaitlin to the hospital and told Eddy and me that the cardiothoracic surgeon wanted to operate on her. The doctor explained that Kaitlin's lung would most likely collapse again with Kaitlin losing more lung function each time unless they operated on her. We were given two options. With option 1, the surgeon wanted to insert a chest tube through Kaitlin's side, into her right lung and re-inflate it. Option 2 was more invasive than open heart surgery where the surgeon would open up her chest, completely deflate then re-inflate her lung, and then staple it to her chest cavity using talcum powder. That sounded so scary. The doctor did mention another option, but he did not recommend it. He said we could wait for the lung to regenerate and re-inflate on its own, and then hope and pray it never collapses again, which was very unlikely. After two spontaneous pneumothoraxes in one week, chances of a recurrence were now up to 60 percent. We had a big decision to make.

Kaitlin stayed in the hospital for three days until her lung re-inflated to 90 percent capacity. I slept on a cot next to her hospital bed during that time listening to her take every breath while she was on oxygen and morphine. I was so afraid that she would stop breathing during the night. No wonder the first morning after she was admitted I literally noticed my first gray hairs. After much prayer, we told the doctor that we were going to try and let Kaitlin's lung heal naturally one last time. I don't think he expected that decision. If we were going to do that, the doctor said that Kaitlin would have to stay home from school and rest at home with absolutely no sports, or physical, or strenuous activity for at least six weeks. She also wasn't allowed to lift anything heavier than a couple pounds. Basically, I would have to keep her in a protected bubble for that time. Kaitlin agreed that we would try this natural healing resting option. If nature didn't take its course, then we would schedule the operation. Kaitlin had been a very active sophomore in high school, playing fall varsity soccer, and junior varsity basketball. She was also taking tough classes, especially advanced chemistry. We knew this wasn't going to be easy.

I called Sister Agnes, Attendance Director, and Father Dan Blout, Principal at Greensburg Central Catholic to explain our situation. They were extremely compassionate and understanding. Father Dan asked all Kaitlin's teachers to send their lesson plans and assignments to the office, where I picked them up, along with all of her textbooks, so Kaitlin could keep up with her classes from home. This was before everything was done on computers. Nowadays, teachers would have emailed their assignment to us. I'll never forget Sister Mary Helen giving Kaitlin an oral advanced chemistry quiz over the telephone. The faculty and staff went above and beyond to accommodate our situation. Kaitlin dutifully stayed at home for six weeks, read her books, did her assignments, took the tests, and kept up her grades. She was and has always been an honor student. She continued to follow doctor's orders, rested, and didn't overexert herself.

During those six weeks, I prayed for Kaitlin's lung healing, so that she would be spared that serious invasive operation. I continuously prayed the rosary for Kaitlin, along with novenas to the Blessed Mother and St. Jude. Also during those six weeks, I met a woman who owned an embroidery shop in Greensburg who gave me a novena to Saint Theresa the Little Flower. I figured I'd pray to St. Theresa as well, especially since she was a young girl saint, twenty-four years old when she died.

That woman, Debbie Rua, had assembled a small shrine to St. Theresa in her Greensburg shop called *Embroidery Express*. As a member of our GCC Girls' Basketball Parent Club, my job was to get the gifts for the senior girls to present to them during Senior Night that February. Their gifts were fleece throws embroidered with their names and a basketball. Ray and Debbie Rua embroidered gifts for many of the local high school sports teams. Anyway, when I asked Debbie why such a devotion to Saint Theresa, she told me and allows me to share her story.

Debbie was 38 years old when her mentally retarded sister passed away at the age of 40. Her sister had been getting treatment for rheumatoid arthritis, when she should have been getting chemo for cancer. It was a very sad ending to a very sad life. Debbie became bitter and blamed God. She quit going to Mass and quit receiving the sacraments for many years. This was the same woman who took herself to church as a child, and never made her First Holy Communion until fifth grade after her kind hearted step-dad realized she had missed it when she was supposed to have made it in second grade like most other young Catholics. Apparently, her mother was too consumed with her mentally disabled sister to even notice.

Fast forward, years later, to the 100th anniversary of the death of Saint Theresa, the Little Flower . . . Debbie's friends, Carol Gaffey, who owned a dress shop in Greensburg, and two others, Becky and Cindy, invited her to join them on their trip to Europe to visit the St. Theresa Shrine in Lisieux, France, a popular pilgrimage site. Debbie told me that she had never even heard of St. Theresa before that, but agreed to go along with her friends as she loved to travel, and since it was right before the Christmas season, she felt it might be a much needed break from their embroidery business's busiest and most stressful time of year. The four friends went to Mass in the small church that Saint Theresa attended during her time in the convent. Debbie didn't go to Communion, because she hadn't been to Confession. After Mass, her friend Cindy said that she would go back into church with her, so she could make her confession, and then go to communion at the next Mass. There were many Masses, one after another, at this pilgrimage site. So after many years of being estranged from church and the sacraments, Debbie went to confession and then received Holy Communion.

Middle Years

When they came outside the church, it was a rainy and cloudy day, but the friends wanted to get a picture of themselves nonetheless. Carol Gaffey took a photo of Debbie and Cindy in front of the shrine. When she had the film developed and enlarged the photo to give to her friends as gifts, she noticed something very unusual. There were rays of light directly above Debbie's head, even though there was no visible sunshine that rainy day in Lisieux. Perhaps these were rays of God's Grace being showered down upon Debbie after her return to him. Maybe Saint Theresa's intercession helped Debbie find her way back to Jesus. When Debbie finished telling me her story, I then understood her devotion to Saint Theresa. After that story, I was compelled to pray to Saint Theresa the Little Flower for her intervention with Kaitlin's lung healing as well. I did pray the novena that Debbie Rua had given to me in her embroidery shop that cold winter day. I'm happy to report that we did get blessed with our own little miracle. Kaitlin went back to school the second week in March, and never had another lung problem. That summer, she was able to resume playing basketball and soccer. Nobody could believe it, especially the doctors! Well, I could believe it. After all that prayer, we had the intercession of the Blessed Mother, Saint Jude, and now Saint Theresa on our team. Talk about a trifecta!

So we went back to cheering on our daughters at their basketball and soccer games. At this time, Bridget had graduated from Greensburg Central, and was a freshman playing on the girls' basketball team at Washington and Jefferson College where she was majoring in political science in hopes of going on to law school. Kaitlin continued with basketball and soccer during her junior and senior years at Greensburg Central Catholic, and Tierney played those same sports in the Norwin community leagues while an eighth grader at Queen of Angels. Tierney then followed suit and attended Greensburg Central where she played soccer, and earned leading singing roles in her high school spring musicals, *Footloose* and *Oklahoma*. We logged many miles on our odometers traveling to practices, and to game after game, year after year. Dinners were on the fly as we raced home from work to either drive daughters to and from practice, or travel to their home and away games. In spite of the hectic schedule, we had fun, and enjoyed watching our daughters play sports that they loved while meeting and socializing with families doing the same thing as us.

There were lots of parties during these times. There were celebratory parties after we won games or made the playoffs, elaborate sweet sixteen parties, themed birthday parties, and our teenage children's high school graduation parties. Pool parties down the street at Maggie and David's house lasted until the wee hours of the morning. We lounged around their pool chatting, drinking, and eating while *Earth, Wind, and Fire* CDs played over and over in the background on those hot summer days and nights. Our other friends, Jon and Mary Kay, even started having February break the winter blues parties. Their children, Jenna and Jonathan, were in the same grades as Kaitlin and Tierney. Their parties became famous and fun annual events on our North Huntingdon community calendar.

CHAPTER 9

The New Millennium

ASIDE from our daughters' high school graduation parties, the most exciting party we've hosted at our house has to be the Turn of the Century, Happy New Year 2000 Millennium Party. We must have had over a hundred people in our home to usher in the new century. We invited our family, friends, neighbors, and fellow parishioners. Grandparents, teenagers, and children were also included. There were people of all ages and generations. Our house was bursting at the seams. Everyone was joking about whether our computers would crash at midnight, or how many gallons of bottled water they had stashed in their cellars just in case all the systems really did crash! It was designated Y2K, and the massive computer glitch was supposed to happen and bring civilization to its knees on the first day of 2000! We all watched the television and chanted the New Year's Eve Countdown as the Time Square New Year's ball descended. It was a night of celebration exploding at midnight with champagne bubbly, balloons, and confetti. The Balmert children had started a New Year's Eve tradition of making their own homemade confetti by cutting up tiny pieces of colored construction paper that they generously shared with all the other kiddos, which everyone then threw all over the house at midnight transforming it into a kaleidoscope of color. We didn't mind, because everyone was having such fun, and we were welcoming a new century. Incidentally, it seemed like it took years to clean up all that colored confetti that had fallen behind furniture, under the sofa and loveseat, and in between couch cushions. And the years just kept flying faster and faster.

I had been teaching Third Grade at the now-closed Pennsylvania Avenue School in Irwin the first year of the millennium. My students and I had been trying to think of a unique way to commemorate the new millennium, and we finally decided what to do at the end of the school year. In June of the year 2000, my Third Grade students and I assembled a collection of memorable items to include in a time capsule. We gathered items such as newspapers, yearbooks, music CDs, and personal mementos, and placed them inside a waterproof time capsule. We dug a deep hole outside in the school front lawn, where we place a plaque indicating that the time capsule could be opened in 15 years. At that time, 15 years seemed so far away.

Little did I know at that time, that 15 years later, a 24 year old former third grade student, named Evan, who was working for Norwin School District, would seek me out in my fifth grade classroom at Hillcrest Intermediate, and ask me whether and when we were going to open our time capsule. That meeting seemed to come out of the blue, and felt a little like life coming full circle again. Meanwhile, what we both didn't know was that the school district had already been making plans to open the time capsule which now was buried on the property of the Golden Heights Personal Care Home. Norwin School District had sold the Pennsylvania Avenue School during its rebuilding and renovating years to developers building that Senior Care Facility. So, administrators from Norwin School District and Golden Heights Personal Care Center were working together to plan a ceremony to open the time capsule that we had buried to commemorate the millennium. That came as such an unexpected surprise, and I was to be a big part of it. A lot of change occurred between 2000 and 2015, so I'll continue my story in chronological order before getting to the time capsule opening in 2015. Note to self . . . life is a series of continual changes, and the new millennium would bring many more.

My mom retired from the bank in 2000, after an illustrious career, and my sisters and our families were invited to many, too many, ha-ha, retirement parties in her honor. Mom had quite a career and served on many boards, so lots of different groups wanted to honor her. Daddy had retired from Port Authority Transit in 1996 without any fanfare, and spent most of his time perfecting his golf game. I was grateful to still have them, and that they were in good health. I thanked God for them, and prayed for their continued good health daily. Our family had much to be grateful for that year. We were especially thankful for the joyous birth of Denise and Eric's millennium baby, Rachel Lynn.

The New Millennium

The new millennium seemed off to a good start. Unfortunately, my optimism didn't last long. It came to a crashing halt on September 11, 2001, when terrorist hijackers crashed two planes into the World Trade Center in New York City. It was the end of an age of innocence. Most people remember where they were and what they were doing that infamous blue-skied sunny September morning. I was teaching fifth grade at Stewartsville Elementary School in the Norwin School District. During my prep period that morning, I went downstairs to the main office to check my mailbox and copy. As I walked into the office, I saw our school secretary and principal watching something intently on the television in the corner of the room. They had looks of horror on their faces, and I knew instantly that something was very wrong. When I asked them what happened, they both turned and told me that our country was being attacked! For the next 30 minutes, we watched the tragic events unfold in front of our eyes. Skyscrapers were crumbling in flames and falling down. People were jumping out of windows to their death. We couldn't believe our eyes! New York City, The Pentagon in Washington, DC, and then a small rural town 65 miles southeast of Pittsburgh called Shanksville, in Somerset County . . . all disasters! It was getting too close for comfort. When would it stop?! Where would they strike next?! Then, the parent phone calls started, and one by one, our students were called over the intercom system to report to the office for an early dismissal. If our country was going to war, and we didn't know where else they were going to attack, our parents wanted their children with them. Families wanted to be together. Businesses around the United States were sending their employees home. At the beginning of that school day, I had a full classroom of students, but by the end of the day, only a few of my students were still left. I couldn't go home. I had to stay with them. When my students started asking me questions about what was wrong, and why almost everyone else was going home, I gave as little information as possible to assuage their curiosity, and left the devastating details to their parents.

I was worried about my parents. They were in route to Naples, Florida to meet my Aunt Sheila and Uncle Bob for their annual September trip to the beach. My parents were at the Greater Pittsburgh International Airport sitting on the runway, ready to take off, when the pilot announced to the travelers on board that all United States flights had been grounded immediately, and they would be returning to the airport terminal. There my parents would retrieve their luggage, and then drive home. Aunt Sheila and Uncle Bob's airplane had already taken off from the Hartsfield-Jackson Airport in Atlanta when their pilot made an announcement that a couple planes crashed into skyscrapers in New York City, and that all United States aircraft were being grounded. Then the pilot announced that they would be making an emergency off-landing in Tampa. When they arrived in Tampa, the airport was closed, but Delta Airlines had rented a bus and drove the passengers and their luggage to the old Naples Airport which was also closed. Uncle Bob met a nice guy there who drove him to the rent-a-car to get a car to drive to the Edgewater Beach Hotel where they had reservations. Uncle Bob said Naples was like a ghost town and not a soul was on the beach. Aunt Sheila and Uncle Bob stayed overnight, and drove home to Atlanta the next morning.

After we ascertained that my parents, aunt, uncle, and children were ok, we worried about Eddy's relatives who lived in New York City. Since all the lines were down, it took a while, but we were soon reassured that all our Guarascio relatives were well, at least physically. Many of them knew people who died in the disaster. So many lives were tragically shattered that day.

Veterans Day had more meaning that year for all of us Americans, and I wanted to do something special to honor our veterans and soldiers. So, I invited U.S. Army Reserve Major Yvonne Bryan, the mother of my student, Megan Folio, to talk to my class about the national situation following the September 11th terrorist attacks. That forum allowed my students to express their fears and share their feelings with a member of the armed forces. The students also wanted to talk with a soldier about the war in Afghanistan. After hearing Major Bryon speak, I was reminded of my own childhood experience during the Vietnam War when my fifth grade class sent letters and gifts to our troops there.

After talking it over with Major Bryon and the other three fifth grade teachers, we decided to make sure our servicemen and women got a little early holiday cheer. All of our 120 fifth graders participated in our service project in lieu of a Christmas gift exchange for each other. The students collected and then we mailed care packages of candies, health care items, bath and beauty products, stationary, and pen pal letters. Fun Party Services in Jeannette and World of Values in Norwin Hills Shopping Center donated Christmas stockings to put our pen pal letters in. Scozio's Shop 'N Save grocery store donated candy canes. In addition, many parents sent money in lieu of donated items. We collected $330 for sundry items and the expensive overseas postage. When all was said and done, we had $60 left over for a student reward pizza party. The children demonstrated great maturity giving up their gift exchange party, and were so generous with their donations, and the time it took for packaging that we wanted to reward their kindness. We ended up mailing six large packages to soldiers in Afghanistan, Bosnia, and aboard a navy vessel, the U.S.S. Fife. Two of our boxes were sent to Major Bryon's sister, Air Force Capt. Tammy Abbett, in Ramstein Germany, where they were forwarded to troops flying food drop missions over Afghanistan. Major Bryon made sure all our packages were sent to her military contacts, so there would be no worries about the packages being rejected, because of anthrax or other terrorist concerns at that time. I think the most important lesson my students learned participating in our service project, was that much *goodness* could come out of the most terrible situations. Just as our heroic police officers, firefighters, EMS workers, doctors, nurses, and average citizens modeled compassion and the goodness of humankind during that dreadful time in our nation's history, our students felt they were able to make a little difference in some small way. We eagerly awaited our pen pal letter responses, and were thrilled to get many letters of gratitude for our modest efforts that January. Time has passed, life moves on, people carry on, but we will never forget.

The following year brought more bad news. Uncle Denny O'Grady passed away on May 28, 2002 after a long hard-fought battle with lung cancer. He endured much suffering, had months of chemo, and lived through an operation where doctors removed one of his lungs. Aunt Lynne remained by his side as his devoted wife and loving primary caregiver. His siblings visited them in Marietta, Georgia, and prayed for his survival. Even little Tierney had her fellow classmates pray for her Great-Uncle Denny. She mailed him a paper *frog* with the acrostic message that he should be *Faithfully Relying On God*. Apparently, God wanted him back home. We took comfort that his suffering was finally over. Aunt Lynne made arrangements to fly his body back to Pittsburgh, and have him buried at All Saints Braddock Catholic Cemetery where his parents have been laid to rest. His bright light, smile, quick-wit, and master storytelling would be sorely missed. Uncle Denny and Aunt Lynne historically would *hold court* to entertain us during family functions. We would gather around them like they were celebrities, and listen to their travel tales and amazing adventures. It took a long time to process that Uncle Denny would no longer be with us during the family holiday celebrations. To this day, every time I hear Uncle Denny's favorite song, "Celebrate Me Home," by Kenny Loggins, I can't stop the tears.

In April 2004, my parents celebrated their 50th wedding anniversary. My sisters, Sheila and Denise, and I planned a spectacular reception. We invited our large extended family and our parents' friends. Aunt Sheila and Uncle Bob, and our cousins Diane and Mariane, all flew in from Atlanta. We had a music D.J. play their favorite songs while we all danced the night away. We hired a local photographer to make a video, using photographs, of the highlights of their 50 years together. It was a beautiful tribute to a great couple, and to their commitment. As I watched my parents cut their anniversary cake, I thanked God that he had richly blessed them, and that they were both still in good health.

Our next big celebration, commemorating Eddy's and my 25th wedding anniversary, occurred during the summer of 2004, AKA, *The Summer of Love*. We proclaimed it such to our family and friends, and much to our delight, everyone jumped on board the Love Boat. Our first destination was back to New York City to reenact the engagement proposal on a horse and carriage ride in Central Park. Bridget took our picture just as Eddy proposed a second time with a new upgraded two carat diamond solitaire. And yes, she did capture my look of surprise. Then, we were whisked off to St. Patrick's Cathedral where Eddy had arranged for the priest to give us a special marriage blessing. Again, our daughters were witness as we knelt down at the altar to rededicate ourselves to each other. It wasn't a Mass, but it was a beautiful ceremony just the same. Later that night, we took our girls to see their first Broadway show, which was *Wicked*. We, along with all the critics, all thought it was a spectacular production. I couldn't help but make personal connections to the show that mirrored my Junior Miss Talent Award oral interpretation of the Wicked Witch of the West's version of the story, *The Wizard of Oz*, some thirty years earlier.

After our return from New York, my parents invited our immediate family members to join us for an anniversary dinner at The Monterey Bay Restaurant atop the Jonnet Building which overlooked the lights of the shopping district along Route 22 in Monroeville. It was such a nice evening with all of our loved ones gathered around to help us celebrate our love and commitment. But the festivities didn't end there. The Love Boat sailed us onward to a tropical island.

The highlight of the *Summer of Love* was our trip to beautiful Bermuda. Bermuda with its pink sandy beaches, stone walled European-looking winding roads, coconut palm trees, and elegant ambiance was everything my Grandmother O'Grady told me it would be and more. I had dreamed of going there since I was a little girl. Bermuda is a tropical paradise. The sapphire blue ocean waters were crystal clear, and the fish were colors of the rainbow. If you looked down at your feet while you were standing in the water waist deep, you could actually see your toenail polish. The temperature was perfect the week we were there, with low humidity, and a balmy breeze. Again, we took our daughters with us to celebrate and vacation. We stayed at The Fairmont Southampton Princess Resort perched on Bermuda's stunning south shore amid miles of pink sand and towering palm trees. The resort is truly palatial and the summit of luxury. We swam, sunbathed, shopped in Hamilton, the capital of Bermuda, and dined in fabulous restaurants. Our favorite restaurant was The Aqua Seaside Restaurant, owned by Michael Douglas and Catherine Zeta Jones. Pictures of them were everywhere on the walls as we waited to be seated. We decided to dine outside down on the beach. The waiter took a family photo of us with the azure blue Atlantic just a few feet behind us.

My favorite memory of Bermuda was when we went to Sunday Mass at St. Anthony's Church, a small Spanish mission looking church nestled in a rural hillside amid the red roofed native Bermudian homes. It's always a comfort being a Catholic, that no matter where you go to Mass in the world, whether it's in the United States, Europe, or the Caribbean, the Mass is basically the same. The language might be different, but the prayers, components, and order of the Mass are universal. My magic moment occurred during the recitation of the Our Father prayer. The entire congregation, mostly native Bermudians and a few tourists, sang the most glorious rendition of the Our Father that I had ever heard. We sang together with such fervor, love, and conviction. I was overwhelmed with a sense of peace and gratitude, that all felt right with my world. My husband, children, and I were all holding hands, praying and singing the Our Father, and we were in paradise in beautiful Bermuda. I felt such a connection with God the Father at that moment. I was so filled with gratitude for all his many blessings. I remember thanking him for my husband and children, and that my parents were still alive and healthy in their retirement. It was a magical ethereal eternal moment, where I actually felt the love of God the Father, and I'll always remember it as such. Our week in Bermuda ended too soon, but our *Summer of Love* would continue back home.

Our friends had jumped aboard the bandwagon of the *Summer of Love* as we all partied by the Balmert's pool many a weekend the summer of 2004 to celebrate a summer of lovin. The *Ya-Yas*, friends, family, and neighbors hung out in the Balmert backyard until the wee hours. I don't know if I ever thanked Maggie and David enough for hosting all those great parties. They made many happy memories for all of us.

Unfortunately, not all memories of the summer of 2004 are happy ones. A week after Kaitlin graduated with high honors from Greensburg Central Catholic High School in early June, she was diagnosed with Crohn's Disease. She had been suffering with stomach pain and symptoms for quite some time. A colonoscopy confirmed the diagnosis which took me by surprise. I kept thinking she had colitis like my father, or a collagenous colon like me. The Soltis's genes carried a history of gastrointestinal issues. Kaitlin was prescribed oral medications which sustained her until she went on intravenous Remicade her sophomore year at the University of Pittsburgh.

The summer's end brought another diagnosis which wasn't good either. My dear friend, and future teaching partner, Karen Dvorsky, and I were supposed to go out with our husbands in early August to get together for a night on the town before we went back to work. Karen called to cancel our date as her husband Mike was rushed to the hospital. Karen's husband, Mike, was diagnosed with a rare form of appendix cancer. He suffered stoically, and underwent a brutal, yet effective, revolutionary *chemo bath*, which put his cancer in remission for six years. About five years after his chemo bath, the producers of the popular television show, *Grey's Anatomy*, called his doctors to research his type of cancer as they were going to write it into a story line on the show. Mike Dvorsky was then called to do a television interview with his doctors on the network nightly news. We teachers watched Mike on that television interview and were praying that his remission would last. Mike appeared healthy and cancer free for many years. He founded and was a board member of the PMP (Pseudomyxoma Peritonei) Research Foundation, and was dedicated to raising funds for research to find a cure for Appendix Cancer. We almost forgot what he'd been through, or that his doctors told him his cancer would likely return, as the years flew by without incident. During that time of wellness, Mike and Karen traveled to Hawaii, Las Vegas, Kennebunkport, Paris, and London. They also hosted wonderful wedding celebrations for three of their four adult children. Life was good.

In January of 2005, Bridget Rose graduated a semester early from Washington and Jefferson College with a degree in Political Science, and set her sights set on law school at Duquesne University in Pittsburgh. While at W & J, she received a Presidential Scholarship, was on the Dean's

List every year, and was a member of the Political Science Honor Society (Pi Sigma Alpha), the Honorary Scholastic Fraternity (Order of Omega and Gamma Sigma Alpha), and the pre-law society. In addition to these scholastic honors, Bridget served as a School Ambassador. She was also a member of the Kappa Kappa Gamma Sorority, and the Assistant Philanthropy Chair, PanHellenic Counsel Representative, and Fraternal Leadership Conference Representative. She also played on the girls' basketball team her freshman year. Throughout college, Bridget interned at Dickie McCamey Chilcote Law Firm. Consequently, Bridget proceeded to take the LSATs and planned on starting Duquesne University Law School in August 2005.

Since Bridget completed her undergraduate degree a semester early, she decided to spend the six months in between finishing college and starting law school in Naples, Florida with her beloved Aunt Julie, per her invitation. Bridget got a job as a waitress in Tommy Bahamas Restaurant in Naples, and had the time of her life working there. She also earned enough tips to offset tuition costs. Bridget treasures the memories she made with her Aunt Julie during that special time.

I would be remiss not to mention what a wonderful and loving aunt Julie Guarascio has been to our children. Aunt Julie (Aunt JuJu), as she's affectionately referred to, has been like a fairy Godmother to all three of our daughters since they've been babies. She is actually Tierney's Godmother, but treats all our girls with equal amounts of spoiling and generosity. Julie has always gone above and beyond gifting our girls with their back to school shopping sprees, Christmas presents, and their birthday gifts. Sometimes, she takes them shopping for simple retail therapy for no particular reason, other than to have fun and spend time with them. She's also the first person who introduced them to manicures/pedicures and spa treatments. She has loved all of her nieces unconditionally, like they were her own daughters. She's invited each of our daughters to bring their friends to stay with her in her beautiful carriage house in Naples, Florida many times over the years. She continues to open her heart and home to her family and friends all the while maintaining an illustrious career as a candy brokerage National Sales Representative. Julie has had a remarkable career and has been rewarded several times as the National Sales Representative of the Year! It's always nice when good things happen to good people who deserve it. Most importantly, Julie has managed to be there for her sister, brothers, and mother whenever they've needed her. Her lifelong strong work ethic and devotion to her family have been wonderful examples to her nieces and nephews. Now back to Bridget.

Bridget started Duquesne University Law School in August 2005. Her law school activities included being a student bar association representative, a chairperson for the Barristers' Ball, and a member of the Women's Law and Sports and Entertainment Law Society. In law school, Bridget interned with the Honorable Judge Joy Flowers Conti in US District Court. After graduation from law school, Bridget went on to pass both the Pennsylvania and Florida Bar. She worked at smaller area firms in Pittsburgh gaining experience before obtaining a role as a Trust Advisor with PNC Wealth Management. Then in 2011, Bridget joined K & L Gates LLP, an international firm of more than 2000 lawyers practicing in 47 offices located on five continents, where she steadily advanced through their Office of General Counsel. Bridget was responsible for addressing high-level conflicts of interest issues for every major industry group represented by the firm.

Despite the rigors of her profession, Bridget became an outstanding Pittsburgh community leader volunteering for many charitable organizations. She is very dedicated to the American Heart Association. She served on the 2013–2014 Go Red for Women Executive Leadership for the Western Pennsylvania Heart Luncheon and Conference. In addition to her work on Go Red for Women, she served as the Heart Ball's Auction Committee Co-Chair, and as a Heart Walk Team Captain. Bridget's other charity work included supporting the Champions of Hope as committee member on the annual Pittsburgh Gala benefiting St. Jude Children's Research Hospital and its mission of finding cures for children with cancer. Additionally, Bridget occasionally distributes food for the Greater Pittsburgh Community Food Bank through the South Side outlet, and participated in the Emerging Leaders Kickoff for the Auberle Home, national agency of the year group, dedicated to healing families and empowering youth throughout Southwestern Pennsylvania. We are so proud of our first-born daughter. She'd always set such a good example for her sisters. My parents were very proud of her as well. My sisters and I started calling Bridget "Mary Pat Junior" as we thought she was going to follow in our mother's community service footsteps. But I digress, back to the autumn of 2005.

Shortly after Bridget started law school, my dear father was diagnosed with prostate cancer. My parents kept it as private as possible, but my dad was never the same after the operation. My mom and dad dealt with it as stoically as possible, and my sisters and I weren't really that involved with helping them. Side effects after the surgery took its toll on them, but they kept the faith that the cancer was curable. We were all relieved that daddy didn't need radiation or chemotherapy. The cancer could have been worse. The only visible evidence of his condition to the rest of the family was the package of Depends in the corner of their linen closet, and the change in my dad's disposition.

My dad wasn't the only man is our family having health problems. In 2006, my brother-in-law, Dom, started having neuromuscular symptoms such as deep muscular twitches, called fasciculations, which progressed from his arms and legs to his chest, and back. At first they attributed this to side effects from Lipitor, but that wasn't the case. Unfortunately, the symptoms continued to get worse. Dom told us that it felt like there was a motor in his body that he couldn't shut off, and it seemed to get worse at night. Dom and Sheila couldn't even get a good night's sleep. Sheila said that she could even see his muscles move. You could actually put your hand on his arm and feel his muscles jumping. Everyone in the family started to worry that this was something really serious. Sheila, being a nurse, knew all too well, the horrible diseases that it might be. Thus began their quest to find a good doctor and a diagnosis. Dom was seen by his PCP who sent him to a neurologist who had tears in his eyes (as he worked with Sheila) when he advised them, Dom's EMG (electromyography) and physical exam were very suspicious of a motor neuron disease, namely ALS. ALS, or amyotrophic lateral sclerosis, is a neurodegenerative motor neuron disease, which has no cure and an average life expectancy of two to five years after the diagnosis. It is more commonly known as Lou Gehrig's disease. We all started praying like crazy that Dom didn't have it, and would recuperate.

In the next nine months, Dom and Sheila would travel to see noted ALS specialist, Dr. Zachary Simmons, at the Hershey Medical Center where they did MRIs (magnetic resonance imaging), EMGs, which tests nerve conduction to the muscles, a muscle biopsy, and a great deal of blood work. Eventually, Dom was told they believed him to be in the early stages of ALS. Dom was then seen at the John P. Murtha Neuroscience and Pain Institute in Johnstown, as it was a new center associated with Hershey Medical Center and Dr. Simmons, and closer to their home. There Dom was given monthly pulmonary function tests to assess the progression of the disease in his lungs. When the doctor discussed starting Dom on Rilutek to slow the progression of ALS symptoms, Dom refused telling the neurologist, "I know something horrible is wrong with me, but I know it is not ALS."

My sister Sheila began praying the Divine Mercy Chaplet given to her by her friend, Debbie. Sheila shared that every time Dom had needles put into his skin, she would imagine Jesus holding his arms around Dom, and would pray the Divine Mercy for a healing for her husband. Dom was coaching baseball that summer, and as a man of great faith, believed he would be okay. In the meantime, Sheila, our mother, Dom's mother, and I started going to Healing Masses for Dom. Finally, the night before they had an appointment with the renowned Dr. Eric Pioro at the Cleveland Clinic, Dom and Sheila attended a Healing Mass at St. Paul Catholic Church in Greensburg. When the priest prayed over him, Dom had an experience of total peace, and he fell backward in the spirit without touching the ground. The next day when the EMG was repeated by the head neurologist at the Cleveland Clinic, Dr. Pioro told Dom he would not say he had ALS, but that the symptoms could progress to ALS in time. He advised Dom to return if he started to get worse. It has been 14 years since then, and while Dom deals with constant cramping and fasciculations, he is alive and active, and a testimony to God's healing graces. Sheila tells anyone who will listen that Dom is a true miracle. Our community of believers, our church, our work places, and our sister Denise's church were participants praying for that miracle.

My entire immediate family joined them, their children, Dom's mother Molly, and my parents at the first Healing Mass at Our Lady of Joy Church in Plum Boro, Pennsylvania, to pray for Dom's healing. We all drove there in a blinding torrential summer thunderstorm, to pray, and support Sheila and Dom. My mother later joked that the sheeting rain was Satan's way of trying to prevent us from going there, but we made it. It was the first time any of us had been to a Healing Mass, and it was such a beautiful spiritual experience. It began with the priest guiding us through the most moving examination of conscience. Father Bill Kiel was the main celebrant. In brief, Fr. Bill was a high school biology teacher before he was called to the priesthood. He was ordained in 1993 in the diocese of Greensburg, Pennsylvania. He made his first pilgrimage to Medjugorje, Yugoslavia a year later, where he received his gift of healing from The Holy Spirit.

Medjugorje is the site of the longest series of Marian apparitions in church history, from 1981 until the present day. The appearances of the Mother of God in Medjugorje have been accompanied by a number of miracles, including over 360 physical healings, reports of the sun dancing or spinning in the sky, rosary links and medals changing from silver to gold, and other phenomena. Millions of pilgrims from all over the world have traveled to Medjugorje since the 1980s.

Author, Fr. Richard J. Beyer shares the story of one such miracle in his daily meditation book, *Medjugorje Day By Day*:

> "A striking miracle occurred in Medjugorje involving a 43 year old Italian secretary and mother of three, Diana Basile. She had been diagnosed with multiple sclerosis in 1972, along with urinary incontinence, perineal dermatitis, blindness in one eye, difficulty walking, and a severe clinical depression. In May of 1984, Diana joined a pilgrimage group going from Milan to Medjugorje. On the evening of May 23rd, she was in the church and a friend helped her climb the steps to the side chapel where the apparitions were then occurring. From the records kept at the parish in Medjugorje, here are her own words:
>
> "At that point I no longer wanted to enter the chapel, but the door was opened and I went in. I knelt just behind the door. When the children came in and knelt down, I heard a loud noise. After that I remember nothing, except an indescribable joy and certain episodes of my life passing before my eyes as though on film.
>
> When it was all over, I followed the children, who went straight to the main altar in the church. I was walking just like everybody else, and I knelt down just as they did. It didn't actually occur to me that anything extraordinary had happened, until my friend came up to me in tears."
>
> Diana's cure had been instantaneous. Later that night, she found that she was no longer incontinent, and the dermatitits had completely disappeared. Her right eye, useless for twelve years, had regained perfect vision. The following day, she walked the six miles from her hotel in Ljubuski to the church in Medjugorje, and later climbed Mt. Podbrdo."

Fr. Bill Kiel's Healing Masses are probably the closest most of us faithful will ever get to a miracle in Medjugorje. In our local Pittsburgh and Greensburg dioceses, people come from all over to attend Fr. Bill Kiel's Healing Masses, in hopes for a cure, knowing the Holy Spirit works through him to heal people with terminal diseases and illnesses. It was during this Healing Mass at Our Lady of Joy, that I first witnessed people *resting in the Spirit* after Fr. Kiel laid hands upon their heads. The church was packed with very sick people. There were people in wheel chairs, and many of the faithful were clearly suffering with some sort of disease or affliction. Fr. Bill would lay his hands on the heads of the faithful, and pray. Many of them would fall back unconscious into the arms of appointed *Catchers*. It looked a little scary. I had never seen anything like that before, and I have to admit, that at that time, I was lacking faith, skeptical, and fearful. I just didn't know if what I was witnessing was real, but I did feel filled with the grace of the Holy Spirit at that first Healing Mass.

Afterward, Dom's condition seemed to stabilize, and so we continued to pray novenas to the Blessed Mother and St. Jude, and recite the Divine Mercy Chaplet. My mother gave Sheila and Dom a lawn statue of St. Jude to place in their front yard, and I bought a statue of the Blessed Mother for their yard as well. We figured they needed all the help they could get, and so, we continued to storm heaven with prayers. Dom has since been diagnosed with a neuromuscular disease called *Isaac Syndrome*, (fasciculation syndrome), and although he is not symptom free, he has remained fairly stable since then. I do believe our prayers have been answered as doctors have since confirmed that Dom does *not* have ALS.

In May of 2007, Eddy and I were getting ready for Tierney's graduation from Greensburg Central Catholic High School. We had both Bridget's and Kaitlin's graduation parties at our house, and were happy to be planning our last high school graduation celebration. We hired a local landscaper to trim the shrubs and trees, lay fresh mulch, and basically to help tidy up the yard. Pitt Rental had already been contacted to erect their festive white party tents in our backyard. We were expecting a couple hundred guests. Eddy painted walls, and I cleaned, cooked, baked, and prepared for the party weeks before graduation day. We were so excited for this momentous occasion. Our baby girl would be graduating high school. It would be the end of an era. All three daughters would soon be in a college or university at the same time. Yikes! Financially, that was a frightening thought! Bridget was finishing her second year of Law School at Duquesne University, and Kaitlin was completing her junior year at the University of Pittsburgh. Tierney had been accepted and would start her freshman year at St. Vincent College in Latrobe, Pennsylvania. FYI ... Latrobe is famous for being the home of two beloved men, children's iconic television host, Mr. Fred Rogers, and golf legend Arnold Palmer. Also, St. Vincent College is the home of the Pittsburgh Steelers Summer Camp.

The New Millennium

Tierney wasn't the only person in our family graduating in May of 2007. I had just completed two years of study and earned my Master Degree of Education in Curriculum and Instruction from Gannon University. I had been attending weekend classes at a satellite location in Monroeville, Pennsylvania, about a half hour from our home, while still teaching at Norwin. This would be a nice bump up the salary scale for me in my school district, and earn me more money to help finance our daughters' educations. Everything seemed to going along as planned.

It was a sunny Saturday afternoon, May 22nd, and I was outside pulling weeds and planting flowers getting ready for Tierney's graduation party, when I heard the telephone ring. I ran inside to answer the phone, and it was my sister Denise. Her voice was shaking, and she said she had some really sad news. John Barbarino had passed away that morning. He had recently been diagnosed with prostate cancer, was in the hospital with complications, and was sent home to recuperate. He died of a blood clot to the heart. He was home sitting in his favorite chair when he died. We were all in shock. John was such a wonderful man, husband, and father. He and Anna Marie were Godparents to my sister Denise. John was a devout Catholic. Our Barbarino cousins had lived next door to my parents for over fifty years. The memories of our childhood flooded over Denise and me as we talked on the phone. I remembered how kind John was to me as a child. Every Friday evening on his way home from work as a body and fender man at Baumann Chevrolet, he'd stop at Irene's Pizza in East McKeesport and bring home a large square pizza for his wife and five kids. If I was playing with Kathy at their house around dinner time, he'd always offer me a piece of that pizza, which was such a treat in those days. I can still see him carrying that pizza out of his station wagon, after he'd parked his car in their driveway, and walked across the yard into the house. It was his Friday routine. And now John was gone. I just kept walking in circles around our backyard basketball court trying to let it sink into my brain. John was gone. Life would never be the same for Anna Marie, their daughters and sons. A week and half later, we went through with Tierney's graduation party, but dearly missed having Anna Marie and John there. It was another reminder that life goes on.

In mid-June, I finally had the opportunity to travel with Eddy to Europe. During his previous business trips there, I was always teaching and unable to join him. This time I was out of school, and the timing was finally right. He had business in Amsterdam, Netherlands, Brussels, Belgium, Paris, France, and Cologne, Germany, and he would be taking me along. We flew out Monday, June 18, 2007, on USAir from Pittsburgh to Philadelphia. We had such a close call connecting flight that we missed our flight to Amsterdam, and were rerouted to Manchester, England. When I heard the English accents of the people in the airport there, I thought of my Great Grandmother Katherine Rochford, who was born in England. During my childhood, my mother would tell me stories about her, and of the close bond between them. Because of that, I felt an instant connection to the people there, and didn't mind that we ended up at their airport for the day. We eventually boarded a KML Airplane and flew from the UK to Amsterdam. I made a point of keeping a travel journal to help me remember my first trip to Europe.

We finally arrived in Amsterdam, Netherlands, which is commonly referred to as Holland. Amsterdam is the capital, a bohemian liberal city, known for legalizing marijuana. We stayed at the old and elegant Grand Hotel Krasnapolski, facing Dam Square, which lies outside the royal palace. (Years later, on April 30, 2013, Queen Beatrice of the Netherlands stood on the palace balcony, and abdicated the throne after a 33 year reign as tens of thousands of people crammed into Dam Square to cheer the continuity of the monarchy, and show their loving support.)

Dam Square is a gathering place for all sorts of people. When we were there, café tables surrounded the square where thousands of people relaxed and watched the various kinds of entertainment, everything from jugglers to musicians. In the center of the square was this large World War II obelisk monument where people were constantly taking pictures. It is usually so crowded, we had been told, that the pickpockets have a field day there. I narrowly escaped one myself after spinning around as one came dangerously close while reaching for my purse. He smiled acknowledging my vigilance, nodded his head with respect for my quick reaction, and walked away. From then on, I tried not to act like an awestruck tourist.

To the left of our hotel was the infamous *Red Light District* known for its legalized prostitution. We made sure to steer clear of this area, and decided to walk around this lovely city. It was a perfect 75 degree day. Amsterdam is a city of canals, houseboats, and bicycles. There are approximately seven major canals, and hundreds of smaller ones. Boats coast along these canals while people aboard dine and party. Outdoor cafes line these canals, stone arched-bridges rise over the waters, and it makes for a beautiful sight. Bicycles were everywhere, and cars were few and quite small. The majority of the population ride bicycles to get around. Amsterdam is known for *a million people and two million bikes*. We enjoyed learning about the traditional courtship etiquette of bicycle riding. In general, the people seemed laid back, happy, smiled a lot, and were friendly, helpful, and warm. Even though the official language is Dutch, pretty much everyone speaks English which made it easy to explore and communicate.

We walked to see the house where Anne Frank hid with her family from the Nazis for two years during WWII before they were reported to the authorities. There was such a long line wrapping around the building that we decided not to wait to take the tour of her hiding place. We did stop and pay tribute at the small statue of her outside the building, which is simply a tall canal home. After that, we walked to the Vincent Van Gogh Museum which held the majority of his artwork, the largest collection of his paintings. His pieces were breathtakingly beautiful. It was such a shame that someone as gifted as he, led such a sad and tragic life. We continued to meander through the city for the remainder of the afternoon into evening. Then we went and ate a delicious dinner at Dauphine's, where we feasted on steak, veal, and cannelloni. After dinner, we retired to our room for the night.

Eddy had a business meeting in the afternoon on Wednesday, while I was left to shop, and tour the city by myself. I decided to lunch at the Esprit Restaurant/Café on Spui Street about five blocks from our hotel. The food was delicious there as well. I ordered a goat cheese and honey sandwich on brown bread with fresh spinach, avocado, and tomato, and made a mental note to make one for myself back in the States. I went shopping after lunch in the Mozart Plaza which was the first enclosed shopping mall in Amsterdam. That evening, Eddy and I had dinner at D'Thee Boom, a quaint little French restaurant with delectable food, particularly the white chocolate mousse dessert.

Thursday afternoon, we caught the 2:30 train to Brussels, Belgium. We arrived in Brussels about 5:30 p.m., and checked into the magnificent Hotel Metropole. On the way to our room, we noticed a plaque on one of the room doors with an inscription stating that Sarah Bernhardt, the world famous actress, had stayed there in 1919! I cracked up remembering how my mother or Grandmother O'Grady would call me Sarah Bernhardt whenever I was overly dramatic. After dropping off our luggage, we immediately headed out to the Grand-Place, a huge public square plaza surrounded by the city tower and a range of gorgeous 300 year old buildings with spires, statues, and cathedral-style gothic architecture. A web of narrow, cobbled streets convenes onto the Grand-Place, which has been the economic and social heart of Brussels since the Middle Ages. We dined at one of the many outdoor cafes on delicious soup, cheese, and croissants before shopping for chocolates and other delicacies. People were swarming everywhere. Most speak French, the many people we met in both countries, spoke two and three languages, and almost everyone speaks English. We took a short walk to one of the famous Brussels' landmarks, and one of Eddy's favorites, the Manneken Pis. The Manneken Pis is a small bronze statue thought to represent the *irreverent spirit* of Brussels. It is simply a statue of an angelic child performing one of Nature's most basic functions (peeing). Belgians have created hundreds of outfits for this adorable statue, and there are many legends that have inspired the statue's significance. We heard stories about everything from peasant boys extinguishing fires with their urine, to a father finding his lost child and striking a statue of the boy in the exact pose in which he was found, to a boy driving away an invading army from a tree, and finally to a witch who turned the boy to stone for peeing on her property. In any case, it is a most charming statue.

My favorite statue was nestled in one of the narrow cobbled streets off the square on the way to the Manneken Pis. I thought it was a gold life-size statue of Jesus, lying dead after the crucifixion. His pain was palpable. The statue was a smooth shiny gold metal. I laid my hands upon the body praying that my brother-in-law Dominick would be healed of his affliction. People who gathered around the statue were speechless in silent reverence and prayer, running their hands along the body. Later, I found out that the statue is a bronze, not gold, statue of Everard 't Serclaes, a Brussels liberation hero of the fourteenth century who was cowardly murdered. The last hundred years, people have started to rub the statue for good luck. In any case, it was a most moving statue that motivated many people to prayer.

After it started to sprinkle, we went back to our hotel for dessert, and sat awhile in the magnificent marble lobby. I called my parents back home to check in with them, as they had promised to check in on our daughters while we were away. After talking to my mom, she reassured me that everyone was well, and instructed me to enjoy myself, and not to worry about anyone at home. The next morning, we ran back to my favorite chocolatiers shop in one of the side streets off the Grand-Place to buy homemade Belgium chocolates for souvenirs. Then, we quickly ate a breakfast of eggs and crepes at one of the little cafes, and raced back to our hotel to check out, so we could catch the train for Paris.

The French countryside is beautiful, reminding me of the patchwork quilt farmlands of rural Pennsylvania. We talked to a man on the train from Sweden, who spoke 12 languages, about politics in America. He seemed better informed of the issues than most Americans care to be! We arrived in Paris around 2:30 on a cold and rainy afternoon, so we quickly got our coats and umbrella, and ventured out to explore. Our hotel is the Hotel Ambassador, and the concierge booked our dinner reservations for that evening and Saturday. We taxied to the majestic Eiffel Tower, where the line was too long to wait in the rain to go inside. Instead, we walked under it through a beautiful park toward the Avenue des Champs-Elysees, the capital's most famous thoroughfare. It is a spectacular thoroughfare, lined with cafes, luxury hotels, fine restaurants, theaters, and many of the world's most famous haute couture fashion houses. People from all over the world are strolling along the avenue. It's easy to pick out the Parisians, as they are the effortlessly best dressed in their slim slacks, jeans, jackets, scarves, and fashionable clothing. Shady chestnut trees and colorful flower beds border the sidewalks. We found out there are actually many streets contained within the area of Paris known as Champs-Elysees. We wandered about looking at all the elegant palaces and formal gardens. We ended up at the most famous historic landmark, the Arc de Triomphe, which Napoleon had built after his greatest victory. This huge monument is actually the world's most famous triumphal arch. Many victory celebrations and parades in Paris start there. We just kept walking in the rain around this sensational city of lights until dinnertime. We ate at an authentic French restaurant called Taint Louise, where we feasted on another delicious meal.

Saturday was cool and cloudy with periods of sunshine, perfect weather to explore Paris. Our first stop was the Left Bank of the River Seine, the area known as St. Germain des Pres. Its streets and cafes are crowded with intellectuals, publishers, writers, and executives. We found out this is an older area of the city favored by famous artists, revolutionaries, and writers. It was the regular haunt of a younger Napoleon, philosopher Jean-Paul Sartre, Ernest Hemingway, F. Scott Fitzgerald, Gertrude Stein, Robert Wagner, and many more. Some of their apartments are still marked.

We ate breakfast at Les Deux Magots café, which is across from the oldest church in Paris called St. Germain des Pres Church. Inside, we lit a candle for our special intentions, particularly Dom, in front of the Our Lady of Consolation statue. We felt Our Lady's comforting and loving presence. Back at breakfast across the street, we dined on delicious quiche and omelettes. Seated at the table next to us, we met an interesting woman writer and world-famous philanthropist named Camille Lavingston. She told us that she was planning on writing a book on manners in the U.S.A. She was a lovely, older woman involved in politics and charity work in New York City. She conducted business seminars around the world on business etiquette based upon her previously published book entitled, *You Only Have Three Seconds to Make Your First Impression*. Her conversation held us spellbound.

After breakfast, we headed to the Latin Quarter of Paris, down the Boulevard St. Michel to the Place St. Michel, which is a fountain-statue of St. Michael. This area is also associated with artists, intellectuals, and the bohemian way of life. We discovered many inexpensive little gift shops, cafes, fast foods, boutiques, and theaters along the maze of narrow cobbled streets. After so much walking, we decide to take a boat tour down the River Seine where we were able to jump off and on depending upon which landmarks we wanted to visit.

We decided to go to the Musee du Louvre, possibly the greatest art museum in the world, along the left bank of the River Seine. The artwork in this venue was breathtaking and humbling. The Louvre's treasures include art from BC through the nineteenth century, such as the Winged Victory (Nike) statue from 220 BC, Venus de Milo from 100 BC, and the infamous Leonardo da Vinci Mona Lisa, painted by the artist in 1503. When we were there, one entire wall as devoted to the Mona Lisa, which had major security around it as people swarmed up to the velvet rope. Two armed soldiers stood guard on either side of the painting which was encased behind bullet-proof glass. All of the artwork in this section of the museum was simply magnificent. Besides the art, the grounds and buildings are eye popping, as it is set in a fifteenth century royal palace. We could have spent days in the Louvre, but had to leave to attend 6:30 Saturday evening Mass at Notre Dame Cathedral.

The world famous Notre Dame Cathedral sits on the isle de la Cite in the Seine. The cathedral is a Gothic masterpiece. Pope Alexander III laid the first stone in 1163, marking the start of 170 years of toil by armies of Gothic architects and medieval craftsmen. It was here that Napoleon declared himself Emperor. The cathedral is truly majestic! It features three main doors, golden walls, superb statuary, ornate windows, a central rose window, and its famous gargoyles. Inside were many side altars where we stopped and lit another candle for special intentions. At Mass, we celebrated the feast of St. John the Baptist. Of course, the entire Mass was said in French, but we easily followed along. After practically memorizing the Mass in English, and after my two years of French classes in high school and college, I was able to understand and experience a deeply spiritual service amid such magnificence. I also couldn't help thinking that God must be delighted at mankind's marvelous workmanship.

After Mass at Notre Dame, we caught another cab and went to dinner at a trendy French restaurant which was frequented by celebrities such as Jackie Kennedy, whose photo was framed and signed in the entrance way. We dined on delicious veal and chicken dishes covered with fabulous creamy Moray sauces. Since our restaurant was in St. Germain des Pres, we decided to stroll through the streets to digest our rich dinner. People were everywhere, still dining at little sidewalk cafes. In Paris, people generally eat dinner late at night as it doesn't get dark in the summer until about 10:30 p.m.! The next morning, we took a train back to Amsterdam, because Eddy had a Monday morning meeting scheduled in Mijdrecht.

It was a four hour train ride from Paris to Amsterdam. On the train, we met two delightful young women from Florida. They were best friends and graduate college students from UNC at Charlotte, backpacking their way through Europe to study architecture abroad. What a wonderful way to spend the summer! And all I kept thinking was that in college, I wasn't allowed to go on spring break!

Back in Holland, we arrive in Vinkeveen, which is on the outskirts of Amsterdam. We stayed at a ski lodge looking 1960s type hotel called the Golden Tulip. It was quite rustic and peaceful, situated nicely on a small lake. Our room was located a few yards from the lake where we would watch the lovely ducks swimming in the rain. On Monday, Eddy had a meeting until about 2:00 in the afternoon. I just hung out in our room reading books, waiting for his return, while sort of feeling like a mistress.

When Eddy returned, he introduced me to a lovely and bright young woman named Emma Gosden, a Medrad finance director on European operations. She drove us to Maastricht, about a two hour drive, where she had lived the past two years. During the car ride, they talked a little business, and then she advised us on places to visit in the city, before we bid her farewell. We checked into our hotel, Grand Hotel de L'Empereur

Maastricht, dropped off our bags, and then left to explore the quaint historic city of Maastricht.

We walked down cobblestone streets across the river Maas over the Roman foot bridge to the town square. Cafes, small shops, old buildings, and lots of people are all around us. The shops closed at six, so we decided to find a nice place to eat dinner. Luckily, we find a fabulous restaurant that serves lobster and plays American music. Tony Bennett, Barbara Streisand, and Frank Sinatra were playing on the sound track. There was a gorgeous crystal chandelier hanging in the middle of the ceiling of this small restaurant/café. After dining on a delicious meal of lobster, spinach, potatoes, topped off with strawberry mousse for dessert, we met the young couple who owned the place. They were gracious and warm. After complimenting their restaurant and food, they welcomed us to The Netherlands knowing we were from the States, as our American accents gave us away. We walked back to our hotel, and called it a night.

The next day, we were scheduled to go to Cologne, Germany. First, we had to take a bus to Aachen, where we boarded a train to Cologne. The Dutch and German countryside were so beautiful, as were the small villages that we would pass through on the way. It was raining and cool again, but we had dressed appropriately for the weather. We arrived in Cologne early Tuesday afternoon, and headed directly to the ancient Cologne Cathedral. It is majestic, and so huge that we can't walk back far enough on the street to get it all in the camera. It is even more gigantic than Notre Dame. It took approximately 800 years to build the Cologne Cathedral! Inside it is enormous, with many side alters, with people praying everywhere. We went up to one of the side alters, lit a candle, and prayed for our loved ones. It seemed surreal just to be there. After spending some time inside in prayer, we went out to explore the shops in Cologne.

I knew Paris and Milan were fashion capitals of the world, but I didn't know that Cologne, Germany was one as well. Cologne is a shopper's paradise on a world-class scale. It has all the famous shops you can imagine. We walked in and out of the shops down the main streets. We purchased several of the stylish scarves that all the women in Europe seemed to wearing that summer. We ate lunch at a café famous for its beer. I'm not a beer drinker, but was told I had to try it there. It was smooth, sweet, light, and delicious. It went down well with the cheese and chicken salad and fresh fruit. We met an interesting man from Germany who sat at our table and made good conversation with us. After lunch, we found a religious shop and bought a crucifix for Sheila and Dom, and some souvenir Christmas ornaments.

Before long, it was time to head back on the train to Maastricht. Then, we transferred from train to bus, and arrived in time for dinner. Emma called to invite us one of her favorite restaurants. She took us to another small café across the foot bridge, where we dined on delicious salads, fresh fruit, and brie cheese, followed by an entrée of fresh fish, scallop potatoes, and white asparagus. After a little business talk, Emma asked us if any of our daughters would be interested in working in the organic children's clothing store she owned with a friend back in East Liberty, outside Pittsburgh, Pennsylvania. We told her we'd mention it to Kaitlin, as she was working part time at the Coach Store in Shadyside, not far from there, or the University of Pittsburgh, where she went to school. We thanked Emma for dinner, said goodbye, and walked back to our hotel. Wednesday, Eddy had business meetings all day, and I spent the time shopping at all the unique little shops Emma had advised me to visit. Later in the day, we took the train from Maastricht back to Amsterdam to pack and prepare for our trip back home to the States. What wonderful memories I have of that trip to Europe! I felt like the luckiest woman in the world, married to the sweetest husband in the world. Before we knew it, we were back in the United States for the Fourth of July festivities, and back to reality.

CHAPTER 10

Sad Times

*S*UMMER always seems to come and go so quickly. In September, Aunt Sheila and Uncle Bob came up to my parents' place to visit before they all left for their bi-annual vacation to Naples, Florida. During their stay here in Pittsburgh that week, they and my parents decided to spend a day in Ligonier. Nestled in the Laurel Mountains of Pennsylvania, Ligonier is a beautiful bucolic town listed in 2012 as one of the best small towns in America. It boasts a beautiful town square known as *The Diamond* right in the center of town, is host to the Rolling Rock Races, and home to Fort Ligonier. Ligonier celebrates Fort Ligonier Days every second weekend in October to commemorate the Battle of Fort Ligonier, a key engagement of the French and Indian War, fought on October 12, 1758. We always make it a point to attend those festivities every year. In addition to all that, it's just a great getaway to go for the day for window shopping, antique shopping, and dinner. Eddy and I decided to meet them that day, and walk around town.

After dinner at the Ligonier Tavern, we decided to walk to the local Dairy Queen to get ice cream for dessert. During our walk, I first noticed that my Dad seemed short of breath. This was unusual as he was always in great shape from walking up and down the hills of the Carradam Golf Course where he spent so much time during his retirement. When I mentioned this to my mom and Aunt Sheila as we walked ahead, my mom told me she had made a doctor's appointment for my dad for this very issue. She seemed very concerned like she knew this was going to be serious.

After they returned from their trip to Naples, my mom accompanied my dad to his doctor's appointment. The doctor immediately scheduled a chest x-ray for my father. When the films were read, the doctor called my parents in to relay the bad news that it looked like lung cancer. After additional doctor visits, it was confirmed, and so started his long sad fight against this brutal cancer.

In November, my dad underwent surgery to try and remove some of the cancer in his lung via a chest tube incision. When the thoracic surgeon explained how he'd have to slice into my dad's side to operate on his lung, an image of Jesus flashed before my eyes as the Roman soldier was thrusting a sword into his side. Daddy's suffering was only beginning. I'll never forget the brave look on my dad's face, and his *thumbs up* can-do attitude as they wheeled him into surgery. He was determined that he would beat it. We were optimistic and trying to remain positive as well, until the surgeon came out to talk to us afterward in the waiting room. There he told us it was worse than they expected, and that my dear father had only about one and a half to four years to live. We were devastated! My sisters and I tried to hold back the tears to be brave for our mother. She in turn was trying to be brave for us. We were all in shock, and struggled to process this information. Somehow through the grace of God, we remained hopeful, that with lots of prayer, he would defeat those odds. So we started praying to the Blessed Mother and St. Jude to ask God for a miracle.

Early December, my dad was scheduled for his first chemotherapy treatment. Not knowing what was in store, or the cumulative effects of chemo drugs on the human body, dad declared his first treatment "a piece of cake" when I asked him how it was. My mom accompanied him to every treatment that first round of chemo, which lasted approximately six months. He was scheduled for chemotherapy every three weeks at UPMC McKeesport Hospital Cancer Center. He received excellent, compassionate care from his Christ-like oncologist, Dr. Kevin Kane, and his dedicated team of nurses, Darra, Diane, Deanna, Barb, and Sharon. There he would sit in the chemo chair for several hours with my mom by his side, while the poisonous drugs would flow through his bloodstream trying to kill the cancer cells while damaging healthy cells in the process. After each treatment, he would get a little weaker, sicker, and more tired. The initial evidence of the power of the drugs taking their toll on his body was when he lost his beautiful head of white hair. No longer could his younger brothers-in-law teasingly call him the *Silver Fox*. I tried not to look shocked the first time I saw him completely bald. I told him he still was handsome, even though his face was swollen from the prednisone, and he had started to get that *cancer look*. My mom decided that we were going to have a Happy Christmas that December, in spite of the grim prognosis. So, we all forced ourselves to be strong for each other, and pretended to be happy, in spite of our heavy hearts. We also focused more on the religious reason for the season, the birth of Our Savior, than the gift-giving, than we ever did before.

My sisters and I started to visit our parents after work during the week days. As time went on, and dad kept getting sicker, and mom started getting more drained from being his primary caregiver, we started to take them dinners to give my mom a little break from cooking. We would invite them to our houses for dinner more just to get them out of their house if Daddy was feeling up to it. Sometimes, Eddy and I would take them out for a drive to the country if Daddy was having a *good day* just to have a change of scenery. He loved the Laurel Mountains, and the rolling hills and farmlands of Western Pennsylvania.

After six month of regular intravenous chemotherapy, Daddy was put on maintenance chemo drugs to keep the cancer frozen and prevent it was spreading. It was still there, but the tumors in his lung had shrunken significantly after his six month course of treatment. How we had hoped and prayed for a miracle that the chemo would totally eradicate the cancer, but it wasn't meant to be. We all carried on, but it felt like there was a dark cloud hanging above us. The daily stress of living with cancer was taking its toll on both my parents, and there was only so much anyone could do. Try as we might, nothing any of us did to help could alleviate Daddy's suffering. Some days I didn't know who I pitied more, my dad fighting his losing battle with lung cancer, or my mom watching him fight his losing battle with cancer.

In the meantime, my daughters were continuing with their higher education, and we had some happy news in the spring of 2008. Bridget graduated from the Duquesne University School of Law, and Kaitlin earned her undergraduate degree from the University of Pittsburgh. My dear mother was able to attend both graduation ceremonies, and dinner celebrations. Bridget landed a job as a contract attorney doing document review at Eckert Seamans Law Firm, and had moved into a cute apartment in the South Side of Pittsburgh during Law School, so she wouldn't have far to travel for her new job.

Kaitlin had graduated from Pitt after taking 22 credits a semester to complete three majors: Business, Psychology, and Pre-Medical Studies, which also included three minors in Spanish, Chemistry, and Latin American Studies. On top of her amazing academic course load, Kaitlin worked at the University of Pittsburgh Medical Center (UPMC), and volunteered at the Children's Hospital of Pittsburgh Oncology Unit. She had also been the Philanthropy Chair at her Delta Delta Delta Women's Fraternity where she participated in and organized multiple philanthropy and social events for the UPMC Hillman Cancer Center, e.g., Pitt Dance Marathon. Her past honors include the National Society of Collegiate Scholars (NSCS), National Scholars Honor Society, Beta Beta Beta Biology Honor Fraternity, Golden Key Honor Society, Psi Chi (Psychology) Honor Society, Order of Omega Honor Society, Omnicron Delta Kappa National Leadership Honor Society, and Business Excellence Award and International Scholar Laureate Program Nominee.

Kaitlin was accepted into three prestigious Master Programs: Carnegie Mellon University Heinz School of Public Policy, Georgetown University Public Policy Institute Master Program, and George Washington University for a dual degree program in MPH and MPP. (Master in Public Health and Master in Public Policy). Kaitlin would decide on Georgetown, and start there in August. All five of us helped move her into a rental row house in Georgetown. Eddy and I were so proud of our hard-working and ambitious daughters. There was so much visible change going on in our lives during this time.

Tierney just finished her freshman year at St. Vincent College, and was in the process of deciding upon her major. In June of 2008, Tierney got a summer job working at Johnston's the Florist Country Shop helping to take care of their plentiful plants and fabulous flowers. Tierney enjoyed being surrounded by such beauty, and would frequently share customer anecdotes with us. One day she came home from work, and told me about this nice elderly lady who came to buy flowers for her church. Tierney said the woman asked her what church she belonged to, and if she went to church. When Tierney told her that she was a practicing Catholic, the lady said that she was delighted to hear that, and complimented Tierney profusely. As Tierney helped her choose church flowers, and carried and loaded them into her car, the woman kept blessing Tierney and saying what a nice young girl she was, and thanking her for all her help. Tierney told me that was one of her best memories of working at Johnston's. I reaffirmed her helping this lady, and forgot about it for a while.

That weekend, I decided to go to Sunday evening Mass (last chance Mass) at St. Barbara's Church in Harrison City, a sister parish to St. Agnes. As I was reading their weekly bulletin after Mass, I noticed an interesting piece on information. A traveling statue of the Virgin Mary, which had been blessed in Medjugorje, would be visiting St. Barbara's Church that week. Parishioners were being invited to come pray the rosary in front of the statue for special intentions in hopes of special blessings. I made a mental note to tell my mother about it, knowing of her devotion to the Blessed Mother. When I mentioned it to my mom, she said, "Let's go!" When I asked my mom when she wanted to go, she said that Monday would be the best day for her. Tierney was off work that Monday, so she offered to go with us to pray for her Pappy. So the three of us went to St. Barbara's to pray the rosary for my father the first day the statue was on display.

When we walked into the narthex at the entrance to St. Barbara's Church, we looked around to find the statue of the Blessed Mother that had traveled all the way from Medjugorje. We immediately saw the tall statue of Our Lady, dressed in a white gown trimmed in gold, elevated on a make shift altar. In front of her were beautiful flowers, which were still being rearranged and put into their vases. Monsignor Paul Fitzmaurice was pastor at St. Barbara's Parish at that time, and he was helping a few elderly ladies carry more vases of flowers to the small altar. We walked toward them to explain why we were there. Before I had a chance to speak, one of the three elderly ladies called out to Tierney, saying, "Tiffany, is that you? Aren't you the nice girl who helped me choose our flowers last week at Johnston's Greenhouse?!" The lady continued to tell me what a sweet girl Tierney was when she helped her with the flowers. I thanked her, and explained to them that we came to pray the rosary for my father who was suffering with terminal lung cancer. Then I made formal introductions. The ladies introduced themselves and asked if they could pray for him with us. Monsignor Paul set up two kneelers in front of the statue of Mary, and my mother, daughter, and I knelt down and began to pray the rosary. The four of them stood behind us, and prayed the rosary with us for my father.

After the rosary recitation, I thanked Mgr. Paul and the ladies for praying with us. As we started to say our good-byes, one of the ladies asked me if I would like to buy a smaller replica of the statue of Mary for only $99 which had also been blessed. I declined the offer saying that we had several statues of Mary at our home, as did my mother. We both have lawn statues of the Blessed Mother, and several small statues in our bedrooms. So we left the church, went into the parking lot, and got into our car. As we were circling around to leave the church parking lot, one of the ladies ran up to our car waving her arms in the air for us to stop. I said, "Mom, what is she doing?" And my mother said, "I don't know, but you better stop." So I stopped the car, and rolled down the window. The lady said that we couldn't leave before she gave a present to Tierney. She said that she understood that my mother and I had statues of Mary, but we never said Tierney had one. She then lifted a two foot replica statue of the Blessed Mother out of the trunk of her car, and handed it through our car window to Tierney who was sitting in the back seat. I protested, and said that I would pay her then for the statue. She adamantly refused, saying that you don't pay somebody when they give you a gift. She only asked Tierney to find a place of honor for the statue in our home. Tierney said that she would find a special spot for Mary in our home, thanked her again, and off we drove. My mom and I teased Tierney on the way home, saying that the Blessed Mother was determined to watch over her, so she better be good!

When we arrived home, we immediately knew where we would place our new statue. We have a beautiful hand-painted floral hall table upstairs in our hallway that Tierney and I picked out together in a specialty shop called *Oh, Heather*! Now I know why I bought that table! Situated between the girls' bedroom doors, it's the perfect place for Our Lady to stand, and watch over my daughters. And every time I walk out of my own bedroom door, she's the first person I see every day. So Mary stands on my own make shift altar, where I've placed a silk flower arrangement in front of her to honor her, reminiscent of my days back in elementary school when I was Child of Mary. Everything old is new again! And one way or another, I think that statue of Mary was meant to be in our home. What a coincidence that the lady customer at Johnston's the Florist turned out to be the woman from St. Barbara's Parish who would give Tierney a blessed statue of The Virgin Mary from Medjugorje! I also took it as a sign that the Blessed Mother was hearing our prayers for my father. The maintenance chemo regimen that my father had been on, seemed to be keeping his cancer in check. Thereafter, I continued to pray to Mary for her help and intercession in front of that blessed statue daily.

The UPMC McKeesport Hospital Foundation Annual Fashion Show fundraiser has always been the last Sunday in July at The Youghiogheny Country Club, in Elizabeth, Pennsylvania, for as long as I can remember.

My mother has been on the hospital Board of Directors for many years, so every year we look forward to attending and participating in this big event. Over the past years, my sisters and I, and our daughters have all been models in this gala affair. Every year there is a different theme for the fashion show. In July 2008, the theme was Pink and White in support of Breast Cancer Awareness, so we were all encouraged to wear those colors to the fashion show. My mom didn't like leaving my dad for long periods of time that summer, and was reluctant to go shopping for a new pink and white outfit to wear. I told her I'd help her find something quickly, and that Daddy would be fine for a couple hours while we were at the Monroeville Mall.

We quickly walked into Macy's determined to find a pretty pink and white outfit for my mother. She also wanted new white pumps to match. So, off she went to look for her clothing, and I told her I'd look for her shoes. While I was perusing the stock in the shoe department, I turned around and was surprised to see two women wearing pretty pink and white striped blazers right behind me. They were both blond and almost looked like sisters. I complimented them on their jackets, and asked where they bought them, explaining why I was asking. I also asked them if they were twins, since they were dressed exactly alike. They said they dressed alike on purpose, because they were the *Angel Ladies*. When they asked me if I had ever heard of them, I unfortunately had to say no. They explained that they had a radio show where people called in to have them do *readings*. They said they channel spirits and relay what is being told to them by *angel guides* to the people they are reading. Their names were Eileen Miller and Charlotte Ramsey. The next thing I knew they handed me their business card with their pink angel wings logo and these words: Angel 2 Ladies, Insightful Readings on Angels Wings, By Appointment, Kindly Call, Angel 2 Ladies, Eileen & Charlotte, their phone number and email, Angels Be With You! I still have the card! Being raised a good Catholic girl, I was always taught that it was a sin, and against our religious beliefs to engage in fortune telling ventures, since God is the only one who can know the future. Although, I believe this to be true, I also believe the Holy Spirit gives some people gifts in this area.

Being that I didn't seek them out, I let them talk. They told me that I looked sad, and then proceeded to give me a reading, right in the middle of the Monroeville Mall Macy's Shoe Department! They said there was a man in my life, named John, who was suffering with terminal cancer. I replied, "Yes, that would be my father." They told me his Grandmother was in heaven praying for him, and so was somebody named Anthony, who had been in his life. I said that there wasn't anybody close to my father named Anthony, who would now be in heaven praying for him. Then, right after I said that, it dawned on me, that my dad's favorite uncle was my Great Uncle Tony, who would come visit us when my sisters and me were children, bringing us blessed Easter baskets filled with candy every spring! Then the Angel Ladies told me that my dad's cancer in his lung was *frozen*, and would remain so for several years. They said they would pray for him, and as I was thanking them, my mom came into the shoe department. I introduced them, paraphrased what they told me about my father, and then bid them farewell. I never did tune into the radio station that carried their broadcast, but I've always thought what a coincidence it was that I'd run into these 2 Angel Ladies who came out of the blue, wearing pink and white pinned striped blazers on a summer afternoon when we were shopping for a pink and white outfit for my mother. Was I supposed to run into them? Was that meeting meant to be? I took it as a positive sign, a God Wink, with hopes that real angels were watching over my family, and just maybe, my Bubba, and my Great Uncle Tony were in heaven watching over us, and praying for my father. When my mother and I arrived back home that afternoon, my dad was sitting on their front porch in his favorite white wicker rocking chair. As I relayed to him the encounter with the Angel Ladies at the Mall, tears streamed down his face. He was so fragile and emotionally spent, and in need of all the hope and spiritual help he could get. So whether the Angel Ladies were legit or not didn't matter to me, what mattered was maybe there were two more people praying for my dear father.

The UPMC McKeesport Hospital Fashion Show was a huge hit once again, and quickly came and went. Suddenly, it was August, and August brought more bad news. Eddy's sister, Terri Sowerby, was diagnosed with kidney cancer at the age of 46, after several months of feeling sick, tired, and losing weight. She was operated on at UPMC Shadyside Hospital in Pittsburgh, where her doctor removed her right kidney, hoping that the cancer was contained. When caught early enough, if kidney cancer is contained, the kidney is removed, and typically there is no further treatment with an excellent prognosis. We were all hoping and praying that this would be the case with Terri. I remember visiting her in her hospital room that August trying to reassure her and her husband Tom, sister Julie, and mother Beverly that she would be fine. I recalled how Becky, our previous Camelot neighbor, had the same diagnosis many years ago, and was now perfectly healthy and in complete remission. Everyone looked relieved and said how grateful they were to hear that good news. We all remained hopeful.

Unfortunately, that would not be the case with Terri. When she went back for her three month check-up in December, her CAT scan showed that the cancer had spread. It has been over fourteen years now, and Terri has endured many surgeries, and much private suffering. In the past fourteen years, in addition to losing a kidney, she has had part of her lung removed as the cancer began to spread, and a few years later, a tumor removed from her brain. After doctors unsuccessfully used a Cyber Knife at UPMC Shadyside to excise the tumor, Tom took Terri to Memorial Sloan Kettering Hospital in New York City for the brain surgery. They found a brain surgeon, Dr. Viviane Tabar, willing to perform the risky operation. Knowing how traumatic it is for a woman to lose her hair, the female surgeon complimented Terri's head of thick brown hair and compassionately informed Terri that she would only have to shave a thin strip for the incision to operate and remove the tumor. Terri was put in a twilight sleep during the hour-long operation so the skillful surgeon could periodically talk to Terri during the surgery. It was miraculously successful, and the entire brain tumor was removed! Terri woke up from surgery, with the only complication being a loss of perception, the doctor noting that she would never be able to be an architect! Terri shared with us a dream she had while undergoing back to back MRIs. She dreamed that while in the arms of Mary, she saw her dad Rick, my dad John, her brother Bruce, and her cousin Johnny all standing in a row on a stage with their arms around each other sort of like the Radio City Music Hall Rockettes. They were laughing and smiling, and together they all said, "You're welcome, Terri!" Then, they all took a bow! Terri had been praying to all of them for their heavenly help and assistance prior to her surgery.

In addition to dearly departed family members, Terri had been praying to her favorite patron saint and namesake, St. Theresa the Little Flower. During Terri's brain surgery, Eddy, Danny, Julie, and Beverly all went across a little side street to the Church of Saint Catherine of Siena to pray for Terri's successful surgery. Tom remained with Terri at the hospital, and has been with her every step of the way. The emotional support Tom has provided for Terri is a beautiful testimony to their love. It might be important to note here that Eddy told me their brother Danny prays for Terri, when he attends daily Mass, in front of a statue of St. Theresa at his local Catholic church. Danny told Eddy and me that he has seldom missed a day since Terri's diagnosis to pray for Terri in front of that statue. Terri has also mentioned to me how grateful she's been for Eddy's research and guidance during her ordeal. Eddy researched renal cancer advanced drug therapy options, and advised Terri and Tom on questions to ask her doctors. Initially, I connected Terri with our neighbor Becky, which led her to Dr. Hrebinko, the surgeon at the UPMC Hillman Cancer Center in Pittsburgh. We've all rallied our energies for the counterattack on Terri's cancer. Tom's love, Julie's love and home care when needed after surgeries, plus all of our prayers may very well be the reason that Terri is surviving and thriving in spite of this wicked renal cancer that has been wreaking havoc in her body. Once again, the power of love and prayer prevails, and miracles happen. We all continue to pray daily for Terri. A follow up scan did show spread to the left kidney, and a successful surgery to remove part of that kidney was done in 2018. The latest drugs and our prayers are continuing to manage this disease. Terri is an inspiration, and an amazing and courageous survivor. Terri is a miracle!

In September 2008, the first of the baby Ya-Yas got married. Ginny's daughter, Jessica, married her own Eddie in a beautiful church ceremony at St. Vincent Basilica in Latrobe. The reception at the Greensburg Country Club was a joyous and fun occasion. It's always fun when the Ya-Yas get together. Many of our North Huntingdon neighbors and St. Agnes Church friends were also in attendance on this happy occasion. We feasted on filet mignon, toasted with champagne, and danced the night away until well after midnight. The day after the wedding, my feet were really hurting, and I remember thinking for the first time that I wasn't as young as I used to be!

A month after Jessica's wedding, my feet were still hurting and I thought that was strange, so I decided to make an appointment with a podiatrist to see if I did something to my feet when I danced all night in high heels. Dr. Donnie Beck was a year ahead of me at Serra Catholic High School, and since he had a reputation as a good podiatrist, I decided to make an appointment at his office in McKeesport. So after teaching one day in November, I went to my appointment to inquire about the pain in my feet. Dr. Beck gave me a prescription to get my feet x-rayed to make sure I hadn't broken any bones. I made a follow-up appointment before I left, and went back to work the next week. Things were very busy at work, and I was staying late after school most days, so I called to cancel my follow-up appointment with Dr. Beck. The office secretary put me on hold, then got back on the phone and said that Dr. Beck still wanted to see me about my feet x-rays. So, I decided to go to the appointment after all.

Dr. Beck proceeded to tell me that the radiologist noticed lesions on my feet in the x-rays. He relayed that the radiologist had concerns that these lesions on my feet might be indicative of cancer elsewhere in my body! I had never heard of such a thing, and felt so completely shocked that I burst into tears right in front of him! Dr. Beck reassured me that this probably wasn't the case in this instance, because he said that I looked healthy and fine. I told him briefly that my father and sister-in-law were suffering with cancer, and that my family and I couldn't take much more. He kindly said he understood, but recommended that I follow up with my family doctor and get a good check-up just to be sure.

Actually, I wasn't so sure that I was fine. I hadn't been feeling well for quite a while. I felt exhausted most days and emotionally drained. On top of that, I thought I had pulled a muscle in my rib cage area while digging out my dead lawn flowers the first week in November, and carrying the large loads of debris and weeds to the garbage cans. I had been having pains in my right side under my breast in my rib cage area about a month. I decided it would be best to see my primary care physician.

I made an appointment the first week in December. On December 10, 2008, I had an appointment with my primary care physician at his office building in North Huntingdon. After the doctor examined me, he said that I looked healthy and fine, and that it was probably stress that was making me feel so exhausted and tired. He said that I probably pulled a muscle in my rib cage and that it takes months to heal. In addition, he also said that he never heard of lesions in your feet indicating cancer elsewhere in your body. He gave me a script to get my blood work done to check my CBC, and to get a chest x-ray. A week later, I called his office, and the nurse said that my blood work came back fine. Right after that, I went to UPMC McKeesport Hospital for a chest x-ray, and that also came back clear. That was good news, except for the fact that every week I felt sicker and sicker.

Christmas came again, and I just remember feeling so tired and exhausted wondering how I was going to do it all again that year. Eddy and I had started hosting an open house Christmas Eve buffet dinner at our house for our extended families a few years earlier. I loved doing it, and our relatives seemed to love coming to our home, so I knew we couldn't cancel. My mother must have sensed something was wrong, because she kept telling me to take better care of myself. She said that I looked like

I was losing weight, and that she couldn't worry about me, because she had her hands full taking care of my father. I reassured her that I would be fine. The week after Christmas, we celebrated New Year's Eve with the Ya-Yas at Sally and George's house, and toasted the New Year 2009 to good health and happiness. I thank God that we can't see into the future, because 2009 would become one of the most difficult years of my life.

In the beginning of January 2009, I started having horrific night sweats. The sweats were so bad, that I would have to get up in the middle of the night and change my nightgown a couple of times. The bed sheets were drenched, so I would put down a large bath towel to sleep on the rest of the night, so I didn't have to change the sheets. I asked several teacher friends who were older than me, and had already gone through menopause if their hot flashes ever occurred at night, and if they were as severe. When most of them said no, I figured it would be best to make an appointment with my gynecologist. I had missed a couple periods in the past six months, so I thought I was beginning menopause. In the middle of January, I had an appointment with my OBGYN (Obstetrician/Gynecologist). After an exam, he recommended that I try hormone replacement therapy to address the night sweats. When I mentioned the pain under my rib cage that I thought was a pulled muscle, the doctor advised me to make an appointment for physical therapy to deal with the muscle pain.

So, the next thing I did was make an appointment for physical therapy. By this time, it was the beginning of February. During my second or third appointment, I had a different physical therapist who seemed very concerned when I showed him the area on my body that I thought was a pulled muscle. When I laid back on the exam table, the area protruded where the pain had been. As the therapist touched my rock hard skin, he must have realized that it wasn't a pulled muscle, but a large tumor! He told me that I should immediately get myself to a hospital emergency room! Not knowing what he was thinking, I told him that I'd made another appointment that coming Monday with my PCP, because I hadn't been feeling well. He said he didn't want to scare me, but that I better keep that appointment, because he didn't think my problem was a pulled muscle.

As I was leaving that Thursday evening appointment on February 12th, I promised to keep my Monday doctor's appointment. I explained that I had to attend the Norwin PTA Outstanding Educators Dinner the next evening as my teaching partner, Karen, was being honored, and

I had to give the presentation speech. Again, the physical therapist reminded me that nothing was more important than my health, and I reassured him that I would take care of myself. So, I went home that evening, finished writing my speech, and made chocolate-covered strawberries for Karen, and for my mom's card club the next night. Once again, that night, I awoke in a drenching sweat, changed my nightgown, put a towel on my soaking wet sheets, and got up for work the next day. This was becoming a ritual since the beginning of January.

The other symptom I've neglected to mention was the total exhaustion I was feeling every day, no matter how much sleep I got during the night. I remember walking down the school hallways some days those past few months thinking I wished I could just lie down and go take a nap somewhere. Somehow, I made it through those work days, but would come home and lay down for a nap after work, before I'd get up to make dinner, and then go visit my parents. I felt like I was running on empty, and adrenaline was getting me through most days.

It was a huge relief after I gave the presentation speech at the Outstanding Educators Dinner. Karen and Mike seemed touched by my kind and complimentary words, and many people came up to congratulate me on my speech, including our superintendent. After the dinner was over, I bugged out as soon as possible. As I walked to my car in the parking lot of the Stratigos Banquet Hall, I looked up in the sky and promised God that I would do something now to find out one way or another, what was wrong with me. I was glad the weekend was upon us, and hoped that I could get a little rest.

Saturday morning, February 14, 2009, I awoke after another sleepless night of drenching sweats. Since I was too sick to go out to celebrate Valentine's Day, Eddy made us a veal and crab dinner at home. When I could hardly eat the delicious looking food he made, he said we should finally go to the emergency room. So I packed an overnight bag knowing instinctively that I wouldn't be coming home that night.

We drove to the emergency room, where the emergency room doctor listened to my list of symptoms, and then examined me. He knew that I was really worried because I told him I sensed that something was very wrong with me. He told me not to worry, and that it probably wasn't cancer. Then he left the room. Why wasn't I feeling relieved? The next thing I remember was the doctor coming back into the room. All he said was, "I'm sorry, you do have cancer." After that, all I remember is grabbing

Eddy's hand, and feeling as if someone had just sucked the life out of me. Then, I collapsed into him, and everything went **black**.

Since I don't have much recollection of the next few weeks, I've decided to include the notes that Eddy wrote and saved on his computer the next seven days. I'm copying them exactly as he wrote them. Here are his words:

> Susie
>
> Thought it best to keep a log of activities to better understand and support associated cancer treatment and care. Keeping personal sentiment largely out of these entries except where thoughts and opinions might be relevant to our actions.

(FEB 15 - SUN)

I'll call this Day 1 because it's the first day of the disease and I know there will be a final day of the disease, maybe 120, 150, or 180 days from now but there must be full remission . . . we can look forward to late Summer! In actuality . . . the situation first commenced in November 2008 or sooner.

The trip to the Emergency Room occurred at approximately 10:00 pm following yet another worsening night of lethargy, loss of appetite, etc. The difference tonight was she passed on a great Valentine's evening dinner and she had spiked a fever of 101 and rising. We could no longer ignore the signs we had attributed to a pulled rib muscle (pain) and change-of-life (tiredness and night sweats).

The lump on her lower right side had become increasingly evident and, just the prior week, Anna at PT had advised that there was something beyond a muscle tear. The hospital completed a CT scan, and it was an enlarged liver filled with numerous masses. Dr. Gunther had advised that it was probably not cancer but, for the first time, Susie and I suspected otherwise. The doctor had downplayed the matter stating there were three small tumors (3–4 cm); in actuality, there were 5 – 7 and the largest at 12–14 cm. I knew little of cancer at the time (other than research for Terri) but observed that they were very round and neat . . . knew that might be lymphoma and the doctor suggested the same.

Susie was very sick and getting sicker by the minute. We checked into the hospital and were aware that Sunday would be a wasted day (until everyone returned on Monday). The oncologist on call stopped by to allude to the fact that the masses were most probably cancer and that the disease did not start in the liver. They planned to scope the GI tract to find the origin . . . first the lower tract (colonoscopy) then the upper tract (endoscope). I knew they suspected stomach or pancreatic cancer. [Eventually, just the endoscope was performed.] All Susie's vitals were monitored as temperature fluctuated and an IV was started with fluids, Dilaudid (pain), and Ativan (anxiety).

Your mind races in all directions but clear thinking is needed as you evaluate options and push for maximum, accelerated medical attention. Slept at hospital.

Day 2 (FEB 16 - MON)

Oncologist Dr. Kevin Kane visited and appeared very concerned; he ordered an endoscope to identify the origin of the disease. Dr. Sudhir Narla performed the procedure (Sheila observed) and, as suspected, found a large irregular growth (4–5 cm) in the small intestine/duodenum. The growth and surrounding area were extensively biopsied. The findings were forwarded to Pathologist James Primavera (strongly recommended by Dr. Kane as one of the best . . . results were to be available in 48 hours). Slept at hospital.

My mind was racing and the pain of Susie's fear was the worst . . . she repeated that she wanted to attend the girls' weddings and be around for grandchildren. My thoughts were quite opposite (looking back) as most of our dates, starting with the very first party date, distractively flashed through my mind. I also convinced myself that there was no time for self-pity or crying and began to gear up for a long fight.

Day 3 (FEB 17 - TUE)

Nothing new . . . everyone was suspecting the worse, e.g. pancreatic cancer, etc. I had run home and, reluctantly, researched the matter online. I determined that there were four main types of small bowel cancer: (1) Adenocarcinoma, (2) Sarcoma, (3) Carcinoid, and (4) Lymphoma . . . the first was the worst and Lymphoma was the best. I specifically asked if it could be Lymphoma and Dr. Kane indicated no . . . he was almost certain it was the worst, carcinoma (the difference is this one starts in the lining and is untreatable whereas Lymphoma starts in lymph tissue and is highly treatable).

Dr. Kane suggested we go home and rest since we would be better off at home. Real glad to do so ... antsy about the pathology report. Susie was given prescriptions for Dilaudid (pain), Oxycontin (pain), Ativan (anxiety), and Ambien (sleep).

Had a random thought that my grandmother would have been 100 today since she was born on February 17, 1909. I'll bet no one thinks what life is like 100 years after their birth ... what your grandson and his wife might be enduring.

Day 4 (FEB 18 - WED)

Home and feeling a little better ... Susie's able to come downstairs but definitely not interested in seeing anyone. I'd get a few calls and visitors that I had to put off. Nurse Dara called to check in and said that the path report should be back later that day. Once, the diagnosis is clear we can proceed with further testing, including a heart Doppler, a MUGA (heart test), PET-CT scan, bone marrow test, etc. Received no call so I called after dinner ... report still out (expect a very thorough analysis). I remember telling Bridget ... "we're really due for a break."

Day 5 (FEB 19 - THU)

Just got that first real break we needed ... Dr. Kane called at 11:30 am to indicate that the path report has taken a 180-degree turn and they are onto something good ... Lymphoma markers. This takes the cancer out of the GI tract and makes it much more treatable. Not final but the report should be conclusive tomorrow (Friday). Things were looking up (somewhat) and my crazy prayers were getting answered.

Day 6 (FEB 20 - FRI)

1:00 pm – Dr. Kane calls and is very excited, happy, and utterly shocked to report that the pathology report is complete and does indeed indicate fast growing, **Diffused Large B-Cell Non-Hodgkin Lymphoma**. I had read enough to know that this was the best of the worse cases and the fast growing B-Cell NHL was highly treatable and curable and Dr. Kane reiterated the same. I knew immediately that fast growing is actually better as it does not linger like slow growing lymphoma. At my request ... he agreed to verify all of this with the Hillman Cancer Center (Shady Side) and said he was in discussion with a Dr. Raptus (a Greek doctor specializing in Lymphoma). Dr. Raptus was equally surprised by the findings.

Dr. Kane went on to describe the plan of action that included all of the above testing (or staging to determine how widespread the disease is) and a chemo drug regimen referred to as R-CHOP. This is very harsh chemo and includes Rituxan (antibody therapy), Cyclophosphamide, Doxorubicin, Oncovin, and Prednisone (blast of steroids). Susie would need six treatments at three-week intervals (over 4 ½ months). Will detail further on day of first chemo. Of course . . . Susie would experience harsh side effects including hair loss, etc.

Interesting note . . . it was Mr. Tomei's, Mickey Law's, and Richard's birthday and all said the above news was the best gift they could have got. The outpouring support of neighbors, friends, and family is most incredible.

My spirits are high!

Day 7 (FEB 21 - SAT)

Sorry . . . I don't want to do this anymore.

End of Eddy's notes.

I don't remember too much about my first few days in the hospital. Dilaudid, Oxycontin, Ativan, and Ambien were a blessing, and an escape from my misery and pain. I do remember the looks of pity from the kind nurses at UPMC McKeesport who came into my room in the middle of those nights to change my night gown and soaking wet bed sheets after my drenching night sweats, and help me try to maneuver my way to the bathroom with an IV pole attached to me. And I do remember waking up for the first time, and turning my head to see Eddy sitting on a chair in the corner of my hospital room, and what a comfort it was that he was there. I reassured him that I wasn't ready to die, and that I would fight for my life. I wanted to grow old with him, and see our daughters get married, and have grandchildren. I told him that I wanted the whole life experience. Then, I told God that I wasn't afraid to die, I just wasn't ready.

How in the world could I have cancer?! Susie Snowflake had lived a clean life. I always followed all the good health rules! I ate my fruits and vegetables, walked two miles a day for exercise, wasn't overweight, never drank, never did drugs, or smoked cigarettes. Something was wrong with this picture! There was no rhyme or reason for this to happen to me. I rationalized my father and grandmother getting lung cancer, because they had both been smokers in their youth. That wasn't fair either, because they both quit smoking soon after the Surgeon General told America that cigarettes were hazardous to your health. It just wasn't fair. But then, I realized for the first time, that life wasn't fair. Did anybody ever deserve to get cancer, even the people who didn't follow all the good health rules? Was it fair for babies and children to get cancer? Was it fair for frail elderly people to get cancer? Was it fair for good people to get cancer? Was if fair for babies to be born with diseases and disabilities? None of it is fair! And nobody deserves any of it! After this realization hit me, I thought about the crucifixion. Was it fair for an innocent, good man, the Son of God named Jesus, to suffer horribly and die for our sins? These were some of my first conscious thoughts coming out of my merciful fog, or my medically drug induced state of mind. It was early on that I decided not to ask God, "Why me?" I asked myself instead, "Why not me?" I wasn't better than anyone else. I had it too good for too long. It was just my turn to suffer. There had to be a reason. So I figured out I better make it count, and decided to offer it up to God for whatever intention He saw fit. Of course, I suggested many of my own intentions, and begged Him for His mercy and healing grace.

My first chemo treatment was scheduled the end of February. The doctor and nurses had told me a little of what to expect, but naturally didn't want to frighten me any further about the horrors of chemotherapy. Plus, if they'd never experienced the physical and psychological pains of chemo, then they really couldn't explain how horrible it is. They were giving me little bits of information at a time. We teachers call it, *chunking the information*. I was still trying to process everything that was happening to me. They told me that I would lose all my hair, and that it would start falling out about ten days after my first treatment. They warned me about the mouth sores, sore throat, loss of appetite, lack of energy, weight loss, and peripheral neuropathy. They didn't tell me how each subsequent treatment would make me weaker and sicker, because the effects of chemo are cumulative.

The morning of my first chemotherapy treatment was a cold, and sunny blue-sky February morning. I didn't sleep much the night before, worrying about what to expect. As Eddy and I pulled out of our garage, and backed down our driveway, we both looked out the front windshield of the car, up into the sky to see a perfectly shaped cross, out of thin clouds. There were no other clouds in the sky that morning. I took it as a sign from God that he would be with me that morning and throughout my ordeal. That *cloud-cross* gave me the strength I needed to get me through that day. Sometimes God will manifest himself to us through non-magnificent ordinary things. And we must see these things through the eyes of faith.

The UPMC Cancer Center in McKeesport Hospital is where I would go for my chemotherapy treatments. In the cancer treatment center there, I could choose to lay in a lounge chair, or a bed. The nurse suggested a bed the first time, and said I might dose off during the hours long treatment. Several IV bags were attached to a pole beside me, and each one would deliver a different poisonous drug into my veins. My chemo regimen was referred to as RCHOP chemotherapy, an acronym for Rituxan (antibody therapy), Cyclophosphamide, Hydroxydaunorubicin, Oncovin, and Prednisone (steroids). They told me it was potent, AKA brutal, but extremely effective. Dr. Kane said that we were going for the *cure*. I figured I could endure anything that would cure me of cancer. I was determined to live whatever the cost!

The needle went into my forearm veins quite easily the first time. The nurse told me that I had good veins to choose from. I felt a burning sensation as the poisonous chemicals circulated through my bloodstream. I was given lots of fluids through another IV, and soon had to relieve myself. The nurses told me how important it was to drink plenty of water during and after chemo treatments to help flush the poisonous chemicals out of my body. The chemo turned my urine red, and it looked ominous in the toilet. I was told to flush twice, since it's so poisonous. The nurses told Eddy to try not to use the toilet at home right after me. I never slept or dozed off during that first treatment. Looking around the room, it all seemed so surreal. The other lounge chairs and beds were full of sick people getting chemo just like me. Most looked older than me. Most were either bald, or wore scarves or hats on their heads. I knew that's what I'd look like the next time I came for treatment.

After not sleeping the night before, I was hoping to go home and get a good night's sleep. That wouldn't be the case. That first night, I became violently ill and threw up what little food I had eaten that day. I hadn't had an appetite for months, and had lost lots of weight. It took much effort to eat small portions of food. I vomited up the Italian wedding soup, and everything else I had eaten that day. I haven't been able to even look at wedding soup since then. After that, I started shaking all over, and my heart began racing out of control. I was nauseous, and had a terrible headache. I tried to relax and control my heart rate, but it was futile. So, Eddy took me back to the hospital that night, and they admitted me again. The next thing I knew, they called in a cardiologist named

Dr. Awan to treat me. I endured another sleepless night worrying that I might be having a heart attack on top of everything else. And I was still having those horrific drenching night sweats. Again, the nurses had to change my soaking wet sheets and help me change my hospital gown in the middle of the night.

Dr. Awan came to see me first thing in the morning. My sister Sheila had worked for him as a cardiac nurse years before, and had the utmost respect and affection for him. It was easy to see why. He immediately allied my fears, and reassured me after testing, that I wasn't having a heart attack, and that my heart was healthy. He hugged me and told me that I would be fine. That's the first time somebody said that to me, and it was golden. He prescribed a Lopressor which would slow my heart rate during my time going through chemo. My racing heart was my dear little body's reaction to the poison chemicals that were being introduced into my system. All I wanted to do was sleep, but the prednisone wouldn't allow it. It made me feel wired, wide awake, and all jumpy inside when all I wanted and needed was rest. I was becoming so weary. The next day in the hospital, I remember trying to put mascara on my eyelashes, so I would look better if anyone came to visit me. My hand was shaking so badly that I could barely do it. As I look back, I realize what a pitiful sight that must have been since my sickly appearance was the least of my problems. At least the Lopressor was working, and my heart rate became regular again. I would take that prescription for the next year and a half until I could be weaned off of it. After a couple days of monitoring me, I was discharged from the hospital.

Like clockwork, my hair became very matted, and started falling out in about ten days. A few days before it started falling out, my mom, daughter Bridget, sister Denise, hairdresser Heather, and myself took a drive to *Wigs 'N More* boutique in Latrobe. The shop is located directly across from St. Vincent College Basilica, so it was easy to find. It caters to cancer patients. The women who work there, were very compassionate and helpful. When we walked in, it felt surreal that I was looking for a wig. My hair was still thick and long, below my shoulders. It was overwhelming, as there were literally hundreds of wigs to choose from. I didn't know where to start, so I just sat down in a chair and let my loved ones bring me random wigs. I wanted one that looked like my hair, same length, same dark brown color. The first wig I tried on was the one I bought. Strangely enough, it was named *the Susan*! All the wigs had women's names, and this one was exactly what I was hoping to find. Coincidence or not, I call it a *God Wink*. I bought wig shampoo, conditioner, and a wig brush, and off we went.

Heather came back with us to my house to cut my hair into a pixie cut, so it would be less traumatic when my hair started to fall out. After she was done, I looked in the mirror, and was nicely surprised at what I saw. I looked younger, and everyone started calling me Audrey Hepburn. Eddy came home from work, and said the same thing. He gave me a little card with a note that said, "Love the hair." It was a brief little morale boost, but it wouldn't last long.

Not long after that, I started to lose the *Audrey hair*, and it was devastating. I called Heather, and she came back to my house, and shaved my head in our kitchen. It would be too painful to watch it fall out clump by clump. When I looked in the mirror this time, all I saw was a cancer patient with a white bald head and sunken dark-circled eyes. Feeling exhausted all the time, I still wasn't sleeping thanks to the effects of the prednisone. I was starting to get that *cancer look*. I already looked emaciated, like skin and bones, and with a bald head, remember thinking to myself that I looked like a concentration camp victim. For somebody who had been frequently complimented on her good looks throughout their life, this was just another bitter pill to swallow. It is quite humbling. You realize quickly that we are not our physical self. It's unfortunate that our society continues to define women by their physical appearance. This woman in the mirror was not me, but I realized that that's how people would see me. I felt adamant that I wouldn't let it define me. When Eddy came in from work that day, he looked at me, tried to hide his shock, and asked me if my hair would grow back. Then, he quickly regrouped, and said I had a nicely shaped head. After reminding him that the nurses reassured me that it would, I said a prayer that my hair would grow back quickly. I kept telling myself that this was only temporary. Someday, I would look and feel like me again.

Just when the effects of the first chemotherapy treatment were wearing off and I was starting to sleep and feel human again, I was scheduled for my second round. Chemotherapy would be three weeks apart for six treatments. That meant I should be done in June. I had to keep my eye on the ball, put on my armor, stay positive, and keep praying that I would be cured.

After the second chemo, I was beginning to get to know my doctor and nurses better. Dr. Kane was so Christ-like in dealing with me and his other patients. He treated us like people first, asked us about our families, and what we did outside the confines of the cancer treatment center. He was extremely positive and hopeful. His unique sense of humor would help to alleviate the seriousness of what we were all about. His sense of comic relief was a welcome reprieve. And he wasn't just kind to me, because my mother was on the board of directors at the hospital, or because he had been my father's doctor as well. I witnessed him exhibit the same excellent care, concern, and compassion toward all his patients, even those who appeared to be real characters.

The nurses who worked with Dr. Kane seemed to pick up on his demeanor, too. Their names were Dara, Diane, Deanne, Barb, and Sharon. If Dr. Kane, was the Christ-like physician, his nurses were the Angels. They were compassionate and gentle as well. They all knew the right things to say, and what not to say to us patients. They got to know our families, and cared about us as people. Every time, I would leave a chemo treatment, the nurses would tell me they loved me. It was something nice and encouraging to hear. They were my cheerleaders in my battle against cancer. They would smile when you needed a smile, or hold your hand, when you didn't think you could hold on yourself. They made the dreaded cancer center not such a dreadful place to be. They kept reminding me that with each chemo treatment, I was closer to a cure.

The only place I went those first few months besides the hospital was church once a week if I was having a good day. Basically, I just stayed in my bed and rested, because I felt so sick and weak. I couldn't believe how weak I was. It took great effort just to get up out of bed and go to the bathroom. I had no strength. I struggled to eat, and had no appetite. We stocked up on a nutritious drink called Fuze. I drank it daily, and often only wanted hot tea and toast. I often wondered if all cancer patients felt this sick, or was I that sick because I had a blood cancer that zapped all my energy. It took such great effort and energy just to get a shower. After that, I was done. I'd crawl back in my bed and nap. And then I'd wake up and pray.

All I did for days on end was lay in my bed and pray. I prayed the rosary daily, novenas to the Sacred Heart of Jesus, the Infant of Prague, the Blessed Mother, St. Jude, St. Theresa, St. Anthony, and St. Peregrine. I prayed like it was my job. I prayed in my bed with my door closed, and felt the loving calming presence of God with me during those times. I prayed so intensely and passionately, that several hours would go by and I didn't even realize it. I grew to treasure that time I had alone with Jesus. During this time, I guess I developed a personal relationship with him. I felt being personally loved by God. I wasn't just praying for myself either. I prayed for everyone I knew who needed or asked for prayers. I prayed for people on the news who were hurt in accidents, or were victims of natural disasters. I had a long list of regulars, mostly family and friends, on my prayer list, and it didn't seem like work. It brought me great comfort and peace. It was my only escape from my pain. The more I prayed the better I felt; if not physically, then certainly, emotionally. Something else interesting to note here, is that I couldn't cry. For some reason, even when I was alone for hours on end when Eddy and Bridget were at work all day, and Tierney was away at St. Vincent College, and Kaitlin was living in Georgetown, I still couldn't cry for myself. I knew I had every reason to cry, but just couldn't. I think I knew instinctively that if I started, then I wouldn't stop. Maybe I just didn't want to open the dam, and release all those waters.

Bridget moved back home from her apartment in the Southside of Pittsburgh to help Eddy take care of me. I was too sick at the time to even feel guilty for that. I knew I was fighting for my life, and needed all the help I could get. I was too sick to cook meals, or do the other many household chores that need done when you're running a home. I truly appreciated her self-less act of love and sacrifice for me. Bridget and Eddy cooked dinners, brought meals upstairs to my bedroom, cleaned, did laundry, shopped for groceries, supported each other, and helped take care of me. She never complained about it, or about getting up earlier in the morning to go catch a bus to ride back to her law firm in the city. Eddy was my rock, always remaining steady and calm, at least in front of me. During my sickest days, when I was in the most pain, he made sure I took the right pills in the proper doses on days that I was so medicated, I didn't know which way was up. Most mornings he would take the extra time before he left for work to make me delicious looking *Grand Slam* breakfasts, and bring them upstairs to our bedroom on a tray. He did this particularly on my worst days when I couldn't get out of bed after the effects of chemo would hit me hard several days after each successive treatment.

Msgr. Paul Fitzmaurice had been reassigned from St. Barbara's in Harrison City, and was now pastor at our home parish of St. Agnes in North Huntingdon. He called our home, as I had been put on the parish prayer list, to see when he could come to our house to give me the Sacrament of the Sick. This was in the first few weeks of my illness. So he came one evening and I got dressed in sweats and came downstairs to our family room to greet him. Bridget, Tierney, Sheila, and my niece, Meghan, were there, too. Msgr. Paul said some powerful prayers over me, and read some scripture from the Bible. He blessed me with holy oil and stayed a little longer to visit with us. We sent Eddy out prior to this to play basketball to relieve some stress. Msgr. Paul mentioned when he was leaving that he had invited Father Bill Kiel to our parish in March to conduct a Healing Mass. I put it on our calendar in hopes I could attend.

CHAPTER 11

My Miracle & Transformation

THE Healing Mass was scheduled for March 10, 2009 at St. Agnes Church in North Huntingdon, a week before my second chemo, so I felt well enough to attend. Eddy and I went into our church and sat in the back. I didn't know if I'd be well enough to stay. The Mass was conducted by Father Bill Kiel with Monsignor Paul concelebrating. The Mass began with a soul-searching examination of conscience, and then the usual ritual of scripture readings, gospel, offertory, consecration of the Eucharist, Our Father, sign of peace, and Holy Communion. At the end of Mass, Healing Service instructions were given followed by prayers for healing. We were instructed how to exit from our pews to come to the center of the altar if we wanted to be blessed and participate in the *laying of the hands*. Catchers were standing on either side of the lines of people who were standing in front of both priests. The church was filled with sick and disabled people and their families who were there to support them. I decided I wanted and needed this blessing. Not knowing what to expect, I walked down the aisle with Eddy behind me to stand in front of Father Bill Kiel on the altar of God.

I was shaking as I walked down the aisle toward the altar, but I felt compelled to do this. I walked toward Fr. Bill Kiel, and stood directly in front of him. Eddy stood behind me, and two catchers were on either side of me. Fr. Bill laid his hands on top of my head. I didn't even care, or notice if his hands moved my wig. I closed my eyes, folded my hands in prayer, and prayed silently that the Holy Spirit would hear my plea, come to me, and heal me. I begged him. Fr. Bill started to pray aloud. At first, I heard him in English, and then it sounded as if he switched to praying in

Latin, and then he sounded like he was praying in gibberish. I thought, "Is this Greek?" Suddenly, I realized that he was speaking in tongues! And he sounded like he was praying faster and faster. Even though my eyes were closed, I could see bright ovals of lights going round and round in front of my eyes. And the next thing I felt was my body going down, floating down, and resting on the ground. I laid there on the altar floor, floating in an unconscious state. I felt the pure peaceful love of God enveloping me, holding me, and warming my body. It was pure ecstasy! Heavenly light was all around me. I just laid there (Eddy said it was about 10 minutes, but I had no sense of time.) relishing the feeling of the warm and loving embrace of the Holy Spirit. I was literally and physically feeling God's love! I knew he came to me, and I was basking in his glow and glory. I could have lain there forever, but too soon, I felt Eddy shaking me to wake up and get up. I opened my eyes and realized I'd been crying. Tears were rolling down my face. They were tears of joy! Tears of relief! Tears of humble gratitude! I had a hard time getting my balance as I stood up, so the catchers and Eddy helped steady me. Eddy put his arm around me and guided me back to our pew. I tried to process what just happened to me and couldn't. I said some prayers of gratitude, and then Eddy helped me walk outside to our car. There was a sacred silence in the car on the ride home. I couldn't find the words to describe what had just happened to me, because it's too much for words, and so I decided to savor the silence and reflect on the spiritual blessing I had just experienced. After being anointed by the Holy Spirit, I felt the joy of being personally loved by God. Words will never be adequate enough to describe my ethereal experience and what took place in my soul at that Healing Mass. This profound encounter with God was like my own Personal Pentecost. It transformed me forever, and I would never be the same.

That experience also helped me to better understand the mystery of the consecration at Mass when the priest blesses the bread and wine transforming it into the Holy Eucharist. I had a hard time understanding that the bread and wine actually become the Body and Blood of Christ until then. I realized that if God could send his Holy Spirit down to physically transform me, then he could just as easily send down his Holy Spirit to change the bread and wine into the Body and Blood of Jesus Christ. It's all such a mystery based on faith, but now more easily believed and understood. I no longer think that the bread and wine *represent* the Body and Blood of Jesus, I truly believe that it *transforms*, and when we receive Holy Communion, we take in the Spirit of God.

The next week I was scheduled for my second chemotherapy treatment, and another CT scan. Sheila protectively told me not to expect much in terms of positive results on the CT scan, as I'd just had only two chemo treatments and I had been polluted with large liver tumors. Best case scenario, we were hoping to see the tumors had shrunk, that the chemo was working, and that my body was responding positively to the chemo. Dr. Kane appeared to be in shock as he put my CT scan results up onto the computer. He waved us over to the counter to see the screen for ourselves. After only two chemo treatments there was absolutely no sign of the cancer! Every tumor had completely disappeared! These were nothing short of miraculous results! Dr. Kane was elated to announce to us loud and clear, "Complete remission!" Then he declared, "It's a miracle if I've ever seen one!" Eddy, Sheila, and the Cancer Center nurses had tears in their eyes. Eddy and Sheila were so happy! Once again, I felt numb. I was so sick and exhausted that I wasn't processing much information those days. This was something they didn't typically see, especially in a case as serious as mine. I knew then and there immediately why my scan was clear, but I felt too overwhelmed and not yet ready to try and explain my experience at the Healing Mass. Once again, the Hand of God had worked with medical science to produce another miracle. This time, I was the one who was blessed.

Dr. Kane explained to us that I would still need to continue the entire chemotherapy regimen. With four more treatments to go, every three weeks, I would be done with chemo in June. This was only March, but I had just received good news, and it gave me the encouragement that I needed to sustain me.

My clear scan wasn't the only good news that March. My daughter Kaitlin had some good news of her own. Kaitlin was working on her Master Degree in Public Policy (Health Care) at the Georgetown University Public Policy Institute at that time. Since arriving in Washington, DC the previous year, Kaitlin had been very active with studies and work at the Washington Division of the URS Corporation (Government Affairs), where she performed research and prepared legislative briefings. She had also been elected and was serving as the 2009 Georgetown Public Policy Institute Conference Chair addressing four major policy fields: health care, energy/environment, education, and homeland security. Speakers included Chief Economic Advisor Jared Bernstein, Secretary of Homeland Security, Michael Chertoff, Washington Post Columnist, E.J. Dionne, and health care panelists Judy Feder, Charlie Kolb, Christopher

Jennings, and the Honorable Thomas Daschle. The GPPI Conference was scheduled for March 20, 2009, in Washington DC. Kaitlin had worked so diligently to make the conference a success, and she invited us hoping that some of her family could attend. Unfortunately, I was too sick and extremely disappointed that I wouldn't be able to attend the conference. However, Eddy, Bridget, my Mom, and Uncle Tim drove to Washington, DC to support her, and attend the conference. My sisters checked in on my dad and me, as we were too weak to make the trip. The conference was highly attended and considered a huge success. We are so proud of Kaitlin, and all of her accomplishments as she builds herself a career in health care policy and politics. A formal framed photograph, with names and the date of the conference, of Kaitlin arm in arm with Thomas Daschle, Judy Feder, Charles Kolb, and Christopher Jennings still stands on top of her childhood dresser in our home.

Kaitlin had a longstanding interest in health care since her undergraduate days at the University of Pittsburgh. During the fall 2009 semester at Georgetown, Kaitlin joined the Senate Finance Majority Committee as a Graduate Associate on the Health Care Team. She was thrilled to work with all the dedicated members of the committee under the leadership of Senator Max Baucus as they drafted the Affordable Care Act (ACA) and made United States history. She would tell me how she would literally jump out of bed in the morning because she was so excited and couldn't wait to get to work. She told stories how they would work until the wee hours of the morning unaware of the time, because they were all so passionate about what they were drafting. Kaitlin received Christmas cards from Senator Baucus that were delivered to our home address for many years since then.

Kaitlin has shared with me her most memorable moments from her time working on the Affordable Care Act. Her fondest memories include: eating Georgetown cupcakes with Senator John Kerry at midnight while they were all still working, accidentally getting into the *Senators Only* elevator with Senator John McCain, who didn't even scold her, and instead was kind enough to ask her how her day was going. Despite initially being on opposite ends of the aisle in the battle for the passage of the Affordable Care Act all those years ago, Kaitlin has said she will forever hold Senator John McCain in the highest esteem. She knew he was a kind man that day in the elevator and, roughly seven years later, she learned that he was also a man of great character. With his iconic *thumbs down* vote to block the repeal of the ACA in July of 2017, he shocked the Republican Party and the nation, having come full circle to defend the legislation he once fought so hard to prevent. Amidst his own battle with terminal cancer and just days short of his final year on earth, in true *Maverick* spirit, Senator McCain chose to put country over party by casting his historic vote. He must have realized how many American lives were at stake should the legislation be repealed. Perhaps we all learn to see things a little more clearly when facing our own mortality.

The American Cancer Society conducts a *Look Good Feel Better Seminar for Women* undergoing chemotherapy cancer treatment. I received an invitation to attend the local event that was held at the Arnold Palmer Cancer Center at Mountain View in Latrobe, Pennsylvania the end of March. I decided to attend, and my daughter Bridget was kind and compassionate enough to join me. When I walked up to the receptionist, she asked me if I was looking for the seminar, and I immediately knew she knew I was a patient, because I knew I had the *cancer look*. Maybe she could tell I was wearing a wig. It saddened me for a moment, but I regrouped and went inside the conference room. There were about a dozen other women there. Most looked much older than me, and there were a couple who looked my age. All I kept thinking was, "I don't belong here." The old Sesame Street song sounded in my head. "One of these things is not like the others, one of these things just doesn't belong." I immediately wanted to leave, but did not. The women presenters showed us cancer patients how to wear makeup and do our wig hair. They gave us free samples of makeup and hair products, and pep talks on how we could still look good during our ordeal. They did a nice job, but their presentation really depressed me. I couldn't wait to get out of there. It wasn't good for me. Guess I'm not the type for something like that, because it really made me feel like crying. But once again, I couldn't cry. I was the girl who used to cry at sentimental Hallmark and Kodak commercials, but I still couldn't cry. Maybe because I had done so much crying over what my parents were going through, that I just didn't have the energy for any more tears.

After my third chemo treatment, I felt sicker, weaker, and more exhausted. The nurses were like my cheerleaders announcing that I was halfway home. Eddy would take the mornings off work, and come to all of my chemo treatments with me. He sat by my side, and never made me feel like he'd rather be somewhere else. Getting me back to good health seemed like his number one priority. Eddy always said the *right thing* to me when I needed it the most. He remained calm, kind, and loving on my most difficult days. Every sick person should have a *patient advocate* as knowledgeable, optimistic, and supportive as Eddy. His love gave me the strength to keep fighting on days when I suffered the most. He is truly my hero, and the love of my life!

The months seemed to go very slowly, as I would get weaker and more exhausted feeling sicker with every subsequent chemo treatment. The side effects of each new chemo treatment would hit me several days after the poisons were injected and circulating through my bloodstream. The prednisone would prevent me from sleeping when I needed sleep so badly. Sleep was my only escape. The mouth sores and neuropathy came like clockwork. Dr. Kane adjusted one of the chemicals in my chemo medicine, instructed me to drink plenty of fluids, and the neuropathy in my feet seemed to improve. But that sick feeling got worse after each treatment. And every month as I got further away from the chemo treatments, just when I felt like I was starting to get my strength back, they would hit me again with another chemo treatment. And each time the cumulative side effects got worse.

Besides praying all the time, I had a lot of time to think about things. I sort of came up with a bucket list of things I had wanted to do in my life, but never got around to doing yet. Top of my list was playing the piano. I had always wanted to play the piano when I was a child, but never had the opportunity. In addition, I thought that learning to read music would help me combat *chemo brain*. I was so afraid of developing that side effect of chemo, and had read that learning new things, and exercising the brain would help. So one day that spring, I called Karen Dietrich, Kaitlin's and Tierney's former piano teacher, to see if she was still giving lessons. After I explained why I was calling, and asked her if she gave adult piano lessons, she quickly agreed to take me on as one of her students. We scheduled my first piano lesson in May 2009. I drove myself to my first lesson, which was only ten minutes away at Karen's home in Irwin. She greeted me with warmth, compassion, and enthusiasm. We developed a close friendship over the next four years that I took lessons with her. She was an excellent pianist who loved music, and loved teaching piano, and sharing her passion with her students. Karen Dietrich was another blessing I received during this difficult time in my life. She was a bright spot. She was another angel that God had put in my life, as she helped me get back in touch with the land of the living. I had felt more in touch with the spiritual world for so long, and music was a soothing transition back to reality. Karen was always encouraging and positive, even on days when I didn't have a good lesson. She was flexible with our schedule and very understanding if I ever had to cancel a lesson due to not feeling well.

Karen Dietrich had lost her husband David to melanoma a few years before I started my lessons, so she had known all too well about the effects of chemo, and how fighting cancer is such a roller coaster ride. She had been a loving and supportive wife taking care of her husband until the end of his life. She had her share of heartache, and carried her cross with dignity and grace. She was a true lady in every sense of the word. And it wasn't until I had taken lessons with her for about three years that she revealed to me that she had nonalcoholic cirrhosis of the liver disease. She had lost her hair the third year of my lessons, and she had asked me where to get a good wig. We learned a lot about each other those four years, and we kept each other abreast about the members of our families, as she had taught my daughters piano when they were younger, and I had taught her grandson Nathan, at Hillcrest. My last piano lesson with her was July 23, 2013. We decided to take a temporary break from our piano lessons as I started a new teaching assignment in August, and she had begun going in and out of the hospital as her health worsened. Karen was eventually put on the liver transplant list in hopes of getting a transplant to save her life. We kept in touch with phone calls and I sent her greeting cards and flowers during her wait for a new liver. She never did get that transplant. On May 1, 2014, Karen Dietrich passed away peacefully at her home. I found out from my mother who had called to read her obituary in the Pittsburgh Post-Gazette. I loved her dearly and hope she knew what a difference she made in my life, and in the lives of my daughters. I know without a doubt, that she is an angel in heaven playing her precious piano, surrounded by a choir of cherubim and seraphim, giving honor and glory to God.

By the time the summer of 2009 came, not only didn't I have any hair on my head, but I didn't have hair anywhere else on my entire body. I felt naked and exposed and very vulnerable. I missed my thick eyebrows and eyelashes, and even my arm hair that some boy made fun of in eighth grade! It seemed strange that I no longer had to shave my legs. Guess that was one perk. I also developed a love-hate relationship with my wig that summer. I realized it was a blessing to have a wig, and it was better that being bald, but the wig was hot, the weather was hot, and since the chemo put me in instant menopause, I started having hormonal hot flashes. Hot flashes are horrible when you're wearing a wig! Especially when you are out in public, and you can't rip it off! When I was alone in the house, I wouldn't wear the wig, but I wore it when Eddy and our daughters were around, as I tried to look as normal as possible for them and me. I really missed my hair! I missed feeling like a natural woman, as Carol King used to sing. It's a shame that so much of our sense of attractiveness and feminine identity is tied up in our hair.

I felt embarrassed every time Eddy saw me without my wig. When we went to bed at night, I didn't wear the wig, and wondered if he was repulsed by how I looked. (Eddy told me after he read this . . . "I never felt that way, and looked at you the same . . . beautiful.") I wondered if I would ever feel pretty or sexy again. I wondered that for a long time . . . years! He never said anything to make me feel that way, it was something that came from within me. I guess too much importance had been placed on my looks in my life. I realized that I didn't want that to be my only value. Would I ever feel normal again? When would I start to feel like the old Susie? Then, I realized I would never be the same. I would never look at life the same way. I felt more like a spiritual being than a physical being. I felt more like a part of the spiritual world than the physical world around me. It was strange. Then, I read a quote from the French philosopher-priest, Pierre Teilhard de Chardin: "We are not human beings having a spiritual experience. We are spiritual beings having a human experience." That about summed it up better than I ever could have.

The first time I was allowed to drive after being weaned off of many of my pain meds, I was terrified to get back behind the wheel. I was shaking. Even when other people would drive me, I felt very anxious. Those feelings stayed with me for a long time.

My sisters, Sheila and Denise, were with us every step of the way in this long journey. Sheila would stop on her way home from work almost every day to check in and see how I was coping. If I had a particularly bad night and was scared, she even stopped at our house on her way to work a few times to help reassure me. Every time I had an MRI or a CT scan, she was always helping to get my reports quickly, as we all worried waiting for results during those stressful times. She would stop down to see me in the Cancer Center when she could get away for a few minutes. Her colleagues in the hospital, and contacts in radiology, made sure I got prompt results, and excellent attention. Denise would come to my house in the day, and bring lunch, run errands for us, pick up meds at the drug store, or just sit and visit. She even drove me to some of my follow up appointments which were every three to four months after my last chemotherapy treatment. She came with me when I went to get my wig, and drove me to get head scarves, and skull caps. The day of my last chemotherapy treatment, Denise, Rachel, and Luke showed up in the Cancer Center with a bouquet of helium balloons that said "Congratulations!" I couldn't have gone through what I did without the love and support of Eddy, Bridget, Sheila, and Denise. They were part of my *Inner Circle* that helped me survive the nightmare. I know it killed Kaitlin and Tierney that they couldn't be there, but Eddy and I insisted that they remain at Georgetown University and St. Vincent College during this difficult time.

Denise was with me at my house the day the *Teachers Basket of Caring* was delivered to my front porch. My teacher friends at Hillcrest had put together a basket of cheer to help support me during this difficult time. Denise carried the heavy basket of gifts up to my bedroom, where she opened every present for me on my bed, and recorded who sent what on notepaper, so I could write thank you notes when I felt stronger. This show of support touched my heart and lifted my spirits. The teachers sent perfect presents such as: daily prayer books, religious medals, novenas, enrollment in spiritual societies, spring magazines, flower pots with seed packets, wind chimes, inspiration books, novels, bath and body products, angel statues, bracelets, healing stones, nail salon gift cards, Giant Eagle grocery gift cards, restaurant gift cards, Macy's gift cards, and sincere and loving well wishes in handwritten notes and Hallmark get well cards. It was all wrapped in cellophane and sealed with a big beautiful pink bow. I felt so loved by my dear colleagues.

In addition to all those presents, my fellow Hillcrest teachers once again went above and beyond the call of duty and cooked dinners and delivered them to my house every Wednesday from the end of February until the end of May, and they never missed a week! No matter the winter weather, or how tired they must have been many of those evenings after work, they never missed a week. They must have had a sign-up sheet in the mailroom, because there was such a nice variety of delicious foods and no repeats from week to week. So for four months every Wednesday, my dear teacher friends cooked and delivered dinners for my family, and always made enough so that we had those leftovers on Thursdays. Their selfless gift was priceless, as my poor husband and daughters knew they didn't have to worry about making dinners those days of the week. I'll always remember the phone conversation I had with Rose, our Hillcrest principal, several months after my diagnosis. She called to ask how I was doing, and wanted to relay to me these words, "Susie, you are loved!"

Those words meant the world to me. I felt their love and support. It was love, prayer, and faith that helped me survive cancer.

My teacher friends had also put me on their various church prayer lists. Our faculty and staff belong to many different churches and denominations, and I was put on all of them. With all those prayers storming heaven, I just knew God had to be listening. So many people were praying for me, including Sister Michaelette, my beloved fifth grade teacher, who put me on the Vincentian Sisters of Charity intentions prayer list. I do believe the nuns' prayers aided my recovery and remission.

My Taylor Ridge neighbors were also supportive and helpful. My next door neighbor, Kristin, sent around a sign-up sheet to my neighbors to cook dinners for my family. They cooked and delivered dinners to my home on Mondays during those months I was on chemo. They also sent greeting cards, religious prayer books, novenas, religious medals, and books of daily meditations. I felt surrounded by love and support.

During my illness, I saved every get well card, thinking of you card, and novena that came in the mail. I lost count at about 450 cards. I've saved them in a large shoebox in my bedroom closet. Someday, I might reread them, but I'm not ready to do that yet. Someday I will. Those cards represent the love that came back to me. People sent cards with messages in them of how I had touched their life in some good way or another over the years of my life. People who had been in my life years earlier, people who I hadn't seen, or spoken to in years and years, were suddenly coming out of nowhere to send their love and support, and tell me that they were praying for me. Childhood friends, high school friends, college friends, old neighbors from previous neighborhoods, former colleagues, acquaintances, past coworkers, club members, former teacher friends and partners, former students, and even parents of students I had taught over the years sent their well wishes. Lots of church parishioners, from our regional churches, also sent prayer cards, novenas, and messages of love and support. It made me think of the old adage, that you get back in life the love that you give. Or as Oprah says, "You receive from the world what you give to the world." What a blessing it was to live to witness all that love coming back to me! Not many people get to see that while they're alive! And I'm still astounded by all the people who told me that they prayed for me!

August of 2009 came, and I knew I was still too sick and weak to return to work. The poisons would be within my body for a long time before I felt well enough to resume my rigorous teaching job. I needed to protect my immune system, and get my strength back. It was too soon to expose myself to all those classroom germs. I was on a short term disability leave. Our wonderful teachers union, the NEA, (Norwin Education Association), established a Sick Bank policy that I was fortunate enough to utilize during my recuperation period. Our then Superintendent, Dr. Jack Boylan, announced on the first teacher back-to-school in-service day that I needed to "Power Up" before I returned to teaching. The Norwin School District administrators, NEA, and fellow teachers were a true blessing to me, with their support and understanding during that difficult time in my life.

Autumn arrived, and with each month I felt a little stronger. In October, another local Catholic Church, St. Edward's, nearby in Herminie, Pennsylvania was hosting another Healing Mass with Fr. Bill Kiel. I read about it in our St. Agnes Church bulletin, and was debating whether to go again. I was wondering whether what had happened to me at the St. Agnes Healing Mass in March could ever happen again. Was it a one-time miracle? Should I go again to another Healing Mass? What if I went and didn't have the same experience? I asked Eddy if he would join me, and he said that he would. So off we went to St. Edwards Church to participate in another sacred Healing Mass. The church was packed with people again that evening. Once again, we sat in the back pews and participated in the Holy Mass prior to the Healing Service. The church was packed with faithful sick and disabled patients and their loved ones who were all praying for grace, healings, and cures. After Mass, those participants wishing to be blessed during the laying of the hands processed down the aisles to the altar. I walked down with Eddy behind me. I was trembling as I walked up to Fr. Bill Kiel to have him pray over me once again. This time I closed my eyes as I had done before, folded my hands, and prayed for the Holy Spirit to come to me. This time as soon as I heard Fr. Bill start to pray over me with his hands on top of my head, I felt a strong wind-like push, and immediately felt myself going down, floating down, once again, until I was resting in the glorious light and love of the Holy Spirit. He came to me once again, this time to reassure me, that what happened to me was real, and reaffirm my faith in the miracle of my healing. I rested once again in an ethereal, euphoric state until Eddy and the catchers started to help me get up off the altar floor. I felt shaky as Eddy led me back to our pew to say prayers of gratitude and compose myself before we left the church. The experience gave me the extra faith and confidence I needed as I faced my fears and fought to remain in remission.

I am in awe at the power of the Holy Spirit. Now at Mass, when I recite our Profession of Faith, otherwise known as the Nicene Creed, and pray the words . . . "He came down from heaven, and by the Holy Spirit was incarnate of the Virgin Mary, and became man," the mystery makes more sense to me that this is how Jesus was conceived. It was by the power of the Holy Spirit that the Virgin Mary conceived a child and gave birth to the Son of God. I get it now. The Holy Spirit is the love of God. So many pieces of the faith puzzle were falling into place.

I was on track to return to my teaching position at Hillcrest, as a fifth grade Literacy teacher, the second semester. I was willing myself to be well enough to return by January. In December, Sally and George invited Eddy and me to spend a few days with them, and Ginny and Bill, at their time-share condo on St. Maarten's Island in the northeast Caribbean. Since Eddy and I had been to St. Maarten's with them several years before, we knew it would be the perfect place to relax and rest before starting back to my rigorous teaching job. I was still wearing my wig when we boarded the plane in Pittsburgh in December, but knew I wouldn't be able to wear it in the tropical heat of the island. I was nervous about letting my friends see me without the wig, but they were so sweet and complimentary when they saw me, that I quickly got over my embarrassment. I felt liberated, free, and natural, and unconditionally loved by our friends.

St. Maarten's Island is a constituent country of the Netherlands, and so its culture creates a laid back lifestyle. We had no set schedule there. We just lounged on the beach, and floated in the warm Caribbean waters. It was wonderful letting the ocean waves wash over my weary body. There were several native women who walked the beach offering visitors body massages as we laid on our beach towels. At the time, I had developed frozen shoulders, probably from the chemo, and so I paid for an arms and shoulders massage to help me relax my muscles. Although, it felt good, I eventually needed three months of physical therapy three evenings a week to help get my mobility back in my frozen shoulders after we came home. I was sad when we drove back to the airport to return home. My friends kept reassuring me that I shouldn't wear my wig anymore, but I put it back on for the plane ride. I wasn't ready to go out in public without it yet. I felt like people would look at me, and know right away that I was a cancer patient. I thought with my wig, they couldn't tell. But looking back, I bet they probably could.

Christmas came and went, and we were grateful for another Christmas with my father. He was on a maintenance chemo schedule which was keeping the cancer inside of him from growing or spreading, but was making him sick in other ways. He started to tell us that December that he didn't know how much longer he could continue with the chemo. He kept saying that it was probably his last Christmas with us, and tried to discourage us from getting him presents. But we did anyway. I bought him a Keurig Coffee Machine, and he enjoyed drinking the different k-cup flavors that next year. Simple pleasures were so appreciated. We kept trying to get him anything he wanted or needed as we tried to distract him from his misery. We just kept praying for God's guidance and mercy, day after day, night after night.

One night, during the week between Christmas and New Year's Eve, I awoke in the middle of the night with the realization that I was going to write this book. Never in my wildest dreams was writing a book among them. I sat up in bed and my mind just kept racing. I debated whether I should go get my laptop, and start writing down my thoughts, but decided to wait until morning. It was then that I sat at my computer and drilled out ten pages without even stopping. Where was this coming from? I never intended to write a book. Then, it all made sense to me . . . why I had been teaching the literacy components of reading, writing, and grammar the past ten years when I had wanted to teach math, suddenly became very clear. *Focus, content, style, organization, and conventions*! These were the writing components I'd been teaching my students for years. Now, I was meant to apply these skills to write a narrative of my own. I'd write my own story . . . *my journey of faith*. I needed a good title for it without turning people off. As I thought about what got me through my own cancer ordeal, and what was getting us through my father's, I knew it was love. *Love was there* . . . every step of the way. When I looked up in the sky the morning of my first chemotherapy treatment and saw the cloud cross, love was there. When I was lying in the hospital bed fighting for my life, and looked over to see Eddy sitting in the chair in the corner of my room, love was there. When my family and friends visited and brought dinners, love was there. When my nurses told me they loved me every time I finished a chemo treatment, love was there. When I went to the Healing Masses and the Holy Spirit came upon me, love was there. When I laid in my bed praying to God for help and mercy and literally felt his presence with me, love was there. *Love Was There . . . A Testimony of Faith*, that would be the title of my book. I'd changed the title of this book several times. So that's what I would write about, the miracles I had witnessed, and/or experienced in my own life, and my journey of faith. But that week flew by, and now I had to get ready to resume my life as a teacher, so I put my writing on the back burner for a while. Little did I know that it would take me many years to finish writing this spiritual memoir about my *journey of faith*.

CHAPTER 12

Normalcy

BEFORE I knew it, it was January, and I was back to work teaching Literacy at Hillcrest. Lori, Amy, and Natalie, my fun fellow Literacy teachers, helped me quickly get back in the groove with our weekly planning meetings. They had worked with my long term substitute and kept her up to speed planning our Literacy lessons. Karen kept me in the know about any new changes in procedure at Hillcrest, and helped acquaint me with our crew of 50 students. I couldn't have asked for a better teaching partner. She was a blessing to me, and remains a dear friend. Her positive can-do attitude made my transition back to work as smooth as possible. Quickly, it became business as usual. I felt a little nervous, but was ready, at least mentally, to be back. It was exhausting keeping the pace I had kept for years before, and it would be a long time before I had my energy level back. Teaching is a very demanding and rigorous profession. But after teaching all those years, it was like riding a bike again.

Some things just come back so easily. I've always felt so comfortable, and in my element in a classroom full of students. There is such a sense of satisfaction when a struggling student finally gets it. That *aha* magical moment is very rewarding for teachers. I missed those moments. I've always felt that teaching God's children, and being a good wife and mother, was my life's purpose, and that I was put on this earth to try and make a positive difference in their lives. This was my way of trying to do God's will, and giving back my blessings. Teachers don't just teach content subjects. We teach values and life's lessons along the way. In a teacher's lifetime, we literally have the opportunity to touch thousands of lives. It's so cool that thousands of people know us. We run into former students in random places throughout our lifetime. It's such a rewarding experience when they recognize me years later, and recall a kindness, a favorite lesson, activity, or some happy childhood memory that I've provided for them. Sometimes, when our students have troubled home lives, their happiest memories are those made at school where they felt safe, accepted, and valued. Teachers have the privilege of touching lives and improving them in ways typically reserved for parents and people in the medical profession. Making a positive difference in my students' lives is intrinsically rewarding. So, my new crop of students, and my teaching friends and colleagues, welcomed me back with love and support. After a short time, it felt like I'd never left.

On March 9, 2010, Msgr. Paul Fitzmaurice concelebrated another evening healing Mass at St. Agnes Church with Father Bill Kiel. This would be the third healing mass that I would attend since my diagnosis. This time I invited my parents to attend hoping that my father would come forward during the healing service after the Mass for the laying of the hands blessing. I wasn't sure if my dad would feel well enough to come, and I didn't want to pressure him, but I was still hoping and praying that Daddy would get his miracle cure. My parents did come, and they sat in the back of the church, while Eddy and I were sitting in the middle section halfway back from the altar. I went through the whole mass and healing service without knowing they were there. The church was packed with sick and handicapped people along with their loved ones like in previous healing masses. Once again, I walked down the aisle trembling with the hope that I would rest in the spirit again during the laying of the hands blessing. Eddy accompanied me to the altar as I walked toward Father Bill Kiel for the third time. As he laid his hands upon my head for the blessing I prayed for the Holy Spirit to come upon me. This time as I heard the priest begin to pray over me, I immediately went down, and rested in the Spirit. There were no oval lights, no praying in tongues, and no wind-like push. It was an almost immediate descent into ecstasy. The warm embracing love of God flooded over me with that ethereal light. Once again, it felt like I was floating on a cloud. It was sheer joy. It is indescribable. When I woke up out of that unconscious state, I was crying again with tears of joy running down my face. Many people who witnessed this have commented to me since then how it has touched their life and increased their faith. I wish I knew what Daddy thought about the whole experience. He was always very private about such things. I found out later from my sister Sheila who was there, that Daddy walked down to the altar for the laying of the hands blessing, but he never rested in the Spirit. I'm not sure if he ever believed that a miracle could happen to him.

Spring 2010 arrived, and with it came the annual overnight Hillcrest camping trip to Camp Lutherlyn. The students were so excited to explore nature via the environmental learning stations set up around the forested mountain campgrounds. The teachers on the other hand, being responsible for groups of over 100 students at a time, just hoped every year that everyone would behave well, stay safe, and not have major accidents. Lori, Wendy, Karen, and I went together as Team 5D Teachers. It was always a rigorous Marine-like schedule for the two days we were there. It was up for a nature walk at 7:00 a.m., breakfast at 8:00, and then a full schedule of activities around the mountain until the campfire at 8:00 p.m. no matter what the weather would bring. We would be so exhausted from trudging up and down those mountain trails on those fieldtrips, but still never slept well worrying about whether any of our students would get sick or homesick or both. We would bunk in the teachers' cabin while the parent chaperones stayed in the students' cabins. I was still wearing my wig, and knew I'd have to take it off to go to bed at night. I was nervous about my teacher friends seeing me with such short boy-like hair at that point. So before we got ready for bed, I told them to get ready for the big reveal. When I took my wig off, they couldn't have been any nicer or complimentary. Karen spontaneously and sincerely told me that I looked gorgeous and shouldn't wear the wig anymore. I felt a big weight lifted from me both figuratively and literally. After talking it through with them, they convinced me to return to school on Monday without my wig. They suggested I tell our students that I went home from camp and decided to get a pixie cut for the upcoming summer. So that's what I did. It was another small victory on my way back to normalcy.

Kaitlin graduated from Georgetown University in May 2010, and I was grateful to be able to attend the graduation ceremony along with the rest of our extended family. The only person that was too sick to make the trip to Georgetown was my dad, but we knew he was with us in spirit. Eddy and I were so proud of Kaitlin's great accomplishments. What we didn't realize was that she was suffering, not only with Crohn's Disease, but with undiagnosed Neurological Lyme Disease symptoms the entire two years she was there studying for her degree in Public Policy and while working full time as a Graduate Associate on the Senate Finance Majority Committee Health Care Team.

Summer came soon after, and before long, we were celebrating the Fourth of July holiday. Sheila and Dom decided to host their annual Independence Day pool party for our family. We would each bring a covered dish to the picnic, and Sheila and Dom would supply the rest. Our family typically overdoes the amount of food we prepare for our get-togethers, but we aren't going to stop anytime soon. That July 4th will always remain a happy memory for our family. Daddy had been having a *good day*, and so he and Mummy came to the party. Daddy had been having more bad days than good ones, so this was a nice surprise. He even seemed like his old happy self. He went swimming in their pool with the rest of us, and even participated in a very physically competitive game of pool volleyball. Mom, Dad, Eddy, me, Bridget, Kaitlin, Tierney, Dom, Sheila, Maura, Meghan, Dominic, Eric, Denise, Rachel, Luke, and Timmy were all there. We were all jumping up, splashing, laughing, yelling, and having fun, just like the good old days. And for a couple hours that day, Daddy and the rest of us, seemed to forget he was fighting terminal lung cancer. He was laughing and smiling his beautiful smile, and enjoying being with us. I can still visualize him jumping up at the net and spiking the ball down on the other team. How he loved participating in sports, and how he loved the water.

Later on in July 2010, I decided to participate in the Norwin Community Relay for Life, the area's largest annual event to raise cancer awareness and funding for the American Cancer Society. Our friends, Maggie and David, who were members of the Norwin Rotary at that time, convinced me that we ought to attend. Maggie and David would be working at the event along with Ginny and Bill, and Jon and Mary Kay, who were also fellow Rotarians. I invited Karen and Mike to join us, as Mike was also a cancer survivor at that time. When we walked onto the track around Irwin Park, it was a sight to behold. The park was packed with people, and filled with white tents, vendors, food stands, health stands, balloons, and thousands of luminary candles that lined the entire half mile walking track. Each luminaria was lit in honor of someone who survived cancer or in memory of someone who did not. Mike and I had registered to participate in the Luminaria Ceremony. We met Karen and Mike and walked into the largest tent to see our dear friends serving food to all the survivors and their caregivers. After we ate dinner and bought our own luminary candle, we walked around the fair grounds and mentally prepared for the Luminaria Ceremony and Survivor Lap. Mike and I had decided to participate in the survivor walk with our spouses next to us. As we walked around the track, the thousands of people who were there all stood up from their lawn chairs that had dotted the park grounds, and applauded us. They kept rising and clapping as we walked the entire lap. At one point during our walk, Mike turned around to Eddy and me, and said, "Not bad. When was the last time you ever got a standing ovation?!" I smiled, and didn't tell him that it was in Reading, Pennsylvania in November of 1973, right after my performance on stage that won me the Junior Miss Pennsylvania State Talent Award. It was a bittersweet moment, and a reality check on how my life had changed since then! After the walk, we left the park, and the four of us went out for ice cream. It was such a beautiful hot and steamy summer evening.

CHAPTER 13

Suffering and Death

*D*ADDY decided to stop taking his maintenance chemotherapy that August 2010. At first, my mother was extremely upset with him for making that decision, but eventually understood that he was becoming increasingly more exhausted feeling sicker with each chemotherapy cocktail, and so tired of the battle he was fighting against cancer. He was simply sick of feeling sick. In addition, Daddy had been listening to an Alternative Medicine Radio Talk Show Host in Pittsburgh, who was an outspoken critic of the medical establishment and pharmaceutical industry. He was also a chiropractor who ran a holistic wellness clinic, and bought radio time to broadcast his own talk show on health topics. His radio broadcasts particularly preached and preyed on cancer patients, advising them to stop taking traditional medicine and chemotherapy. He kept promoting his special vitamin supplements and holistic medicines that he promised would either put patients' cancer into remission, or cure it. Daddy listened to his radio show daily. My dad was grasping at straws at this point in his battle against cancer, and he wasn't thinking clearly. We all tried to talk him out of ordering these holistic supplements, but to no avail. He was vulnerable and wasn't getting any better, and wanted to try something new. We all knew this would be the beginning of the end. Our hearts were breaking for him, but we had to respect his decision to stop his chemotherapy treatment. This talk show chiropractor had somehow convinced my father to try and heal his body naturally using his nutritional supplements. Daddy started the supplements in August in lieu of chemotherapy, and his health went downhill fast. It was painful and heart-wrenching watching someone you love physically deteriorate day by day, week by week.

Daddy was in and out of the hospital many times during the next few months. That September, while I was visiting him in the hospital, he had a mini-stroke right before my eyes. I had asked him if he wanted me to get him anything else to eat, and when he started to answer me, his speech slurred, and his mouth and the left side of his face dropped. Then, he started talking gibberish. At first, I thought he was speaking Slavic, but then I quickly realized he must be having a stroke. Not to scare him, I told him I was going to get a nurse, because he was clearly frustrated and upset that he couldn't communicate with me. The nurse called a code red, and several doctors quickly appeared out of nowhere and attended to him. They sent me out in the hallway as I waited to hear what was next. Daddy's speech came back, and the nurses informed me that he had a TIA, a Transient Ischemic Attack, otherwise known as a mini stroke. That experience further upset and depressed my dad, along with the rest of us.

One of the hardest things to witness, was my dad's total fear of death, and the effect it had on his psychological well-being. He eventually became very depressed, despondent, and desperate. His personality even seemed to change the last few months of his life. He was never blessed with a strong faith, because of his dysfunctional childhood, and didn't seem to find comfort in prayer. One of the times he was hospitalized in those last few months, he was so absolutely terrified of dying, that my dear sister Sheila, slept overnight in his hospital room on a cot next to his bed. He later admitted that he was afraid to fall asleep, so he tossed and turned all night. He also told us how comforting it was that Sheila had stayed with him, and every time he would look over at her during the night, she would "pop her head up" and reassure him that he wasn't going to die that night. My mother, my sister Denise, and I were so grateful for Sheila's strength during those horrible last months. We all relied on Sheila's nursing experience and medical knowledge as she helped guide us through Daddy's dying process.

There were several other times Daddy had to be taken into intensive care where we thought we were losing him. Then, he would rebound and come home. This roller coaster ride was taking its toll on my dear mother as well. Mummy ended up in intensive care for a few days after her heart started racing out of control, until doctors could get it back into a proper rhythm. I remember wondering how much more physical and emotional pain could my dear parents take. I just kept praying for God's mercy.

Suffering and Death

In October of 2010, I decided to participate in the Pittsburgh Annual Light the Night Fundraiser to help raise awareness and money for the Leukemia and Lymphoma Society. Eddy, Bridget, Denise, Timmy, and I drove down to Heinz Field where the walk would commence. Again there were thousands of people there to support us survivors, or to memorialize their beloved family members who had passed away from either of these horrible blood cancers. It was a very emotional experience for me, as I noticed the majority of balloons that were red indicating a person who had died from the disease. We survivors carried white balloons. The people still fighting the diseases were carrying purple balloons. As we walked along the two mile trail, I couldn't help but wonder why some of us live, and others of us die. I felt grateful and guilty at the same time. So many families are torn apart and devastated by the different types of cancers! How I pray that someday cancer is a disease of the past, like leprosy.

I've decided to stop trying to figure out why some people survive cancer and some don't. The following Scripture passage has helped me with that discernment process.

> "But God, who is rich in mercy, because of the great love he had for us, even when we were dead in our transgressions, brought us to life with Christ (by grace you have been saved) raised up with him, and seated us with him in the heavens in Christ Jesus, that in the ages to come, he might show the immeasurable riches of his grace in this kindness to us in Christ Jesus. For by grace you have been saved through faith, and this is not from you; it is a gift of God; it is not from works, so no one may boast. For we are his handiwork, created in Christ Jesus for the good works that God has prepared in advance, that we should live in them." (Eph 2:4–10)

When I reflect on the many miracles in the gospels or at Medjugorje when people are cured, Jesus and Mary both focus on *faith* as the foundation of healing. Two examples come to mind:

> "A woman suffering hemorrhages for twelve years came up behind him and touched the tassel on his cloak. She said to herself, "If only I can touch his cloak, I shall be cured." Jesus turned around and saw her, and said, "Courage, daughter! Your faith has saved you." And from that hour the woman was cured." (Matt 9:20–22)
>
> Richard Beyer recounts in his book *Medjugorje Day By Day*, an instance when a young deaf and mute boy was healed as a result

of his parents' great faith. The seers at Medjugorje had prayed to the Virgin Mary for the boy's cure after his parents had asked that they intercede on behalf of their son. Mary responded: "Have them firmly believe in his cure. Go in the peace of God." (First Years 6-29-81) Little Daniel Setka was cured later that same evening.

So maybe the answer to that long sought out question is a combination of God's grace, plus our prayer with *expectant faith*, along with being a part of his Divine Plan. Maybe the answer is too complex for our mortal minds that we'll never understand it here on earth.

Before we knew it, November came, and Thanksgiving was right around the corner. Daddy could barely walk from his bed to the bathroom. He was on oxygen then 24/7 as his breathing was difficult and labored. He would cough frequently and try to spit up the thick mucus that was accumulating in his lungs. He had breathing exercises where he had to try and blow up a ball in an incentive spirometer, but that only helped for a short while. The cancer had spread to both lungs and his bones since he had stopped taking the chemotherapy. He had indentations in his face from where the oxygen tube laid. His condition just kept deteriorating. It was becoming more difficult to see him suffer so much.

Mummy hoped Daddy could get out of bed on Thanksgiving and come to Sheila's house for the family dinner. She kept hoping he would rally again. Sheila had the oxygen delivered to her home, and set up a reclining chair in her family room for dad. He did come, and it was a total act of love on his part. He was so sick and weak, sitting there freezing with chills, and wrapped in blankets, that my heart ached for him. He hardly ate anything as he had no appetite, and Mom took him home after a couple hours.

December came and Daddy kept getting sicker. He could barely get out of bed. In a moment of desperation, Daddy talked to the infamous chiropractor on his radio talk show, and before we knew it, he scheduled a visit to my parents' home. After he came to talk to Daddy at my parents' house, my dad never mentioned his name again. I think Daddy finally realized that the talk show host's vitamin regimen and holistic medicine wasn't going to cure him of lung cancer. I resented that chiropractor for preying on desperate cancer patients. I believe he exploited people's fears. He frequently criticized medical doctors and claimed it was the chemotherapy poisons killing people. He insinuated that medical doctors didn't really want to cure their patients, because it would put them out of business. He claimed that only he could help people cure their own cancer through his special holistic and expensive vitamin regimen. My poor parents spent thousands of dollars on those products as my desperate father kept ordering the vitamins hoping for a natural cure. It obviously never helped him. My poor mother had to witness all this knowing that my father was not in his right mind.

As I shopped for Christmas presents for my parents, I knew it would be his last. I bought him Pittsburgh Steelers lounge wear which he never would wear. Eddy and I had our annual Christmas Eve dinner buffet for both sides of the family, and neither one of my parents were there. Mummy wouldn't leave him, so Timmy took them their dinner plates when he left. Mom still insisted on having Christmas Day dinner at their house. How she mustered up the strength to cook Christmas dinner while her husband was dying in their bedroom is a testament to her strength and character. Daddy wasn't able to get out of bed, so we all went into their bedroom to sit with him at times during the day. At one point, my sisters and I, and all our daughters were gathered around his bed. He looked around the bedroom at us, and said, "I'm going to miss all you beautiful women." I can't remember what any of us said after that statement, but we all had tears in our eyes. We knew he wasn't going to be with us much longer.

Daddy's physical condition kept deteriorating to the point that he could no longer get out of bed. His oxygen didn't seem to be helping him breathe anymore. The mucus-filled cough was strangling him to the point that he was struggling to breathe. Nothing seemed to be helping him anymore. January 2011 arrived and we knew it wasn't going to be a happy new year. It became very difficult to see my father in so much pain. His suffering was unbearable to witness. My mother was beside herself with grief, and so my sisters and I took turns sitting with Daddy and just being there for mother's moral support. We all started praying for my dad's suffering to end, and for God's mercy. I was having a hard time trying to figure out why my father had to suffer so much.

It wasn't until years later during a Sunday Mass sermon, that I heard an explanation of why we suffer. Father John Moineau, pastor of Immaculate Conception Church in Irwin, Pennsylvania, our regional sister parish, told us that Pope John Paul II preached that human suffering was *redemptive* suffering if we offer it up to God. He said that suffering purifies ourselves from our humanness, and makes us more perfect for heaven. Pope John Paul II said that suffering has a four-fold purpose:

suffering teaches us humility, purifies us, provides us opportunities for charity, and through purgation transforms us from this world to the next. I can certainly attest from personal experience that having cancer teaches us humility. As it destroys your human body, it strips you of all your vanities, leaving you dependent, vulnerable, and humble. The suffering is physical, emotional, and mental. And as a daughter who shared the role of care-giver along with my mother and sisters, I realize my father's suffering provided us daily opportunities for charity as we strived to help take care of my dad's physical, mental, and emotional needs. I also know from personal experience that this type of suffering is soul-transformative. And so, knowing that, I have to believe that my father's three and a half years of suffering served as his purgatory on earth, purifying his soul, so that upon his death, his soul ascended straight to heaven.

On January 13, 2011, a hospital bed was delivered to my parents' home, and my father was put on hospice. He was so weak that he could barely sit up in bed, and no longer could get out of bed to go to the bathroom. He had stopped eating a week before that, and could barely sip his water without help. His breathing was even more labored and he struggled and fought for every breath. Every mucus-filled cough made him gasp for breath. It was heart-wrenching to hear and see. It seemed as if my father was slowly suffocating to death. He was finally put on morphine to help alleviate his pain. My mother, sisters, and I started praying that my deceased Grandfather Henry O'Grady would come somehow and escort my father to heaven. Aunt Sheila Riberich was also praying the same prayer back in Atlanta. We all knew how afraid Daddy always was of death and dying. My saintly Grandfather O'Grady loved my dad like a son. Grandpap had passed away on January 14th, and his birthday was January 16th. We thought that maybe if Daddy died on one of those days, it might be a sign that Grandpap heard us, and God answered our prayers allowing him to escort Daddy into heaven.

The hospice aide was now staying overnight and sitting by my father's bedside. Mummy was sleeping in the back bedroom trying to get a few hours of sleep at night just to function. The weekend came, and my sisters and I took turns staying with my mom and dad knowing that he wasn't long for this world. After one particularly awful coughing jag that Saturday, he tried to breathe into that spirometer tube to loosen the mucus, but was too weak and shaky to even muster up the strength to do that anymore, so Mom just told him to lie back down. It seemed pointless and more painful for him to even try. Somehow, he managed to bless himself with the sign of the cross, and laid back down. That broke my heart.

Sunday morning, January 16th, my sister Sheila was taking our mother to Mass, and I was going to sit with Daddy. Daddy was barely conscious that morning, but was able to lift his head up enough to receive the tiny piece of Holy Communion that Mother brought back from Mass. I was worried that he might choke on the host, but he didn't. His eyes were closed and he seemed to slip into a semi-conscious state. When his eyes were open earlier, they had a cloudy film over them, but were still a beautiful shade of green. His breathing changed from bad to worse in the afternoon. He was so weak that we had to move him into what looked like more comfortable positions throughout the day. He could no longer turn himself from side to side in bed. While Sheila and Mom were at church, Daddy had slid into the railing of the hospital bed, and I couldn't move him back to center until they came back to help. Denise had arrived and Sheila reprimanded us for not moving him sooner. We didn't have her nursing skills, and weren't used to moving patients, and just didn't want to hurt him or cause him more pain. When we did move him, I was relieved to see he was still wearing the brown scapular I gave him under his t-shirt. The nuns taught us in grade school that if you died while wearing a scapular, you went straight up to heaven. How I hoped that was true. His breathing had changed to a slow shallow rhythm, and he lapsed into an unconscious state for the rest of the day. The hospice volunteer came again that evening. Denise said she would stay awhile longer with mom, so Sheila and I went home around 10:00 p.m. that night.

When I arrived home that night, I updated Eddy on my dad's condition telling him that the end was near. Then, I told Eddy how surprised I was that God hadn't taken my dad home that day after all of our prayers for mercy. As I stepped into the shower around 11:00 that night, I reiterated to Eddy how disappointed I was that my Grandfather O'Grady wasn't going to come for my father. Just then, the telephone rang. Eddy picked up the phone on our nightstand, and I poked my head out of the shower to try and hear who called. Eddy said it was Denise calling to say that we better come back to my parent's house ASAP, because Daddy's breathing was slowing down. I jumped out of the shower, threw on my sweats, and we immediately got in the car. The drive only took us about 15 minutes or so, but when we arrived, Daddy had already passed away. Denise and the hospice volunteer had been sitting with Daddy while Mummy was in the back bedroom getting on her nightgown. When they noticed Daddy's breathing changed and became very rapid, Denise went to bring Mummy back to be with Daddy. Then, Denise said that all of a sudden, Daddy's breathing stopped, he gasped his last breath, and looked *startled* by what he saw. We like to think that Daddy saw Jesus! Denise and our mother had been with him when he breathed his last breath. Daddy never had regained consciousness that day, and died around 11:20 p.m. on January 16th, my Grandfather O'Grady's birthday. God had answered our prayers, and I knew, beyond a shadow of a doubt, that my father was now in heaven, and had been escorted through the pearly gates by his father-in-law, Henry O'Grady. It was a God Wink.

The hospice volunteer, a sweet elderly lady, who was with us that night, wasn't a registered nurse, so she had to call a hospice nurse to come and declare my father deceased. My mother, Sheila, Dom, Denise, Eric, Eddy, and I were all there around his bed. It was a blur . . . I remember crying, telling Daddy I loved him. My mother led us in prayer over him while we waited for the hospice nurse to come. Daddy's coloring faded from pink and tan flesh tones to gray and white. It's amazing to see how quickly the body changes when the spirit exits the body. When I touched him, his skin felt cold and hard. We stayed with Daddy until the hospice nurse finally came around 1:30 a.m., which was then January 17th, and so that's the date that she put on his death certificate after she declared him dead. I was so upset, that she didn't write the 16th, but now understand why she didn't. We know it's not the date he died. That is important for me to tell, because the date on his tombstone is January 17th, not the 16th, the day he really died.

Timmy came while we were waiting for the hospice nurse. Then, I guess the hospice nurse called the coroner, and we waited for him to come and take my dad. Sheila and the hospice nurse gave my dad a sponge bath and prepared his body for the coroner. The coroner came with his son and put my dad in a body bag and carried him out of our family home. We couldn't bear to watch that, so we gathered in the dining room, and sat around the table while trying not to hear the squeaking body bag with our Daddy inside being carried away. It was a horrible sound. The next thing I remember was Timmy and Sheila gathering all of Daddy's pills, meds, breathing equipment, etc., and putting them inside garbage bags. We stayed until 3:30 a.m., and then we all went home, leaving my dear mother alone in the house. As I look back, I feel guilty that none of us stayed with her the rest of the night. She said she wasn't afraid to be alone in the house, and that we all needed to try and get a few hours of sleep before we met in the morning to go to the funeral home to pick out his casket, make the arrangements, and go to the florist to order funeral flowers.

None of us slept those few hours, and were back at Mom's that morning after we all called off work. I drove my mom and sisters to Forgie-Snyder Funeral Home in East McKeesport. Bill Snyder met us there and helped guide us through the funeral process. He was compassionate and professional. He also told us that he had golfed with Daddy at Caradam Golf Course, and called him Johnny. He said he was a great golfer, and a really nice guy. Bill commented that he wasn't a good enough golfer to be in Daddy's league. My mom seemed comforted by his kind words. We picked out a black casket and made all the arrangements. It seemed so surreal. We were all still in shock even though we knew Daddy's death was imminent for some time. Next, we drove to the cemetery, and then to the florist. Then, we went back to the house and spend the day together calling people, and receiving calls and visits of sympathy. Anna Marie came over right away and sat with us. She and her adult children, our cousins, visited and brought food. The day is mostly a blur of activity. It was Monday, Martin Luther King Jr. Day. What a sad day it was.

We decided the viewing would be Tuesday evening, and Wednesday from 2:00 to 4:00, and from 6:00 to 8:00. The burial mass would be Thursday. This would give all our out-of-state relatives time to come home to Pittsburgh for the funeral. And they all came, along with all of the rest of our families and friends. We went into the funeral home before our guests arrived. When we first went in to see Daddy laid out in the casket, he looked as handsome as ever. I thanked Bill Snyder for making our father look like he was sleeping instead of dead. It broke my heart to see my mother run up to the casket and stroke Daddy's hair saying over and over, "Oh, Johnny. Oh, Johnny. My poor boy. My poor boy." My parents had lived a lifetime together. Mom had married Dad when she was 19 years old, and he was 24. They had been married for 56 years! My mother has been my dad's family, home, and the love of his life.

Those next three days were a blur. So many people came and went. So many people expressed their sympathy, love, and affection. Flowers were everywhere, food was sent home, and gifts were plentiful. It was such an outpouring of love for the man we all loved. And it was a comfort, and a testimony to the good life my father lived.

Father John Brennan said the funeral mass at St. Robert Bellarmine Church. It was a beautiful mass, and he said many kind words about my father during the sermon. Then, Meghan went up to the pulpit to say a few words about what a great grandfather he was. After that, I went up to give the eulogy to attest to what a wonderful father he was. Here's the eulogy I read at my dad's funeral mass. On a side note, I had mistakenly thought the poem, *Life Is . . .* was written by Mother Teresa, but when I contacted the Missionaries of Charity at the Mother Teresa of Calcutta Center, asking for permission to use the poem in my book, Sister M. Callisita, MC, explained to me that the poem, *"Life Is" . . .*, was not written by Mother Teresa. She regretted to inform me that many other quotes attributed to Mother Teresa are inaccurate or falsely attributed to her. She kindly asked me to not include Mother Teresa's name with the poem, and thanked me for helping them circulate accurate information. She also informed me that the poem, *"Life Is" . . .* was posted on the wall in the home for children in Calcutta with no author mentioned.

Daddy's Eulogy

My sisters and I would like to share a poem with you that we feel summarizes our father's philosophy of life . . . It's entitled . . .

"Life Is" . . .

Life is an opportunity, benefit from it.
Life is beauty, admire it.
Life is bliss, taste it.
Life is a dream, realize it.
Life is a challenge, meet it.
Life is a duty, complete it.
Life is a game, play it.
Life is a promise, fulfill it.
Life is sorrow, overcome it.
Life is a song, sing it.
Life is a struggle, accept it.
Life is a tragedy, confront it.
Life is an adventure, dare it.
Life is luck, make it.
Life is too precious, do not destroy it.
Life is life, fight for it.

And fight he did, for three and a half years, he fought the good fight. My sisters and I witnessed his remarkable courage, bravery, strength, perseverance, and fighting spirit. He taught us that nothing is more precious than the gift of our life. As we reflected on this lesson, we thought of the many other gifts our father has given us...

First, he married a wonderful woman to be our mother, and they with God's blessing, gave us our life.

Then, he gave us each other, which he always said he had fun doing.

He provided us with a happy home and a strong sense of security.

He made us a safe haven, in Fairhaven Heights.

He instilled in us a strong work ethic; nobody was a harder worker than he. In contrast, he also taught us to make time for play, as evidenced in his passion for golf.

He took us on fun family vacations from the time we were little.

He taught us the importance of family as he loved, fed, and welcomed all his in-laws into his home as if they were his own. Our maternal Great-Grandfather and maternal Grandmother lived with us and were taken care of in sickness and in health in our home.

He taught us to be kind to the less fortunate as he always allowed our mother to invite people without family to be a part of ours. We had more than our share of interesting guests at our Sunday dinners and holiday celebrations.

He taught us patience as he allowed us to play pinochle until the wee hours of the morning when he had to get up for work at 4:00 a.m.

He gave us his sense of humor when we took things too seriously.

He shared his wisdom with us and his old-fashioned common sense.

He afforded us an excellent education at the best schools and colleges, and he sacrificed to send us to Catholic Schools to learn about our Christian faith.

He taught us to respect the earth, and to appreciate the beauty of nature. He knew the name of every bird that ever flew, and had a real relationship with hummingbirds.

He taught us to walk, talk, swim, ride a bike, sled ride, ice skate, ride a horse, swing a bat, throw a ball, and golf, just to name a few.

He has taught us so many life lessons, what to do, and sometimes what not to do.

He has given us priceless gifts, but the greatest gift he gave us was the gift of his unconditional love. We value this the most, because we know that this gift is eternal.

Daddy we will love you forever.

Years later, after rereading this eulogy, I realize there were three more very important lessons my father taught us: forgiveness, as he never held a grudge, and forgave his parents for his difficult and motherless childhood; humility, as he remained a humble man throughout his life, as he would often apologize to his buddies when he beat them at golf; and perseverance, for how he never gave up his fight against cancer.

After Mass, we drove in the funeral motorcade to All Saints Braddock Catholic Cemetery, where my beloved father would be laid to rest. It was there that the reality hit me that I'd never see my Daddy again, at least not in this world. Father John said some final prayers, and then military soldiers presented my mother with the American flag that had been draped over my dad's coffin signifying that he had been an Army Veteran who had served our country in the Korean War. We said our final goodbyes, walked back in the January cold to our cars, and drove to Banquets Unlimited in Wilmerding, for the luncheon and wake. As we drove into the parking lot, I couldn't help but think that the last time we were there, we were celebrating my parents' 50th wedding anniversary, and it was such a happy occasion. Little did I know then, that the next time we'd visit would be at my father's wake.

Many people had come to the funeral Mass and then to the luncheon that afternoon. After I thanked everyone for coming to honor our father, Denise and Mariane, Eddy, Eric, and Kippy stood up after the luncheon to say a few words and share their funny stories about Daddy. It was just the comic relief that everyone needed on such a sad and solemn occasion. Afterward, everybody left, and we all went back to my mother's house for the rest of the day. Aunt Sheila and Uncle Bob stayed with my mother the next two weeks as moral support while my mom transitioned from being a loving wife and caregiver to a grieving widow. My sisters and I had to go back to work after a few days, and so it meant the world to us knowing that they would be with our mother during those first couple weeks of Daddy not being in their house anymore.

Daddy's birthday was February 27th, just about six weeks after his passing. Mom decided to invite all of us to dinner to celebrate his memory. My sisters, brothers-in-law, nieces, nephews, Timmy, Eddy, our daughters, and I were all in attendance. Cooking dinner for our family has always been part of mom's *love language*. Mom had asked us to prepare something to say about him. So, we gathered in their living room after dinner, and sat in our *circle of love*, as we all shared either a favorite memory or what we missed most about Daddy. Everyone had touching memories to recall about their special times with him. I decided to write a Top Ten List about the Ten Things I'll Always Remember about My Father. So here's what I said . . .

Top Ten Things I'll Always Remember About My Dad

10. Watching him walk up the steps, after a long day at work, into our house on Hawthorne Street, from my bedroom window, and running into his arms, because Daddy was home . . .

9. Ice skating with him at Alpine Ice Rink on Sundays when I was in grade school, and watching him fly around the rink, and then skate backwards to help me . . .

8. Driving in the car to Tionesta, and stopping along the way to get ice cream . . . driving in the car to Atlanta, Myrtle Beach, Florida, and his singing aloud . . .

7. Getting fresh mountain water out of the mountain spring in Tionesta, getting fresh eggs and butter from Crawford's Farm, swimming with him in Tionesta Creek, spotting deer at night . . .

6. Feeling so safe and sound when he tucked me into bed at night or looked in on us to make sure we were safe . . .

5. Him taking me to see the Sound of Music and My Fair Lady at Eastland Theater . . . going to the Father Daughter Dinner Dance . . .

4. Him telling me to drive safely and be careful every time I left his house . . . him walking me down the aisle and dancing at my wedding . . . him kissing me goodbye . . .

3. Watching him hold, play with, and love my daughters and bond with them over the years . . .

2. How much he loved life, nature, hummingbirds, golf, and me . . .

1. His green eyes, his hardy laugh, his beautiful smile, just Him!

The night before my Dad's first birthday after his death, I had a dream about him for the first time. I figured that since the Bible recounts many accounts of dreams as God's medium to communicate with people, that maybe this dream was God's way of telling me that my Dad was with him in heaven. In my dream, I walked into the back bedroom in my parents' home where my Dad was lying on the bed with his back to me. I was surprised to see him there, and called out his name. "Is that you, Daddy?" He turned around and sat up in bed. He was smiling and glowing with a most magnificent light. He looked healthy, handsome, robust, and young again, like in his mid-30s. I must have been seeing him in his *heavenly body*, because he looked luminous. He said, "Yes, it's me." I asked him how he was. "Are you ok? Are you happy? Where are you? What's it like?" He said, "I'm very happy. I'm everywhere. We have jobs to do here." When I asked him what jobs he had to do, he said, "I do *conscience* work. I work with young baseball players helping them to make the right decisions. I'm that little voice they hear when they're choosing right from wrong." This struck me as an obviously great gift for my Dad that God would allow him to use his talent and love of baseball in the spiritual world, since my Dad missed the opportunity to use it professionally on earth. Baseball had been my Dad's first love. Then, my Dad said, "I just hope that I'm doing a good job, and don't disappoint him." When I asked Daddy, "Who are you worried about disappointing?" He quickly answered back with a look of astonishment that he couldn't believe I didn't know who he was talking about, "Who do you think?" Then, it struck me that he meant God. Then, he said in addition to that, "I'm also very busy watching over all of you. And that's a bigger job." He laughed. Then, I replied, "Well, thank you. We need all the help we can get down here." He smiled again, hugged me, and then I woke up. It was such a gift to feel his physical presence once again, and see him so happy and healthy. I figured that I had just seen him in his *glorified body* which I previously never understood, but now seemed to make more sense to me. He had been transformed, and looked luminous with the presence of God. Perhaps dreams are one of God's special methods of communicating with us. After the dream, I felt assured that my Daddy was ok, with God, happy in heaven, and that in heaven his spirit could be everywhere. However, I continue to offer up Masses for my dad's soul, and pray for him. I still question and don't quite understand how we Catholics are supposed to help pray people into heaven. But, I'll keep trying, just in case I'm wrong, and he's not there yet!

In May 2011, Tierney graduated with honors from St. Vincent College in Latrobe with a degree in Communications. We would finally be done paying tuition for the first time in our lives. It would be a new chapter, and hopefully, a good one!

Tierney had been working part time while she went to college at a local Senior Citizens Care Facility called Redstone Highlands. At first, she worked in their dining room, and then later on got involved in hospice care. She signed up to visit hospice patients in their homes, and seemed to have a gift for it. After college, she got a job as an Assistant Activities Director at another Senior Care Facility called Nature Park Commons in Greensburg. Eddy and I attended their Christmas party that Tierney had planned that year, and were so impressed at what a beautiful event it was. Tierney even led them singing Christmas Carrols with her beautiful voice. It was satisfying seeing her scurrying around making sure everyone and everything was ok that evening. It seemed as if God was steering her into the direction of working with and for the elderly. She has brought so much joy into their lives. She has been a real light in their lives. These jobs all seemed to be leading her up to the position she would be hired to do three years later . . . Director of Community Relations for Juniper Village Senior Care Center, a national senior care facility with local branches, including the one Tierney worked at right next to the Irwin Turnpike exchange ten minutes from our home. I thought back to when Tierney was inducted into the National Communication Association Honorary Society, Lambda Pi Eta, Upsilon Nu Chapter, in the Fred Rogers Center at Saint Vincent College. Little did we know then where Tierney would take her communication skills. Tierney continued to bring joy and light into the lives of her residents there. She was truly making a difference in many lives, especially the Alzheimer's patients and their families who benefited from the music therapy that Tierney had introduced into their program. Tierney would often share sad stories of families torn apart by Alzheimer's. I thank God that my parents had been spared that debilitating disease. How I admire my mother for taking care of my father, and allowing him to die in his own home.

As that first year progressed after my father's death, we all had to get used to life without Daddy. And of course, my dear mother had to adjust to being a widow, and living alone in their home for the first time in her life. We started referring to dates, holidays, and milestones as either before or after Daddy's death. One Sunday afternoon that summer Mom was finally ready to go through Daddy's things. My sisters and I went over to help her. Most of his clothes went to St. Vincent de Paul Society for the poor. Each of us took things that reminded us of our dad. I took a few of his white t-shirts to work out in, and wear around the house. I also took a couple of his warm flannel shirts. I hoped to make a pillow out of one of them. Since Eddy and my father were different sizes, I only took Dad's sport socks for Eddy. Daddy had already given Eddy his watch which didn't fit, so I had the links taken out for me to wear, and his best set of PING golf clubs. My mom needed to keep his favorite sneakers by the garage door, and his personal items which held memories for them. My dad had stored keepsakes in the top drawer of his chest of drawers. My mom hasn't been able to go through those things yet. She tried once, opened it, saw her wedding garter, and closed the drawer in tears. Mom has been so brave both before and after Daddy's death. She has tried not to cry in front of us girls, and has borne her pain privately. We, in turn, have also mourned him privately, in order to protect each other from more heartache. We try to focus on the happy times and remember him laughing and loving life. Nobody loved life more that my dad. That is how he would want it. He used to always say, "Life is for the living. Smile. Be happy, and don't cry. Life is short, so enjoy it."

CHAPTER 14

Faith

*H*APPIER times were on the horizon. The next summer, Kaitlin got engaged to her college sweetheart, the love of her life, Jason Cooke. Jason and Kaitlin had dated at the University of Pittsburgh, were broken up while they attended different graduate schools, and then rekindled their romance the month Kaitlin graduated from Georgetown. During their time apart, Kaitlin earned her master degree in Public Policy at Georgetown, and Jason, now a Lieutenant Colonel in the U.S. Air Force, completed his master degree in Systems Engineering at the University of Dayton. They decided on getting married the following year in Oakland, Pennsylvania, the site of the University of Pittsburgh, where their romance all began. We spent the better part of 2012 happily planning their June 2013 wedding.

For many years after my diagnosis, I continued to have appointments and checkups every three to four months with my oncologist, and twice a year with my gastroenterologist. My gastroenterologist has helped me manage my severe irritable bowel symptoms, collagenous and ulcerative colitis, Celiac Disease, and follow up care after the lymphoma cancer that presented itself in my liver and duodenum. He is also the doctor who diagnosed Kaitlin with Crohn's Disease the week after she graduated from high school. We have been patients of his for many years. He is a good doctor of the Hindu faith. Over the years, we'd had a few conversations about God, religion, destiny, and how sometimes there are no answers as to why good people get afflicted with certain diseases. He mentioned once that maybe my collagenous colon, and its inability to absorb nutrients properly, might be the reason my immune system was compromised enough to be susceptible to cancer. Again, we may never know.

Anyway, I can recall a specific conversation we had once about God. I explained to him that I was Catholic, but respected all religious faiths, especially since reading about how the Blessed Mother told the children at Medjugorje that God respected all religions, and doesn't favor one over the other. I've come to believe God loves all his children equally, and doesn't have favorites. After being enlightened, I've often pondered how Almighty God must delight in the different ways humankind has chosen to worship and honor him. During my conversation with the doctor, I mentioned Mother Teresa of Calcutta, and how she cared for the dying, and loved the sickest and poorest of poor in his homeland of India. The good doctor quickly acknowledged her saint-like acts of kindness, and the sacrifices she made for the sick and dying. Then, when I likened her Christ-like acts of love to Jesus, my gastroenterologist said, "Yes, Jesus was a good prophet. He was a good man." Then he stated that he thought Jesus was a religious leader like Buddha and Mohammed. I understood that people of different faiths refer to their Higher Power by different names, but I reminded myself mentally that Jesus wasn't just another prophet. Out of respect for our religious differences, I decided not to get into a deeper discussion on religion. Driving home from my doctor's appointment that day, I reiterated in my own mind why I knew Jesus was different than these other prophets or holy men, because I knew beyond a shadow of a doubt that he was God.

How did I know this for sure? Faith! I've believed it my whole life. My Catholic faith has been ingrained in me since my infant baptism, first by my mother, and then by the nuns and priests who instructed me in both elementary and high school religion classes. The Catholic Church beliefs are apostolic-based, and can be traced back through eyewitnesses in the New Testament to Jesus and His teachings. As an adult, I had taken a religious education enrichment class sponsored by our parish, St. Agnes Church, reaffirming my faith. *Discovering Christ* is a nation-wide seven-week adult education religious experience evangelization program. Participants watch instructional videos on the essence of who Jesus is, who the Holy Spirit is, the meaning of life, and our call to be Catholic/Christian disciples. After viewing these videos, our parish priests and facilitators opened up these topics for discussion. At the conclusion of all seven sessions, my take-away was simply a confirmation of my faith in Jesus Christ, as the Son of God, who is one with the Father, and that he is God!

Faith

Looking back over notes taken from my *Discovering Christ* experience, the following scriptures helped me solidify my belief that Jesus is God...

Yes, while Jesus was a good man, a great teacher and moral example, he was so much more than a mere human being. The Gospels are filled with examples of Jesus healing people, raising the dead, calming storms, and casting out demons. All his miracles prove that Jesus was no ordinary man. Jesus claimed that he is one with God, and that he is God! "The Father and I are one." (John 10:30) Jesus came to us to reveal God as our *Father*. He wants us to know the love of God the Father personally. If we look at Jesus, then we will know the Father. "If you know me, then you will also know my Father." (John 14:7) "Whoever has seen me has seen the Father." (John 14:9)

> Jesus's behavior on earth, what he said and did is proof that he is indeed God. The proof is:
>
> his authority over nature "They came and woke him, saying, "Lord, save us! We are perishing!" He said to them, "Why are you terrified, O you of little faith?" Then he got up, rebuked the winds and the sea, and there was great calm. The men were amazed and said, "What sort of man is this, whom even the winds and the sea obey?" (Matt 8:25-27);
>
> his authority over death "And when he had said this, he cried out in a loud voice, "Lazarus, come out!" The dead man came out, tied hand and foot with burial bands, and his face was wrapped in a cloth. So Jesus said to them, "Untie him and let him go." (John 11: 43-44);
>
> his authority to forgive sins "One day as Jesus was teaching, Pharisees and teachers of the law were sitting there who had come from every village of Galilee and Judea and Jerusalem, and the power of the Lord was with him for healing. And some men brought on a stretcher a man who was paralyzed; they were trying to bring him in and set him in his presence. But not finding a way to bring him in because of the crowd, they went up on the roof and lowered him on the stretcher through the tiles into the middle in front of Jesus. When he saw their faith, he said, "As for you, your sins are forgiven. Then the scribes and Pharisees began to ask themselves, "Who is this who speaks blasphemies? Who but God alone can forgive sins? Jesus knew their thoughts and said to them in reply, "What are you thinking in your hearts? Which is easier to say, your sins are forgiven, or to say, Rise and walk?" But that you may know that the Son of Man has authority on earth to forgive sins – he said to the man who was paralyzed, "I say to you, rise, pick up your stretcher,

and go home." He stood up immediately before them, picked up what he had been lying on, and went home, glorifying God. Then astonishment seized them all and they glorified God, and, struck with awe, they said, "We have seen incredible things today." (Luke 5:17–26). No other human being or prophet has ever had that kind of power.

No other human being since the beginning of time has had more of a significant cultural impact on the earth than Jesus. We mark time counting the centuries, and our years relate back to when he was born into the world. The abbreviation initials BC stands for *Before Christ*, and AD does not actually mean *After Death* as many people suppose. AD stands for a Latin phrase, *anno domini*, which means *in the year of the Lord*, meaning the year Jesus was born.

Jesus rose from the dead three days after his crucifixion, and then ascended into heaven. Why did he come down to Earth? Jesus came to reveal the personal love of God the Father, and to redeem us of our sins, so that we are worthy of eternal life. Jesus was crucified, suffered for our sins, died on the cross, and rose from the dead to save humankind. The resurrection account is based on first-century, eyewitness accounts confirmed in the New Testament.

> "For I delivered to you as of first importance what I also received, that Christ died for our sins in accordance with the scriptures, that he was buried, that he was raised on the third day in accordance with the scriptures, and that he appeared to Cephas (Peter), then to the twelve. Then he appeared to more than five hundred brothers and sisters at one time, most of whom are still alive, though some have fallen asleep. Then he appeared to James, then to all the apostles. Last of all, as to one untimely born, he appeared also to me." (1 Cor 15:3–8)

No other human being or prophet has ever claimed to defeat death. Jesus defeated death. His resurrection was the proof that love conquers evil, suffering, and death. No other holy human or prophet has ever come back from the dead, or has done for the world what Jesus did.

We can read in scripture how Jesus reveals the Father's love in his actions and teachings. Jesus reveals the personal love of God the Father:

> "When the fullness of time had come, God sent His Son, born of a woman . . . to ransom those under the law, so that we might receive adoption. As proof that you are children, God sent the spirit of His Son into our hearts, crying out, "Abba, Father." So

you are no longer a slave, but a child, and if a child also an heir, through God." (Gal 4: 4–7)

It is this personal love of God and my expectant faith that has sustained me throughout my life, particularly when suffering during my battle with cancer.

Just as I learned in my youth that love is a verb, I've learned along my journey that faith is also a verb. Faith shouldn't just be contained to our belief in Jesus. Believing in him shouldn't change only our thoughts. Believing in Jesus should change our actions. Our faith should change what we do and say, and how we live our life. Jesus expects us to act with charity. St. Matthew (25:35–40) reminds us of these seven corporal works of mercy: to feed the hungry, to give drink to the thirsty, to clothe the naked, to shelter the homeless, to visit the sick, to visit the imprisoned, and to bury the dead. In recent years, giving alms to the poor, and caring for creation have also been added to these charitable actions. These are concrete ways we can live our faith through our actions.

When I reflect on all the love, care, and kindness that my family and friends bestowed upon me during my fight with cancer, I think about all the dinners my neighbors and teacher friends made for me and brought to my house, and all the personal sacrifices my family made to help care for me. I realize that my sickness gave people the opportunity to exercise their faith and perform those corporal works of mercy. In gratitude, the best way for me to thank everyone is to simply pay it forward, and extend that same kind of compassion and Christ-like love to others whenever the opportunity presents itself in my life moving forward. So much goodness came out of so much sadness, because love was always there.

There is something else I've learned along my journey of faith from a sermon given at St. Mary Czestochowa Church in McKeesport on August 15, 2015 to help me better understand the Catholic Church's dogma of the Blessed Virgin Mary's Assumption. It's the biology of *microchimerism*. In simple terms, microchimerism is the process in which a small amount of cells from another individual live within a host body, but are completely distinct from it. In human terms, it's called *fetal cell microchimerism* where every child leaves within his/her mother a microscopic bit of him/her self. Every pregnancy, brought to delivery or not, leaves a small amount of its own cells within the body of the mother, and those cells remain within her forever. This knowledge has helped me understand and explain Mary's bodily assumption into heaven. A small amount of Jesus Christ's cells remained within Mary her entire life. Mary was the true tabernacle in which the Divine Christ did continually reside. According to the Book of Psalms (16:10), we read about how the Holy One will not undergo corruption. Christ's divine body did not decay and undergo corruption. And so it makes sense, that his mother's body, containing cellular traces of the Divinity (particles of God), could not be permitted to decay either. At Mary's Dormition, her body, holding Christ within it, could not remain on earth, but would have to join itself to Jesus in heaven body and soul.

Microchimerism can also support understanding the Catholic Church's dogma of the *Immaculate Conception* of Mary. Mary, the Ark of the New Covenant, would have to be spared the stain of original sin as the carrier through which God incarnated himself in her womb. Her flesh would have to be pure and holy to hold Jesus Christ, the Son of God, throughout life on Earth and into Eternity. It's enlightening when faith and biology can both support these beautiful beliefs. I've tried repeatedly to no avail to locate and get permission from the priest to reference his sermon on *microchimerism*. If I find him, he will gratefully and deservedly get acknowledged in future copies of this book.

Speaking of biology . . . just because I had cancer, it didn't exempt me or my family from having other health problems. In March 2012, I had a complete hysterectomy after living with a prolapsed uterus for 14 years. I'll spare you the graphic details of what a prolapsed uterus is, and just advise you to google it if you're curious. Looking back, I wish I'd had that surgery sooner, because afterward, I felt as if I'd gotten rid of a handicap. I was in pain for days after the operation, and exhausted for about six weeks after the surgery, but it was nothing compared to what I went through with cancer. I'll say this about cancer, it puts everything in perspective. Everything becomes relative. That realization prompted me to share these words of wisdom with my teacher friends when we think we might be having a bad day at work . . . "If you're not lying in a hospital bed fighting for your life, then you're not having a bad day."

I had to remind myself of these words four months after my hysterectomy, when I was rushed to the UPMC McKeesport Hospital Emergency Room once again. Eddy had been on a business trip in Boston the end of July, and I was home holding down the fort while he was away. One night, I went to bed feeling perfectly fine, only to awaken in the middle of the night with horrific stomach pain. I curled up into the fetal position and tried to fall back to sleep, but to no avail. So I lay in my bed until morning, and called my mom to see if she could drive me to the hospital. Aunt Sheila and Uncle Bob were in town staying with her, so they all drove to pick me up and take me there. After an MRI, Dr. Richard Bondi, my surgeon, confirmed that I was having acute appendicitis and needed to have my appendix removed immediately. I called Eddy, who hopped on the next plane back to Pittsburgh, as I was wheeled up to the operating room around 5:30 that afternoon. When I awoke in the recovery room, Eddy was there along with my mom and Aunt Sheila. They had sent Uncle Bob back to my mom's house to wait. The first thing I asked after the anesthesia had worn off was if Dr. Bondi had found any other tumors inside me during the operation. Eddy and my mom reassured me that Dr. Bondi knew my health history, and that he had examined my intestines and other internal organs to make sure everything looked clean. I immediately thanked God for his continued mercy. I was still cancer free! In fact, every day I thank God for his continued mercy, and beg him to allow me to remain cancer free in order to give glory to God and hope to others.

August came around the bend again, and so did back to school time, along with a new crop of students. It was my last year being teaching partners with Karen, and teaching Literacy. I know for sure that people come into our lives for a reason, and that this year would be my turn to be strong for Karen as she had been strong for me. That being said, the dignified and emotional strength Karen exhibited during her husband's illness was simply amazing. Mike was getting sicker every month, as his appendicitis cancer came back with a vengeance. He was in and out of the hospital that summer and autumn on that horrible roller coaster that patients and families are forced to ride when battling cancer. Eventually, Mike spent his last days at their home with visiting nurses coming to help Karen take care of him. In December, Mike was put on hospice, and he finally allowed Karen to take time off work that last week to stay with him. On the morning of December 17, 2012, Karen phoned to tell me that Mike had just passed away about 3:00 a.m. I remember telling her that I hoped my dad was there to meet him when he entered the gates of heaven, and that his suffering was finally over. Mike and my dad were two warriors, who suffered unimaginable indignities and pain, fought the good fight to the bitter end, leaving behind two wonderful wives who cherished them and took care of them until they breathed their last breath. And in the midst of all their suffering, love was there.

Eddy and I went to a beautiful funeral Mass for Mike, after we paid our respects at the viewing. Mike had requested that he be cremated. Karen recounted to us the time during his last days that Mike sat up in bed, turned his head around, looked at her in disbelief, and said, "I'm not going to take up any precious real estate!" And so his wishes were granted. It still seems so surreal. It's hard to believe that Mike is gone. Eddy and I admired and respected him as he was an accomplished and amazing man, loving husband, good father, and dear friend. We were blessed to have known Mike Dvorsky.

CHAPTER 15

Changes, Gains, and Losses

ANUARY 2013 came with the hope of happier days ahead. In February, Norwin School District sends us teachers out an annual checklist each February to see if we prefer to stay in our current teaching assignment, or wish to be switched to teach another subject area, or grade level. Rose, our principal, informed us that the coming 2013–2014 school year, would be one of great change, and so she wanted our input. She asked us for our subject and grade preferences, and told us she hoped to honor them. After teaching fifth grade Literacy for twelve years at Hillcrest, I was ready and eager for a change of subject matter. I had taught fifth grade Math for two years at Stewartsville Elementary in the Norwin School District fourteen years earlier before transferring to Hillcrest Intermediate School, and I loved it. So, I requested a subject area change to Math for the 2013–14 school year. Much to my delight, Rose honored my request, and assigned me to fifth grade Math. 2013 was off to a good start.

Of course, the highlight of 2013 was Kaitlin and Jason's wedding. On June 1, 2013, Kaitlin and Jason were married at the magnificent St. Paul Cathedral where they attended Mass every Sunday together while dating at the University of Pittsburgh as undergrads. The reception was held at the elegant Pittsburgh Athletic Association, the PAA, a couple blocks down the road on Fifth Avenue in Oakland, Pennsylvania. Kaitlin and Jason are a strikingly handsome couple, and their love was visible as we witnessed them recite their marriage vows and profess their love in front of family and friends who came from all over the United States to share in their joy. We were blessed to have our dear Father Larry DiNardo officiate the marriage ceremony and Mass. Over two hundred people attended their reception. And after all those months of planning and preparing, it was over in one night! Eddy and I hosted a bridal brunch at our home the next morning for all our out of state relatives and friends. Kaitlin and Jason arrived as the guests of honor, and then were off to honeymoon in Mexico.

Since Jason was stationed in Washington, DC, the newlyweds found an apartment in Arlington, Virginia. Kaitlin's office for her new job as a Lobbyist and Senior Manager for the American Society of Clinical Pathology was also located in DC. A month after their wedding, Jason bought Kaitlin another wedding present, a red-haired teacup Pomeranian puppy named Cherry Chapstick. Jason already had a beautiful black Great Dane named Maverick, and Cherry became the newest addition to the newly formed Cooke family. Cherry and Maverick stole my heart, and successfully changed me into a dog person. Those pups brought lots of entertainment and joy to our family. Jason is a wonderful husband and son-in-law, who we now love like a son. And so life goes on . . .

That wasn't the only good news we received that year. Eddy was nominated and selected as one of Serra Catholic High School's 2013 Distinguished Alumni. He was honored with six other distinguished alumni on Saturday, September 21, 2013, in downtown Pittsburgh at the Westin Convention Center. It was a great birthday present for me to have Eddy recognized for all his achievements. The evening began with a cocktail hour, followed by a three course dinner, and presentation of awards. Our daughters, new son-in-law, mothers, siblings, and dear friends Sally and George, were all in attendance to witness Eddy receiving this prestigious award. I was so proud of him and all of his accomplishments. His write up and program bio went something like this . . .

> After graduating from Serra in 1974, Eddy earned a Bachelor of Science in Business Management from Penn State University, a Master of Business Administration from the University of Pittsburgh, and a Juris Doctor from Duquesne University School of Law. He also completed extensive leadership training at Carnegie Mellon University, Graduate School of Industrial Administration. With his strong business and law background, Eddy has built a career in global procurement and contracts in both the naval nuclear program at Bechtel Bettis and healthcare manufacturing while at Bayer HealthCare (formerly MEDRAD). Eddy is also involved in many service projects and activities. He is currently on the American Heart Association

Board of Directors and Executive Leadership Team. Through three primary fundraising programs, Go Red for Women, Heart Walk, and the Heart Ball, over $2.5 million is raised annually for needed research, development, and education . . .

After Eddy walked up to the microphone to give his acceptance speech, he went on to mention meeting me at Serra as among the many rewards he received while getting a Serra education. He also mentioned playing sports with his brothers and beating crosstown rival, McKeesport High School, in the annual Neenie Campbell Tipoff Basketball Game. After many years, the Guarascio family remains loyal to the Serra community and committed to supporting the school through Annual Giving. In addition, Eddy and his siblings have reinstated the Bruce Michael Guarascio 1972 Memorial Scholarship to honor their brother. Eddy ended his speech with thanking his family for all our support, and mentioning his gratitude to his parents for the sacrifices they made that allowed him and his siblings to receive a Catholic education. It was a beautiful September evening and a night to remember.

Back to my teaching career . . . My new teaching partners that school year would be Amy Hudson and Heather Champ. Amy and I had worked together on Literacy for many years. She had taught my daughter Kaitlin in fifth grade at Queen of Angels, and we were friends as well. Heather had been my long-term substitute when I was on short term disability battling cancer. Since I had enjoyed working with them in the past, I was looking forward to working with our new team. Amy would continue teaching Literacy, soon to be renamed ELA (English Language Arts), Heather would teach Science and Social Studies, and I would teach Math.

We had the gifted students on our team that year, and the pressure was on us to challenge them along with our regular education students and raise their PVAAS (Pennsylvania Value-Added Assessment System) scores to the next level. Value-added analysis is a statistical method, and a meaningful way, to calculate and measure the influence of a district and school on the academic progress rates of their students from year to year. In 2002, The Pennsylvania State Board of Education passed a resolution to provide statistical analysis of assessment data. The goal identified in this resolution is to bring all students in our state up to the proficient or advanced levels of achievement on their Pennsylvania System of School Assessment (PSSA) tests. PVAAS is just one tool provided by the Pennsylvania Department of Education (PDE) for districts and schools to measure student growth and progress. Taking on this challenge kept me working morning, noon, and night.

In addition, since our Norwin School District curriculum had to be aligned with the new Pennsylvania Common Core Standards, and our outdated math textbook series wasn't yet aligned to those standards, we math teachers had to supplement our curriculum by researching common core math standard lessons that could be found online on such websites as teacherspayteachers.com, which required spending more of our own money than usual, and kept us up working late into the night. We worked hard that year, and our PSSA scores reflected that in July the following summer. I was proud to find out that my team's students' math scores were in the 88 percent, slightly above our fifth grade average score of 85percent. I was also relieved my scores were so good, since these numbers are used to evaluate our teacher effectiveness. Nevertheless, my teaching assignment for the next school year was changed that May, before my administrators waited to see our math scores, and only a couple months before our scores became public. I was extremely disappointed since I had invested a lot of time and energy into planning and creating new math lessons, activities, reinforcement games, and tests. When I questioned our Assistant Superintendent to ask why the change, she explained that she was "planning for the future," and decided that a younger male teacher and I would switch teaching positions. It felt like ageism and sexism, but there was no way to prove it. So, I decided to adjust my attitude for the upcoming school year, and chose to be positive. Life would still present us with occasional disappointments, and I had to remind myself to keep things in perspective. I still loved teaching, loved my students, loved my fellow teachers, and would learn to love teaching my new subjects.

The 2014–15 school year started in August with me teaching fifth grade Science and Social Studies, along with two new teaching partners, Thom Swenson and Allison Bechtold, and a new young principal, Brian O'Neil. Our previous principal, Rose, had surprised all of us teachers at Hillcrest when she announced her retirement that May. That news came as a shock, because Rose loved her job, and we loved Rose. Rose had been our principal since the inception of Hillcrest as an Intermediate School. Rose led by example with wisdom, kindness, and compassion. She gave us no previous indication that she was considering retirement. In any case, the 2013–2014 school year ended with much unanticipated change.

True to character, I ended up loving teaching fifth grade Science and Social Studies. I've always loved teaching United States History, and Science was an exciting and *hands on* new subject. We started the year teaching/learning the *Scientific Method* and the *Engineering Design Process*, and conducted many Science experiments and labs to apply those skills. It was fun and the students were totally engaged. My mother had said to me many times, that things happen for a reason, and that maybe this new teaching assignment would be a *blessing in disguise*. My dear mother's words of wisdom proved to be true. It had been a joy to teach these exciting new subjects alongside my new partners. Another advantage was the fact that there would be less stress on me as an educator, because fifth grade Science and Social Studies are not state tested on the PSSAs. So, after deciding to focus on the positive and embrace the changes, my new position turned out to be a *blessing in disguise* after all.

The summer of 2014 brought many blessings for my daughters. In July, Bridget was notified by the Allegheny Conference on Community Development and the Athena Young Professional Award (AYPA) committee that she had been nominated for the Greater Pittsburgh ATHENA Young Professional Award. Started in 2011, the ATHENA Young Professional Award recognizes an emerging leader age 35 or younger who demonstrates excellence in their profession, contributes to their community, and helps other women succeed. Bridget was nominated by another female attorney, Julie Coletti, who had worked with Eddy at MEDRAD, and had worked with Bridget on the American Heart Association Young Leadership Team, Go Red for Women Executive Leadership Team, the annual AHA Heart Ball, and the annual Pittsburgh Heart Walk. As I mentioned before, Bridget had also supported Champions of Hope as a committee member on the annual Pittsburgh Gala benefiting St. Jude Children's Research Hospital, but I forgot to mention that on June 28, 2013, we attended the event and met former Pittsburgh Steeler Merril Hoge, the keynote speaker at the gala who coincidentally survived the same blood cancer as me, and was kind enough to take a photo with me. Shortly thereafter, I read Mr. Hoge's memoir, *Find A Way*, which inspired me to keep writing my book. Back to Bridget . . . Bridget continued to participate in the Emerging Leaders Kickoff for the Auberle Home, and kept up distributing food for the Greater Pittsburgh Community Food Bank through the Pittsburgh South Side outlet. Bridget was selected to be a finalist, and Eddy and I were invited to the ATHENA & AYPA Nominee Reception on Thursday, September 4th at the Fairmont Hotel in Pittsburgh. It was a lovely evening to honor our daughter along with the other female young professionals for all their contributions to Pittsburgh's charitable initiatives.

Bridget wasn't my only daughter to make the news in Pittsburgh that July. Kaitlin was making news of her own, and came back from Arlington, Virginia to do so. Kaitlin had become politically active since serving as an intern on the Senate Finance Committee during the drafting of the Affordable Care Act while she was in full-time graduate school at the Georgetown Public Policy Institute (GPPI), receiving her Masters of (Health Care) Public Policy.

Kaitlin had dedicated much time and energy in the grassroots fundraising efforts to get Hillary Clinton to run for president, and was instrumental in bringing the Ready for Hillary Bus to Pittsburgh. On July 31, 2014, Kaitlin co-chaired the Ready for Hillary 2016 Pittsburgh is Ready for Hillary Event which was held in a nightclub on Smallman Street in the Strip District. Over 500 people were in attendance, including many of Pittsburgh's top Democratic leaders. Most of our family was able to attend the memorable event, and support the cause. It truly was a night to remember.

Kaitlin went on to follow health reform through to implementation. She worked in health policy consulting helping states design and implement both their health information and health insurance exchanges. Then, she went on to work for Deloitte, where she aided a multi-billion acquisition of a Medicare Managed Care Organization in support of the Dual Eligible Medicare/Medicaid population. After that, she went on to represent 5,000 providers at the University of Pittsburgh Medical Center (UPMC), Physician Services Division, providing regulatory analysis and guidance. Her last job in DC included providing advocacy and regulatory/legislative analysis services to 100,000 members at the American Society for Clinical Pathology. (ASCP)

Not to be outdone by her older sisters, Tierney decided it was her turn to take center stage. She had been bitten by the acting bug, and became interested in Community Theater ever since she performed in high school spring musicals. Tierney auditioned for Rodger's & Hammerstein's *Oklahoma* production at the McKeesport Little Theater that summer. She won the role of Ado Annie which was one of the female leading roles. When Tierney sang "I Cain't Say No," she brought the house down! And when she sang, "All 'er Nothin," she was superb! She has such a beautiful and strong voice, and the audiences must have agreed as she and the ensemble earned many standing ovations during their run. They also received a wonderful review in the local *McKeesport Daily News*. I was so happy that most of our family and friends were able to attend the performances that were spread out over every weekend that September 2014. Joy is truly meant to be shared. Eddy and I had managed to attend every show, trying not act like obnoxious stage parents in the process. I was particularly happy that Kippy was able to attend one of Tierney's performances.

On the extended family front, other major changes occurred that August 2014. Kippy decided to move back home to Pittsburgh after living most of his adult life in Augusta and Atlanta, Georgia. In his early twenties, Kippy would meet and marry Sheila Narbesky. They would have two sons, Michael and Kevin, move to Augusta, Georgia, and build a life there for many years. They lived in a beautiful house situated on a gorgeous golf course in Augusta. Kippy's experience and success in sales, along with Sheila's salary as an anesthetist, afforded them a luxurious lifestyle. For many years, they lived the good life, traveled the country, and earned nice money. Kippy would come home to Pittsburgh for weddings, funerals, and Timmy's annual St. Patrick's Day parties when his schedule permitted. We always loved his visits home. With his quick Irish wit and gift for storytelling, nobody could command an audience, or light up a room, quite like Kippy. Well, on second thought, Uncle Denny could.

Sadly, Kippy and Sheila would divorce after twenty-three years of marriage, due mostly in part to his struggle with drugs and alcohol. Short stints with rehab and weekly AA meetings weren't enough to help him conquer his demons. His battle became a lifetime struggle. Kippy's sobriety was at the top of many of our family members' prayer list. My mother, Aunt Sheila Riberich, and I would pray for him on a daily basis to ask God to help him beat his addiction. Kippy prayed as well for God's help. He had developed a devotion to St. Jude that went way back to the time he prayed for his intersession to save his brother John's life. Johnny's miraculous recovery had impacted all of us. Kippy kept a novena prayer to St. Jude, which my mother had given him, on a bulletin board in his apartment in Atlanta where he lived right before he moved back to Pittsburgh. He brought that St. Jude Novena with him, and told me he prayed it every day. Kippy would experience a lot of loss in his life, and for some of it, he told me, he took full responsibility. But there were two things that he never lost, and that was the unconditional love of his family of origin, and his strong faith.

Kippy moved into his brother, Timmy's house, in August of 2014, until he could get his feet on the ground. Tim and the rest of the family welcomed him with open arms. It was nice having him back in the fold, so to speak, and with us for birthdays, family reunions, and holidays. Kippy was extremely grateful to Timmy for taking him in, and would tell me often how wonderful he was for welcoming him into his home.

Kippy immediately got a job working at the North Versailles Walmart, with hopes of finding a better job, and getting his own apartment. When he wasn't working, he was going to AA meetings. While working at Walmart, his boss would periodically ask him if he was really working as an Undercover Boss. *Undercover Boss* was the name of a popular television show at that time featuring real undercover bosses who would work alongside their subordinates to check out how business was going down in the trenches. Kippy worked hard, and was so professional and personable, that other employees often asked him the same thing. When Kippy left Walmart to take a job selling cars at C. Harper Chevrolet, his boss asked him one more time if he was really working undercover during the months he worked at Walmart. Once again, Kippy would laugh, and say no!

2015 was a year of much change, some sweet memories, and some sad ones. First of all, in February, our Bridget would meet her future husband, after patiently waiting until she found Mr. Right. Bridget's friends had been trying to fix her up on a date with their friend Craig, a handsome Texan who had relocated to Pittsburgh eight years prior to their meeting. Craig and several of his buddies from Texas worked in the gas and oil industry here in Pennsylvania. Bridget had put off meeting Craig for several months until one day, in a Pittsburgh February snow storm, he arrived in his truck to pick her up to meet their mutual friends for pizza. They instantly connected and have been together ever since then. I remember her telling me that when he opened the door to the truck for her to get in, they both simultaneously smiled as the attraction was apparently mutual. And the rest, they say, is history. After a whirlwind courtship, they became engaged the following year. Craig bought Bridget a gorgeous diamond ring, and they began planning their wedding and their future together.

That summer Bridget brought us more good news. Bridget was nominated, and eventually honored in the *Pittsburgh Magazine* November 2015 issue as a winner of their annual *40 Under 40 List* – "men and women who have not yet reached midlife, but have accomplished singular

Changes, Gains, and Losses

things that bode well for the future, both theirs and the regions." Government, industry, nonprofits, and charitable endeavors are honored along with the career accomplishments of the awardees. Winners are chosen on the basis of professional and personal accomplishments as well as their commitment and overall impact on our region.

At that time, Bridget was working as a Conflicts Resolution Attorney at K & L Gates LLP in downtown Pittsburgh. Here's what Dennis Roddy wrote in *Pittsburgh Magazine* about our Bridget in his short bio . . .

> "Sometimes a community leader flies under the radar – leaving traces across the charitable landscape. Meet Bridget Guarascio, a lawyer at K & L Gates who sets the pace in pro bono legal help. Working with the Neighborhood Legal Services Association, she helps low-income couples to resolve custody disputes, allowing each side a voice and sparing children from trauma. Beyond that, you'll find her tracks in places such as the American Heart Association Young Leadership Team, Go Red for Women Executive Leadership Team, the annual Heart Ball Auction (she is chair) and the annual Pittsburgh Heart Walk. She has been part of the Emerging Leaders Kickoff for Auberle in McKeesport, and the Greater Pittsburgh Community Food Bank as well." When asked about her scariest moment, she replied, "Riding horses on a narrow, rocky cliff in Mendoza, Argentina. I alternated between Hail Marys and expletives. Contrary to the language barrier, some words are universally known!"

The celebration to honor the *40 Under 40* winners was held October 30, 2015 at the Pittsburgh Westin Hotel. Fortunately, all of Bridget's extended family members, both grandmothers, aunts, and uncles, were able to join us to honor her, including her new boyfriend, Craig. It was a joyous evening to celebrate Bridget's professional and personal accomplishments, and her commitment to our Pittsburgh region.

In August of 2015, Kippy moved out of Timmy's house and into his own apartment. He hadn't been feeling well for quite some time. In late autumn, he made an appointment at his doctor's, who immediately sent him to the emergency room. Kippy was admitted to UPMC McKeesport Hospital, mid-November 2015.

During his time in the hospital, Kippy had great care from a group of kind nurses who were referred to as the "Dream Team." He had daily visits from his O'Grady family and friends, phone calls, and cards from people who cared, but couldn't be there. Kippy remained personal, charming, and grateful to everyone who cared for him. Kippy and I had long conversations while he was in the hospital. We talked about our youth, his regrets, his faith in God, our wonderful family, and his relentless hope that he would someday finally conquer his demons. Kippy also mentioned to me how afraid he was that he had been in the hospital for a month and wasn't getting any better. His stomach and legs were so swollen and distended that he could barely get out of his hospital bed to walk. His organs were slowly starting to shut down. He was a smart cookie, and probably knew he was dying.

One of our last visits stands out in my memory. Kippy was on the phone with someone asking for his password, so I said I'd go out into the hall for the sake of his privacy. Kippy said no need for me to leave, and relayed his password loud enough for me to hear. It was *Gertrude 8*. This brought tears to my eyes, because *Gertrude* was his mother's middle name, and he was her eighth child, her baby boy.

The last time I visited Kippy in the hospital, I knew instinctively that it was the last time I was going to see him. I told him I loved him and was praying for him, as I said goodbye, and shut his hospital room door. His last words to me were that he loved me, too. As I walked through the hospital, back to my car, I kept praying for God's mercy for Kippy. And now when I look back at the final few weeks of his life, I can see God's mercy in the love, comfort, and care that Kippy received from the doctors, nurses, family, and friends who were there for him.

Kippy passed away on December 12, 2015, after spending four weeks in the hospital. His three older, surviving brothers, Harry, Timmy, and Johnny, along with his sister (my mother), Mary Pat, surrounded him as he laid dying in intensive care. His siblings prayed the Hail Mary together as Kippy breathed his last breath. My mother called me later that Saturday morning to tell me Kippy had died during the night. I had answered the phone in my bedroom, and fell back into bed sobbing as I tried to process her words. It was the second time in my life that I felt like a part of me had died. The first time I felt that way was when my father passed away.

Kippy would often tell my mother and me that God had a plan for him. As my mother held his hand during those final moments, she whispered into his ear, that God definitely did have a plan for all of us, and it was to take him home to heaven. I believe Kippy is in heaven with Jesus, where he has finally found his peace that he could never find here on earth. Rest in peace our beloved Kippy. We will miss your bright light, but we know that someday, we will see you again in heaven.

We had a beautiful memorial mass at St. Robert Bellarmine Church for Kippy on Saturday, December 19th. He was cremated, and his ashes were placed on the altar in front of an 8x10 picture of him. His siblings decided to have a private mass, since his death was unexpected, and so close to Christmas. Then, on Saturday, March 12th, my mother planned another memorial service at St. Robert Bellarmine Church, open to family and friends who lived out of state, giving them an opportunity to pay their respects. The church was packed with people who came to honor Kippy. All of Kippy's surviving siblings were there, along with his ex-wife Sheila, and their youngest son, Kevin, nieces, nephews, great-nieces, great-nephews, cousins, extended family, and friends. Kevin and I both gave eulogies, and nieces and nephews were chosen to do the gospel readings. After the memorial service, Timmy hosted an Irish Wake for Kippy, and invited everyone in attendance to his home. I made posters that we hung on the walls with pictures of Kippy and family throughout his lifetime. It was a bittersweet day. It's still hard to believe he's gone.

The last thing left to do, was to bury Kippy's ashes. We decided to bury him with my grandparents. Timmy found a gorgeous green tombstone and had it engraved with a Celtic cross along with the words, *Beloved Son*. So now, Kippy, Daddy, Uncle Denny, Grandma and Grandpap O'Grady, are all laid to rest in the hills of All Saints Braddock Catholic Cemetery.

Before we knew how sick Kippy would become that autumn, our family had planned to have an eightieth birthday party for my mother at our house in November. We debated on whether to cancel the party, but didn't in hopes that Kippy would be out of the hospital and able to attend. Unfortunately, he was still in the hospital, and insisted that we carry on with the party. It was a beautiful celebration of my mother's 80 years of life. All of mom's other surviving O'Grady siblings, Jessell family first cousins, second generation O'Grady nieces and nephews, daughters, and grandchildren were able to attend. It was such a testimony to how loved she was. I missed having my father there that night, but felt he was there in spirit, and at least featured in all their pictures we had posted in frames on the walls. We had approximately 75 people who came to our party to honor her. It was a wonderful night of celebrating my mother and sharing the favorite memories that each of us had with her. Mom's faith, trust in God, energy, intelligence, kindness, and compassion set the bar for us daughters and the next generation. It was hard to believe she was actually 80! After Daddy died, Mummy was physically exhausted and emotionally drained, but in time, she persevered and started to heal. She still exercised twice a week at a Silver Sneakers gym with our cousin Anna Marie, belonged to a card club and bowling league, volunteered in her community and at her church as a Eucharistic Minister, and still finds time to serve on the UPMC McKeesport and UPMC East Hospital Boards along with the Auberle Board. Her life of service continues as she teaches us all how to survive adversity and remain active, productive, and joyful. It's still hard to believe she's as old as she is! Where has the time gone?

CHAPTER 16

Reflections

SPEAKING of time, May 2015, marked the time to open our Pennsylvania Avenue School Time Capsule. Invitations had been sent out in March by the administration inviting former students, families, staff, teachers, and community members to participate. I was asked to lead the Pledge of Allegiance to begin the ceremony and then to explain the capsule and participate in its opening. The Norwin School District Administrators had asked retired teacher, Mrs. Debbie Kunkle, to organize efforts with the Golden Heights Personal Care Home to coordinate the program on whose site the time capsule was now buried. Our Norwin school district maintenance department had been asked to visit the site prior to our grand opening to help unearth the capsule, and make sure the container would open for us. The director of maintenance was on hand that day to provide any assistance we might have needed. So on Wednesday, May 27, 2015, a large crowd of us invitees gathered on the front lawn of the former Pennsylvania Avenue School, then the Golden Heights Personal Care Home facility, to unveil our millennium time capsule. After explaining that we buried the time capsule on June 5, 2000, as our little way of commemorating the new millennium, several of my former third grade students, who were then young adults, helped me remove our time capsule. Before we opened it, and especially for those people who might have thought 15 years wasn't such a long time, I put together a brief timeline of events to help illustrate just how much our world had changed in this brief amount of time. So here goes . . .

- ◊ January 1, 2000 The world celebrates the turn of the millennium.
- ◊ September 11, 2001 Terrorists attack and crash airplanes into the World Trade Center buildings in New York City, the Pentagon, and a field in Shanksville, Pennsylvania.
- ◊ January 8, 2002 President George W. Bush signs into law the *No Child Left Behind Act*.
- ◊ March 20, 2003 The U.S. invades Iraq looking for weapons of mass destruction.
- ◊ June 6, 2003 Pennsylvania Avenue School closes.
- ◊ February 4, 2004 Facebook, the online social networking service, is launched by Mark Zuckerberg and his fellow Harvard University friends.
- ◊ February 14, 2005 YouTube, the first video sharing website, appears online.
- ◊ August 23, 2005 Hurricane Katrina, the largest and third longest hurricane ever recorded makes landfall in the United States, flooding New Orleans.
- ◊ February 5, 2006 The Pittsburgh Steelers win Super Bowl XL against the Seattle Seahawks.
- ◊ July 15, 2006 Twitter, the micro-blogging site opens with 140 characters maximum per message.
- ◊ August 24, 2006 Pluto is demoted to a *dwarf planet* status.
- ◊ January 9, 2007 Steve Jobs debuts the Apple iPhone, revolutionizing the mobile phone industry, with their multi-media enabled smart phone.
- ◊ November 4, 2008 Barack Obama is elected the First African American President of the United States of America.
- ◊ February 1, 2009 The Pittsburgh Steelers win Super Bowl XLIII against the Arizona Cardinals.
- ◊ June 12, 2009 The Pittsburgh Penguins win the Stanley Cup defeating the Detroit Red Wings.
- ◊ January 12, 2010 Haiti is struck by a devastating earthquake.
- ◊ April 3, 2010 Apple introduces the iPad, another revolution in portable *tablet* computing.

Reflections 181

◊ May 1, 2011 Osama Bin Laden, leader of the 9–11 terrorist attacks is killed.

◊ February 6, 2012 Queen Elizabeth II celebrates her Diamond Jubilee Anniversary as monarch of England

◊ March 13, 2013 Pope Francis is elected Pope in Rome, Italy.

◊ May 13, 2014 Christopher Columbus's flag ship, The Santa Maria, is discovered off the north coast of Haiti.

◊ May 27, 2015 The opening of the PA Avenue School time capsule occurs on the grounds of the Golden Heights Personal Care Home.

Since a time capsule is supposed to be a historic cache of goods, documents, articles, and records of contemporary culture typical of the current period, it was interesting to see what objects our third grade students thought were important enough to include for perusal by citizens of the future. I had kept no record of what we had included 15 years earlier. Thankfully, some of my former students were in attendance to help explain the contents of our time capsule. Each of them introduced themselves and said a few words explaining what they had added. Basically, the capsule contained a local Tribune Review newspaper, Pittsburgh Press newspaper, PA Avenue school yearbook, small toys of the time like Pokeman and Tamagotchi, gel pens, music tapes of Britney Spears and 'N Sync, students' artwork, and personal notes the students had written, and messages of what was popular in pop culture in 2000. Pictures were taken for the local Norwin Star newspaper, and then we were all invited inside the Golden Heights Recreation Room for cake and punch. There, we were informed by the Golden Heights staff that the Senior Care residents were going to make a time capsule of their own and bury it in our same location. It was a sweet memory for my former students, the senior care residents in attendance, and me.

Teaching has afforded me the opportunity to improve lives and create life-long memories for my students in the process. Norwin School District *memory highlights* in addition to creating and burying the millennium time capsule include: assembling and sending care packages from my fifth grade Stewartsville students in December 2001 to our American soldiers in Afghanistan; taking hundreds of our Hillcrest fifth graders on annual overnight camping trips to Camp Lutherlyn where we hiked up and down the mountains attending nature and survival learning stations ending our day singing around the bonfire; conducting whole-school mock presidential elections every four years; and bringing the Fort Ligonier American History Programs along with the Bayer/Covestro Making Science Make Sense Programs to Hillcrest for in-house educational enrichment programs.

But it's the everyday magical *aha* moments where you connect with your students and see the sparkle in their eyes when they finally get whatever concept you're teaching that count as the most priceless memories. It's their smile and excitement when they're totally engaged in a lesson and don't want to leave your classroom, or when we all laugh together at some silly inside joke. It's when you listen to them with care and compassion as they tell you about problems at home. Sometimes students share personal stories of divorce, custody issues, parents who are on drugs or in jail, childhood neglect, emotional or physical abuse, or family members who have passed away. Our students deal with so many sad real life issues that it's no wonder many children in today's society suffer from depression or anxiety. The fundamental challenge for us teachers is trying to cut through all that sadness to help our students focus on learning language arts, math, social studies, and science. Keeping our students engaged in learning is not an easy task. It's hard, and that's what makes it special.

By the 2015–16 school year, 95 percent of American public schools had drilled students on some form of lockdown procedure in the event of a school shooting. Active shooter drills were practiced periodically at Norwin, along with traditional fire drills and tornado drills, due to the prevalence of gun violence in American schools. Our school district enlisted the aid of the North Huntingdon police department to help improve school safety by scheduling active-shooter training into our teacher in-service days. We educators participated in active shooter simulation drills where the police shot blanks, so we faculty members were aware of the sound of a gunshot. The simulation drills were extremely realistic and stressful. Afterward, we teachers learned lockdown procedures along with how to safely evacuate the building. Back in our school buildings, we would practice putting our classroom door-jam locks into place, and gather our students to huddle into a back corner of the classroom out of sight of an active shooter who might be prowling the hallways and peering into the classroom door windows. I would comfort my students by telling them this was the best way to ensure their safety, and that I would protect them as their parents would. This is another example of the kinds of stress our students and teachers have to process. Norwin School District took steps to alleviate the trauma of these active shooter drills by notifying parents, teachers, and students in advance. Parents would have the opportunity to speak to their children in advance to help lessen their fears, and explain that these practices would help keep them safe in a secure environment. I would tell my students they were helping police by participating in the drills. Modeling Mr. Rogers, I would tell children to always look for the *helpers* in an emergency or scary situation, and in these instances their teachers and police would be their helpers.

With full inclusion in our public school district classrooms, we teach a mixture of regular education students, learning support students, gifted students, students with health problems, eating disorders, emotional, mental, and behavioral issues. This is why teaching is a super power, to teach and reach this diverse group of learners. And our challenge is to somehow, someway, connect with these children, enable them to connect with each other, and to grow their learning achievement every year. At some point, after spending so much time together, every classroom transforms into a surrogate family. Students help each other, support each other, and cheer each other on when they succeed. I've witnessed great compassion that my students have shown each other over the years. They grow to care about each other, and form true friendships. I'd like to believe that's a testament to the compassionate culture created by a caring and loving teacher.

Teaching is more than a noble profession, it's a ministry. It's been a lifelong vocation for me. Once a teacher, you're always a teacher. Teachers never really leave their job. We eat, breathe, and sleep teaching. There's always a piece of you that's thinking about your students and teaching them, whether it's planning and researching the next lesson, shopping for supplies for the next Science experiment, buying supplemental materials for math, books for ELA (English/Language Arts), watching the news and reading newspapers for current event topic discussion in Social Studies, creating enrichment activities, designing chapter review games like Jeopardy or Kahoot to prepare for tests, creating tests and checking them, grading projects, reading and evaluating their many pages long writing pieces, attending parent meetings along with guidance counselors, or answering parent emails late at night from home on our iPhones. Imagine doing this for a roster of 84 students a year with approximately 28 students per class. We do all this on top of keeping up with the current educational trends across the country, by way of professional development classes, research, earning graduate degrees, and embracing the latest school district initiatives and directives every new school year.

Teaching is all consuming. When you're in the classroom teaching and meeting the needs of your students, you really can't think of anything else. And that can be a welcome reprieve and an emotional escape from when family members have health problems at home. 2016 would bring more serious health concerns for the people I love.

CHAPTER 17

Adversity, Courage, & Resilience

*E*VERY second Sunday in May, the city of Pittsburgh holds the annual Race for the Cure Marathon to promote breast cancer awareness in honor of those who fought or are fighting that dreaded disease. People come from all over the world to participate, support the cause, and run the race. The race is televised on our local stations, and my family and I frequently tune in to see if we can spot any of our relatives who run the marathon. My cousin Kathy is a survivor, and she and all her siblings participate every year. My dear mother tuned in that year to watch the coverage wondering if she would spot any members of our extended family. After turning off the television, she went to take a bath before getting ready to go to church. While bathing, Mom decided to check herself and thought she felt a lump. Something didn't feel right. So Monday morning she called her PCP, Dr. Rawji, and made an appointment for a check-up that week.

Dr. Rawji took a biopsy of the lump, and sent it to the pathology department. Mom never told us daughters of her fear, and waited the rest of the week to hear back from her doctor. When Dr. Rawji called back, she confirmed that our dear mother did in fact have breast cancer. What a shock it must have been for her to hear, since she had stopped getting mammograms at age 75 after reading literature that they were no longer necessary after that age. So here she was at 80 years old, after dealing with my dad's lung cancer, my dad's and Kippy's death, and my blood cancer, having to deal with her own breast cancer.

The third week in May, Mom called my sisters and me to her house for a family meeting. We knew it wasn't going to be good news from her recent solemn behavior and tone of her voice. We knew something was very wrong with her. As we all sat down on her front porch, my mom said she had something to tell us. My sisters and I started guessing, and breast cancer was the first thing we all mentioned. It was shocking to hear, especially because she had already suffered so much in her life, and I was hoping that it would somehow exempt her from anymore suffering at age 80. But I guess life doesn't work that way. We knew that we needed to be positive and strong for her, that it wasn't a death sentence, and that we would do whatever it took to help and support her. When we eventually left our mother swinging on her porch swing that evening, I looked back at her while getting in my car, and thought of all the happy times we had sitting on that porch. I fought back the tears remembering the poem Kaitlin wrote for my mother back in middle school. She titled it, *Grandma's Front Porch*, and has allowed me to share it with you.

Grandma's Front Porch

The light streams in from two ends and reflects off the wind chimes
There's always just the right amount of a slowly passing breeze
The musty, old green carpet is wet and soggy and squishes between your toes
The swing is rusting and silently creeks when in use
The swing cover is worn and floral with the perfect pre-made indent on the seat for your comfort
A silk spun spider web dangles from the corner post of the swing with an occasional visitor
The fresh smell of gardenias fills the effervescent air
All around you are flowers of all shapes, colors, and sizes
The spinning hanging baskets drip from an early morning bath
Pots of bright ginger, crimson, and golden mums surround you
There's always a faint smell of whatever is cooking in Grandma's oven that never fails in wavering to your nose through the old screen door enticing you to eat more
The cracked red brick lets off a damp coolness much appreciated on a hot summer day
The Virgin Mary protects her grotto which lies in front of the porch almost as if she's protecting its visitors
She's slightly withered, made out of a hard charcoal colored stone with her hands extending out to the sheer display of the beauty of nature in front of her
The innocent chirping of the red-breasted robin somehow overpowers the faint sound of the nearby traffic

> The delicate hummingbird is a frequent visitor to Grandpap's blinding red bird feeder
> The ivory colored petals cover the floor before the old, wicker broom placed in the corner of the porch is put to use
> A tall dark tree is just outside the corner of the porch shading it from any unwanted sunbeams
> Sometimes if you're lucky, you can spot a tiny bird's nest within the mangled branches, or maybe even a filthy mud-covered ball from a kick ball game gone by
> And Grandma's voice, oh, Grandma's voice . . . that is the sweetest sound to ever ring through your little utopia
> The joy and cheer of her happiness from being with the whole family can be spotted in her tone
> The hustle and bustle of a big family meal is echoing all around you, and how could you ever want to get up from that swing!

But my mother did get up from that swing. During the summer of 2016, Mummy endured two lumpectomies to remove the four tumors in her right breast. The first operation was in June, and the surgeon didn't get it all, so she was operated on again in July to make sure the margins were clear. My sisters and I went to every one of her doctor's appointments that summer, and made sure we were there to support her every step of the way on her breast cancer journey. There were many blessings that summer. Most important was that the cancer hadn't spread to any of her lymph nodes. That meant that she didn't have to undergo chemotherapy and all the suffering that it entails. For that I will be forever grateful to God. I had prayed so hard that my sweet mother would be spared chemo, and she would be. However, she had to undergo radiation for the next few months, and take Arimidex, hormone therapy in the form of a prescription pill, daily for five years to help prevent a recurrence. Mummy still deals with the side effects of Arimidex. In spite of all the side effects, she has managed to make a remarkable recovery, soon to end the fifth and final year on the Arimidex. Her perseverance, courage, deep faith, and strength of character during this difficult time set yet another example for her daughters and granddaughters on how to face adversity. And the adversity would keep coming.

In November 2016, our Kaitlin was diagnosed with chronic neurological Lyme disease by a nurse practitioner specialist at her urology clinic in Washington, DC. Kaitlin had been going there to treat interstitial cystitis symptoms when two different blood tests confirmed she had neurological Lyme disease. Eventually, she discovered the link between interstitial cystitis and Lyme disease. In December 2016, Jason was promoted to Major and transferred, so they moved to Boston, while Kaitlin kept getting sicker with the Lyme. Since the Lyme disease had gone undiagnosed for many years, it was too late to treat with standard antibiotics. So, for her first method of treatment, Kaitlin connected with a doctor back in Pittsburgh during their Christmas break where she began a series of holistic supplements. When her chronic migraine headaches, interstitial cystitis, and neuralgia kept worsening to the point where she could barely get out of bed to function, Kaitlin connected with Lyme Literate Medical Doctors who suggested putting a port in her chest with IV antibiotics for several months after telling her that there really was no cure for chronic neurological Lyme disease that had apparently been in her system and gone untreated for years. Knowing that type of treatment wasn't effective unless the Lyme disease is caught and treated early, Kaitlin decided not to risk the complications associated with the months long antibiotic port treatment. But Kaitlin was determined to persevere in her quest for a cure.

This propelled Kaitlin to research Stem Cell Therapy, also known as immunotherapy, the wave of the future in medicine used to successfully treat certain autoimmune diseases and some blood cancers. Kaitlin discovered three Infusio Stem Cell Therapy Clinics, one located in Frankfort, Germany, another located in Toronto, Canada, and the newest located in Beverly Hills, California. After more research, reading, and talking to her medical doctors, Eddy and I decided to take a leap of faith and support Kaitlin in trying the cutting edge treatment at the Infusio Stem Cell Therapy Clinic in Beverly Hills. Eddy was able to accompany Kaitlin during her two week stem cell journey to California where he was also able to work remotely on his laptop. They face-timed me on their iPhones daily, so I didn't have to take off work, but could be kept abreast of how her treatment was going. The type of treatment she underwent there was called Autologous Stromo Vascular Fraction (SVF), which means the medical doctors there used their patients' own stem cells to boost their immune system. Kaitlin's stem cells were extracted from the fat in her back, treated, and returned to her body through five IV infusions per day for two weeks. Ozone Therapy followed where Kaitlin received two 10 pass ozone intravenous treatments while at Infusio Beverly Hills. The doctor, who treated Kaitlin at Infusio, told Kaitlin that 90 percent of her patients felt better and their symptoms subsided with each successive month up to a year and a half post treatment.

When Kaitlin returned to her home in Boston, she drove to the AIM Clinic in New Hampshire, where she continued to receive weekly ozone IV treatments each lasting approximately four to five hours long. Kaitlin was supposed to feel better and her Lyme disease symptoms were supposed to eventually improve after 18 months, but that didn't happen. The second year passed after the stem cell therapy, but Kaitlin was still suffering with symptoms of the neurological Lyme disease. So, Kaitlin altered her diet, water fasted, and took supplements prescribed by the clinic. Kaitlin was so sick with the Lyme while they were stationed in Boston, that she was unable to work, as she could barely get out of bed to function many days. Kaitlin began to feel hopeless and anxious for a cure. The doctors at the AIM Clinic told her this often happens to chronic Lyme disease patients, and so prescribed meds to help her deal with her symptoms. In the fall of 2019, Kaitlin came home to Pittsburgh where she found a new doctor to treat her Lyme disease symptoms with homeopathic medicines in the form of several sublingual drug drops administered under her tongue. As of this writing, Kaitlin is beginning to see some improvements in several of her symptoms. She is determined to persist as she continues to fight the debilitating symptoms of neurological Lyme disease. After battling this incurable disease for twelve years, Kaitlin is praying for a miracle. While she admits her faith has wavered, she most recently had a vision of the Blessed Mother enveloping her with her blue cloak in protection. At first, Kaitlin thought this may finally mean healing, but once COVID-19 hit a few days later, she thinks perhaps she was being protected from that deadly virus in her vision. In any case, I'd like to think that my daughters also have a special relationship with our Blessed Mother Mary as I've tried to nurture a devotion to her their whole lives.

CHAPTER 18

Wedding Bells

*I*N the meantime, we were planning Bridget's wedding to her handsome Texan. The year flew by quickly, and in the blink of an eye, the Big Day arrived. On May 6, 2017, Eddy walked our beautiful Bridget down the aisle of St. Paul Cathedral as Craig awaited his new bride on the altar. Our dear friend, Father Larry DiNardo, celebrated the Sacrament of Matrimony for our family once again. His homily graciously welcomed the many Texans from other religious denominations to our Catholic Mass in honor of Bridget and Craig. After the marriage ceremony, we sprinted through the rain in route to the reception to celebrate their union at the Phipp's Conservatory and Botanical Gardens, a historic landmark set in nearby Schenley Park, Oakland, Pennsylvania. The gorgeous greenhouses protected us from the rain and provided lovely landscapes for all the wedding reception pictures. The Bachelor Boys Band played wonderful music of all genres that had everyone up out of their seats and dancing. The wedding went off without a hitch, and Bridget and Craig were off to honeymoon in exotic Thailand.

Weeks prior to the wedding date, Craig told Bridget that he was offered a job with the awesome opportunity to start an industrial rental company in Houston, Texas, with aspirations to make it nationwide. Needless to say, this was an amazing once in a lifetime offer! As Bridget struggled with how she was going to leave her job at K & L Gates, and abandon her dreams of living in Pittsburgh close to her family and friends, she knew Craig had to take the job, and that they would be moving to Houston, Texas.

K & L Gates was able to transfer Bridget to their office in Houston where she worked the first year of their marriage. Bridget started making friends at a local gym, and met a nice young woman there who also happened to be an attorney who had ties to Pittsburgh. The two girls hit it off, and became good friends. Her new friend told Bridget that her company was hiring an attorney, and offered to take her resume into work if Bridget was interested in the job. After a series of interviews, Bridget was offered the position as Senior Counsel for Loomis Armored U. S., LLC, headquartered in Sweden with its American headquarters in Houston. While Bridget was adjusting to her new position at Loomis, Craig was traveling and opening new offices in cities to grow his business. Bridget learned to appreciate the warmer weather, cultural differences, delicious barbeque, and life in a big southern city. Craig eventually opened a branch office in Pittsburgh with the intention to eventually move them back to The Burgh. After three years in Houston, Bridget and Craig moved back to Pittsburgh in September 2020, six months into the pandemic. Shortly after their move, Craig was offered a new job as Executive Vice President of Sales for a heavy equipment company. We are happy to have them back home in Pittsburgh, while we continue to pray for an end to COVID-19.

CHAPTER 19

Senior Care Compassion

*D*URING this time, Tierney had been building a career in the Senior Care Industry. Tierney developed an affinity working with the elderly way back during her years at St. Vincent College when she worked as a senior living dietary aide to raise money for college tuition. Tierney not only served the seniors their meals, but entertained and delighted them with her bubbly personality, spontaneous singing voice, and silly antics. After graduation, Tierney decided to pursue and advanced professionally in Senior Care as an Activities Director, Outreach Coordinator, Director of Community Relations, Southwestern Pennsylvania Volunteer Coordinator for AseraCare Hospice, and eventually sales. At AseraCare, Tierney coordinated and managed all aspects of their hospice volunteer program, including recruiting, training, and placing volunteers across several counties, marketed the volunteer program out in the community and on social media, instituted and hosted recognition and volunteer appreciation events, and worked with the hospice team to provide excellent and compassionate service to patients and their families. Most impressive to me is that she frequently visits the homes of their patients at all hours including weekends to comfort, sing, and hold the hands of the dying during their last breath. Tierney has been told she has the *voice of an angel* by her patients and their families as she sings their favorite songs bringing them peace and comfort as they approach the threshold of heaven. In addition, Tierney travels throughout southwestern Pennsylvania to attend many of their funerals. Tierney has always had a heart of gold ever since she was a little girl. She was always the child who would be kind to the new kid in the classroom, and would gravitate to help where she saw someone looking lonely or in need.

Tierney interacts with all aspects of the senior care industry in the Pittsburgh region from education (setting up information tables at college job fairs to attract student volunteers), to healthcare for seniors (working with medical professionals), to civic, social, and religious organizations throughout the community. As a result, Tierney became active in leadership roles in the Alzheimer's Association, Mountain View Rotary, and Westmoreland Healthcare Professionals Marketing Group just to name a few. Tierney was named Westmoreland 2016 Spectacular Speaker, and was honored as the AseraCare 2017 Employee of the Quarter for Outstanding Performance. After much persuading by her colleagues to run, Tierney was unanimously elected the 2020 President of the Westmoreland Association of Volunteer Administrators, also known as WAVA.

The latest update on Tierney's career is proof that hard work yields rewards. The Corporate AseraCare Vice President of Sales was so impressed with Tierney after their initial meeting that he immediately asked her to interview for a sales position. After filling out the application online and going through the formal interview process, Tierney was offered the new job as the Provider Relations Manager, basically the Sales Representative for Westmoreland and Allegheny County. This was a job that Tierney had aspired to for several years. When she was told the new salary and incentive plan, she couldn't hold back the tears of gratitude. She kept repeating that she worked hard for years to be considered for this position, and it took one woman from corporate who believed in her to make all the difference. I quickly reminded her that her entire family believed in her, and her hard work and perseverance paid off. Little did we know at that time, that AseraCare would be bought out by another larger hospice company entitled Amedisys, and Tierney's own life would be in jeopardy come June 2020 as she continued to work in the field in the senior care hospice industry that was hit by the Coronavirus extremely hard, and became a global pandemic killing over 450,000 people worldwide. As of this writing, Tierney is currently working in sales at Heritage Hospice as their Community Liaison where she recently received national recognition.

CHAPTER 20

Living the Message

*I*N 2017, McKeesport Mayor Michael Cherepko made a commitment for the city's departments to make major investments in community infrastructure and neighborhoods through a revitalization enterprise entitled *The McKeesport Rising Project*. His hope for the project was to rid the neighborhoods and business districts of blight, while opening doors for new development so that the community could grow. His rationale maintained that as public servants, we are here to uplift our community by improving residents' quality of life. With this in mind, Mayor Cherepko heads the McKeesport Message Committee whose mission is to recognize citizens of all ages and backgrounds who do their part to make McKeesport a better place for everyone. His administration's motto is *Working Together for a Better McKeesport*. In the spring of 2018, Mayor Cherepko's committee selected four *Living the Message* awardees to recognize for their positive impact on the community. The public is invited to nominate four community members who exemplify the qualities: *Respect, Dignity, Hope, and Love*. *Living the Message* awards are meant to showcase these four individuals and describe how each person embodies one of the four characteristics. My dear mother, Mary Pat Soltis, was honored on April 4, 2018 by the Mayor of McKeesport as the *Living the Message* awardee for *Love*. When Mom first called me to share the news that she would be given the award for *Love*, I couldn't help but think how apropos! Mom had been invited to attend the McKeesport City Council Meeting to receive her award, and asked me to accompany her. I was able to take a few pictures on my cell phone of her being presented with the Proclamation award certificate by the mayor that evening in order to share the event with my sisters and the rest of the family. I was so proud to witness her being recognized for her loving contributions to the city of McKeesport throughout her many years of service. In addition, I'd like to share the lovely informational article that Mayor Cherepko wrote about her in the *IN McKeesport Area Magazine Spring 2018 Edition* . . .

> "While she doesn't reside within city limits, McKeesport will always feel, in part, like home for Mary Pat Soltis. Her involvement in McKeesport's many charities has left a lasting impact on Soltis's life, and her kindness has greatly impacted the heart of the McKeesport community.
>
> Today, she serves on the Mon Yough Chamber Foundation and the UPMC McKeesport-East joint board of directors. But her work in the community has extended far and wide to organizations including Penn State McKeesport, the YMCA, Auberle, Allegheny County Airport Authority, and the Allegheny County Library Association.
>
> In the mid-1990s, Soltis got her first taste of politics when she was asked by then-Allegheny County Commissioner Pete Flaherty to serve on the up-and-coming Allegheny Regional Asset District Board, which was to distribute a 1 percent sales tax allotment to cultural assets across the county.
>
> "I firmly believe President Kennedy's statement that without art in our society, we are lacking the true heart and value of our generation," Soltis said. "The symphony, the opera, the ballet – these are all assets that enrich us."
>
> When Soltis reviewed the assets, she noticed there was nothing from McKeesport in the mix. She wanted Renziehausen Park – a recreational hub for communities throughout the Mon Valley – to get the same attention as official Allegheny County parks.
>
> "I wasn't from McKeesport, but I knew the value of it," she said. "What stood out about Renzie Park was how it was utilized by everyone – the garden club, children at the playground, people walking to get their exercise. My sons-in-law had fished in the pond as children. Their families went there for picnics and to watch fireworks."
>
> Soltis shared her own concern as well as that of then-Mayor Joe Bendel when she informed the board she couldn't move forward on a budget that didn't give something to McKeesport. Because of her persistence and commitment to McKeesport,

Renziehausen Park remains a contractual asset for the Allegheny Regional Asset District."

The main reason I share this information about my mother is to impress upon her grandchildren how one person can make a positive difference in other people's lives, and to hold her up as a public servant role model. I want to remind my daughters, nieces, and nephews about the unique contributions their grandmother has made to improve the lives of others, in hopes of inspiring them to use their individual God-given gifts to help make this world a better place.

CHAPTER 21

Pools and Beaches

AFTER growing up with a swimming pool in our backyard on Diane Drive, I just naturally assumed I'd have one in my own yard as a parent someday. Well, that dream took longer to come to fruition than I ever thought it would. When Bob Shuster of RWS Shuster Homes built our new house for us in 1994, he made sure to flatten our backyard after I told him we were planning on getting a pool installed sometime in the near future. Somehow, Catholic grade school, high school, and then college tuition took priority, but I kept reminding Eddy that I wanted a pool. It took approximately 22 more years until that dream of mine came true. On New Year's Eve when Eddy asked what I might like that year, I simply stated that I wanted a pool. There were no daughters getting married that year, and no more college tuition, so it was my turn. Eddy suggested we update our kitchen with new appliances instead. He tried his darnedest to talk me out of a pool. I simple stated, "I want a pool!" every day from New Year's Eve up until he scheduled a meeting with the owner of Westmoreland Pools, in March. After a few meetings, they broke ground in July of 2016. We finally got our own in-ground swimming pool in our own back yard. I designed it exactly according to my dad's advice. It's a free form sport pool with aluminum sides, and dark Caribbean blue liner. The top of the liner resembles the Irish love knot that encircles the pool. The shape of the pool looks very natural in our back yard, like a cement pond, as the Beverly Hillbillies used to call it. The depth of the pool starts at three and a half feet and runs to five and a half feet. There's not a diving board or sliding board. Those days are over. It's perfect for swimming laps, playing pool volleyball, and just lounging on our rafts.

The pool has transformed our backyard into an oasis of comfort. Now it's our turn to host the Memorial Day, Fourth of July, and Labor Day pool parties, and we love every minute of it. My only regret is that we couldn't afford to install a pool when our daughters were living here. The plus side of it is that they love coming home more than ever to relax in our own little resort. Some things are definitely worth waiting for!

When you get older, sometimes it's kind of cool when you feel parts of your life that have come full circle. In June of 2018, Eddy, Tierney, my Mother, and I flew to Tampa, Florida to visit Kaitlin and Jason who was on a six month Air Force assignment there. The weather was sunny, warm, and humid, typical for Tampa in June, so we decided to go to the beaches the week we were there. The first beach we settled on was beautiful Clearwater Beach, which brought back memories of family vacations during my youth with my parents, sisters, cousins, and Aunt Sheila, and Uncle Bob. A couple days later, we ventured down to St. Petersburg Beach. The warm gulf waters and white sandy beaches took me back in time to when I was nineteen years old, and we stayed in the Hilton Hotel right on St. Pete's Beach with the beautiful white sand. The hotel is still there, but now it's the Grand Plaza Hotel Beachfront Resort and Conference Center. Even though the name and owners have changed, the Spinners Roof Top Revolving Restaurant and Lounge remained the same. Jason had to work that day, but the rest of us went inside and rode the glass elevator up to the restaurant. Eddy had joined my family during one of those Florida vacations and remembered taking me to a romantic dinner atop that very restaurant. On the car ride back to Tampa that evening, we phoned Aunt Sheila and Uncle Bob to reminisce about those happy vacations. They recalled my younger sisters and cousins riding that glass elevator up and down, like it was a Kennywood Ride, much to the chagrin of the restaurant personnel. Family vacations to those two Florida beaches were such happy summer memories.

CHAPTER 22

Retirement

When the start of the new school year rolled around in August 2018, I instinctively knew 2018-19 would be the last year I'd be teaching. As the school year progressed and a new crew of students came into my classroom, I decided to approach the year with a renewed appreciation of my teaching profession, and my ability to touch students' lives by making positive differences in them. Instead of thinking I had to do this or that, I adjusted my attitude to feeling grateful that I had the privilege of doing this or that. Eddy had posted a sign in our garage, when our daughters were teenagers, to see every time they came home, since that's the way we typically enter our kitchen. The sign says: "Attitude is everything. Pick a good one!" That sign, still hanging, is also the last thing I saw backing my car out of the garage to go to school every morning.

We were assigned a team clustered with more needy and troubled students than usual my last year of teaching. In our group of 84 kiddos, we had a dozen learning support students, nine students with 504 plans, (According to the US Department of Education, students with a physical or mental impairment that substantially limits one or more major life activities must be protected under the Section 504 Plan and are entitled to a free and appropriate public education.), five students with behavior charts and emotional issues, several with custody issues, and one child struggling to hear with a hearing disability. Years ago, it was rare to have a student who had a parent in jail, in rehab, or on drugs, and if a parent was in jail, it was typically the father. Not so anymore. This particular year, we had students who were living with neither parent, because the mother was either in jail or rehab and the father was out of the picture.

We're seeing more and more grandparents raising their grandchildren, because the parents aren't fit, present, or able to do the job. Two students in particular stand out as having the saddest family situations that year, one a girl, and the other a boy. These students were in counseling with both our school guidance counselors and outside school therapists.

The girl student, I'll call Savannah, (pseudonym), lived with her elderly paternal grandmother who was wheel chair bound after she had a stroke. Savannah was separated from her sister and brother who were sent to live with her maternal grandmother in Ohio. Her mother was recently released from jail and in a rehab facility. Her father, an alcoholic, brought a revolving door series of girlfriends back to his mother's house to sleep with on occasion, particularly on the nights he was drunk, which was often. Savannah's grandmother eventually ordered her son to leave and not return with another woman. But Savannah's father would continue to return to the house alone, drunk after midnight, where he would then wake up and rape his eleven year old daughter.

Savannah had so many unexcused absences from school that the truant officer was sent to her grandmother's home to investigate. Savannah's excuses for missing school were that she was too tired to get up in the morning, therefore missing the bus, and her grandmother couldn't drive her since they didn't have a car and she was disabled. Savannah's medical excuses for being absent from school stated that she was sick with recurring urinary tract infections (UTIs). Recurrent UTIs are usually red flags to doctors and nurses when they occur in children, sometimes indicative of sexual abuse. We eventually informed Children Youth Services (CYS), and they began visits to their home. Savannah began to attend school more frequently, but was still living in an unsafe environment.

Apparently, Savannah's grandmother was also struggling financially as she tried to provide for her. When our students were telling each other before Christmas break what they wanted from Santa Claus, Savannah simply said that she wanted a new coat. Most other students mentioned wanting new iPhones, iPads, electronic toys, and games. When I asked her what kind of coat she wanted, Savannah knew exactly what type of coat she wanted. She wanted a *black, puffy coat with a fur hood, size 16*. She came up to my desk at the end of that particular day to show me her current coat which was ripped, wouldn't zipper, and was too small on her. When I went home that evening, I had 84 tests to check, and told Eddy that I'd like to buy Savannah a coat for Christmas that weekend. A few minutes later, Eddy said he was running to Kohl's and might pick up a coat for Savannah if he saw one like what I had described. When Eddy came home later that night with a Kohl's shopping bag and a grin on his face, I knew he bought Savannah a coat. He relayed to me how he looked at every coat on the store rounder in the girls' coat department, but there were no size 16 coats that fit that description. Then, he pulled out a black puffy coat with a fur hood that said size 12 on the hanger, but when he looked inside the neck area the tag said it was a size 16! He couldn't believe it! I think it was a God Wink, and I think Eddy does, too! The next day, when Savannah came up to my desk to talk to me during dismissal, I told her that Santa Claus left a present for her at my house last night. I gave her the Christmas gift bag, and she lifted out the coat. Savannah cried out with tears in her eyes, "This is exactly the coat I've wanted! How did Santa know? How did he know? I never told him!" I explained that maybe Santa Claus was watching through the classroom window and magically heard her telling me and the class what she wanted for Christmas that year. Savannah wore that coat to school every day until the weather became too warm for it in the spring. That black puffy coat is one of the most appreciated Christmas gifts Eddy and I have ever given, and I mean ever!

Savannah and I developed a close relationship that year as she would often confide in me crying about the situation at home, and I would listen with compassion and help her keep up with her studies academically. Many times I'd have to send Savannah down to the guidance counselor at the end of the school day during Activity Period. During one of the last conversations I had with Savannah before the end of the school year, I told her that if she was being abused physically, emotionally, or sexually, she should tell the guidance counselor and her therapist. She looked at me as the tears rolled down her face, and simply stated, "I can't." That poor child didn't want to tell on her father. It was tragic. I reported this to guidance and CYS. The only good that came out of this sad story, is that Savannah was sent to live with her maternal grandmother in Ohio the summer after my last school year. Savannah was a bright student who could have been earning straight As if she'd had a happy home life with supportive parents. After what she'd lived through that year, it's no wonder she'd missed school, got poor grades, and fell asleep at her desk. Hopefully, Savannah is now living in a healthier, safer, and more secure environment with her maternal grandmother and siblings in Ohio, far away from her abusive father, where she's able to attend school on a regular basis and work up to her academic potential.

The other student with a sad family story that year was a boy I'll call Zane (pseudonym). Zane transferred from another school district after we were already a month into the new school year. At first, Zane was quiet and didn't talk. After a few weeks, it was apparent from his behavior that he was very troubled and angry. He refused to do his school work, was deliberately disruptive in class, and began to have verbal outbursts at inappropriate times. When I'd take him aside to try and help him, quietly correct him, and ask him to pay attention and cooperate with the rest of his group, he would make strange guttural noises and act as if he was not mentally or emotionally well. Zane would usually finish the school day in the guidance counselor's office during Activity Period, and end up lying on the floor in the fetal position. Sometimes he would crawl under his desk and sit there during classroom instruction, obviously not normal behavior for an eleven year old boy.

A few weeks after Zane was at Hillcrest, we found out that Zane's mother wasn't in his life, because she was a drug addict. The man who Zane was living with, and thought was his father, was one of his mother's previous boyfriends. Zane felt abandoned and angry when he found out the man raising him wasn't his real father a month before he started back to a new school. We never found out who his biological father was, if he was alive, or in jail, or rehab. His caregiver, had a job working different shifts, and so Zane spent most of his time at home alone. He had so much anger inside of him that he would periodically explode with verbal outbursts in class. He had a negative attitude about school, and didn't care about anything. He had no friends in school, and didn't care about that either. Zane was bright, but without studying and putting any effort into his school work, his grades were dropping and he was failing most of his subjects. Zane would talk to the guidance counselor daily, and after our intervention, began seeing a therapist outside of school as well. Zane spent many lunch periods eating his lunch in the guidance suite, and then returning to guidance almost every Activity Period at the end of each school day. There were many times when his team teachers and I would skip lunch in the teachers' lunchroom to go check on Zane in guidance, and help him with his overdue assignments. I frequently told him how much we teachers cared about him, and how I believed in him and his ability. After a few months, Zane and I developed a close relationship to the point that he now trusted me, and would sometimes do his assignments just to please me. His guidance counselor saw this progress as well. Positive reinforcement worked wonders with Zane.

Retirement

By the end of the school year Zane was starting to do his assignments independently, and had raised his grades in both my Science and Social Studies classes. I think Zane finally realized that people do care about him, and that ultimately, it was his decision to apply himself to his studies and improve his life. I explained to him that he had a choice about which path he was going to take in life, and I hoped he was going to choose the path to be self-responsible in order to lead a happy and productive life. I told him that he had the power to change his negative attitude from feeling sorry for himself to applying himself in school, getting better grades, and having a positive outlook on life. I even told Zane about my own father's dysfunctional childhood growing up without a mother, and how he made a better life for himself as an adult. Zane hung onto every word as I relayed a little bit of the story of my dad's motherless childhood.

The autumn after my last school year let out, I ran into Zane in the Giant Eagle Grocery Store in our community. Zane approached me as I was turning away from the pharmacy checkout, and said, "Hi, Mrs. Guarascio! How are you?" He smiled and looked happy to see me. I was surprised to see him, and asked how he was. He told me he was "good!" He told me that his new school year was going well. I wished him good luck in sixth grade, and reminded him that I believed in him. Then we both said goodbye and left the store.

When I got back in my car, I asked God to bless both Zane and Savannah with the love and support they'd need to sustain them the rest of their lives. Months later, I found out that Zane had been placed in Learning Support in sixth grade, was prescribed meds, and had been assigned to a Student Assistance Program (SAP) mentor. That was such great news that Zane would be getting the additional help he desperately needed. It was a comfort to know that both of these troubled students were off to a better beginning that next school year.

My last year of teaching had flown by faster than ever. The days became weeks, which rolled into months. After the whirlwind start of the 2018–19 school year, Thom Swenson, my teaching partner, Trisha Brunazzi, our gifted education teacher, and our then Superintendent Dr. Kerr, traveled to China for two weeks as part of Norwin's new cultural student-exchange program. Afterward, a large group of Chinese students and a few of their teachers accompanied our educators back to Hillcrest to attend our classes as part of the exchange program. Trying to teach and include students who didn't speak English, while the rest of us couldn't speak Chinese, proved to be an interesting challenge, but I'm glad to have had the experience. More importantly, it was an authentic way to broaden our students' horizons. Soon after our Chinese guests left Hillcrest, we began collecting nonperishable goods for the Food Bank prior to Thanksgiving, and before long, our faculty and staff were celebrating Christmas at the local Fire Pit Wood Fired Grill. January snows ushered in the second semester, followed by Lent, St. Patrick's Day festivities, Easter, PSSA testing, and the very busy month of May chalk full of fun end-of-the-year activities. As my last year of teaching progressed, I tried to savor every memory as the last time I'd . . .

Norwin School District Administrators request that teachers notify them of their retirement plans by the beginning of April. So on April 1st, I emailed my letter of intent to our Director of Human Resources to make my retirement plans official. In my letter, I mentioned that during the course of my lengthy teaching career, including the past two decades at Norwin, how I've had the privilege of instructing thousands of young people who have gone on to benefit society in big ways. This truly leaves me with a great sense of accomplishment with my career choice and my teaching performance as well. Every year, it seems that more of my past students and their parents either come to see me, or contact me to tell me how their lives were touched and/or changed in a positive way because of my influence. This is why teaching has been the most rewarding career I could have chosen. Teaching has afforded me the opportunity to improve lives and create life-long memories for my students in the process. I look back at how I strived to make school a happy place for my students to learn, and am filled with gratitude for the chance to make a difference. Now, I look forward to new adventures making memories with my family and friends as I begin a new chapter in my life.

And so it was official. As May approached my retirement seemed more real. The Norwin Education Association (NEA) Teachers' Union hosted their annual retirement dinner that year on May 9th, so I decided to attend. Bridget wasn't able to fly in from Houston, but Eddy, Kaitlin, Tierney, my Mother, Sheila, and Denise all came to honor me for my years of service along with my teaching partner, Thom. After a delicious dinner at Banquets Unlimited, there was a short program where our teaching partners introduced us with a few kind words. Thom had touched my heart when he mentioned my *versatility* as an educator. He also bought me a sharp and spacious travel tote bag for when Eddy and I go on future vacation trips. The presenters were followed by us retirees expressing our gratitude and sharing some favorite teaching memories. The NEA did such a great job including our personal accomplishments into the program booklet, there wasn't much left for me to say when they called me up to the microphone. Then, the NEA presented us retirees with a beautiful white embroidered throw, flowers, and a bouquet of blue and gold balloons. I was grateful for my family to be there, especially for my mom, as it was a milestone in my life, and in hers, and such a happy occasion.

The last week in April, I had posted invitations in the mailroom and teachers' lunchroom at Hillcrest inviting all my teaching friends and colleagues to help celebrate my retirement at a pool party at our house the end of May. Eddy had designed a cute invitation which included a picture of me teaching my first year at St. Robert's in 1978! Everyone got a big kick out of it, and seemed excited to celebrate with me, but I didn't know who would be able to attend since May is such a busy month filled with many obligations. My retirement party on May 23, 2019 turned out to be one of the happiest memories of my life. The weather was perfect for a pool party, even though nobody swam. It was sunny and warm, and we all sat around the pool, under the patio table umbrella, or on the back porch to reminisce and toast to my retirement, and the end of another successful school year. Eddy had taken a half day off work to help me host the party. He had ordered all the pizzas, and had all the drinks and snacks put out when we arrived after teaching all day. I had made an antipasto salad the night before which he had put out in the kitchen. Eddy also put blue and gold balloons on our mailbox, and threaded lights through our rod iron pool fence that sparkled at dusk. There was even a full moon that night. It was perfect! Almost all of my teacher friends came to celebrate my retirement, and presented me with the most beautiful and meaningful gifts. Karen and Eleni brought a delicious retirement sheet cake, and a beautiful Irish bowl. Several other gifts stood out to mention. Amy and Lori parodied a *Miss Nelson Is Missing* (and she isn't coming back!) picture book with my name replacing Miss Nelson! I'll cherish it as a reminder of our friendship, especially during the years we taught Literacy together. They also presented me with a beautiful Hawaiian planter for around the pool. Laura and Mandy brought a beautiful butterfly solar powered garden table that lights up at night. The Hillcrest Celebration Committee, of which I've been a member since its inception, presented me with a pretty retirement garden stone. There were so many bottles of wine, flowers, and gift cards that I can't remember them all now, but sent thank you cards for them at the time. It was such a joyous occasion sharing teaching memories and funny stories celebrating my retirement with my fellow teachers. Their love and support touched my heart. We are truly a sisterhood. I love those girls. Only a teacher can understand the life of another teacher. We teachers have a special bond, and I think it's universal.

The highlight of the party was when Eddy announced there was a surprise present on our front porch. Lo and behold, my dear daughter Bridget had sent *Millie's Homemade Ice Cream* served to us by the owner, Millie herself, standing in front of her pop-up ice cream parlor. Millie is famous for owning ice cream stores in Pittsburgh, Oakland, and Squirrel Hill. The pretty pink tablecloth advertising the yummy ice cream flavors was the icing on the cake. Everyone loved it. The delicious ice cream was the hit of the party, and it was so sweet and thoughtful of Bridget to arrange that all the way from Houston. The party continued late into Thursday night, but by 11:00 pm, everyone had gone home as we had to teach the next day. TGIF was the general sentiment the next morning!

And just like that, it was over. The last few weeks of May I had given away teaching materials, books, subject files, projects, games, learning centers, tests, posters, bulletin boards, and just about anything I thought was useful to various teachers who had expressed an interest in my educational stuff. I said goodbye to my students on their last day for the very last time. I was just about to burst into tears when I heard the calls to come out of our classrooms. So, all of us teachers walked out of our classrooms like we do every *last student day* to watch as Lori Ryan did her annual cartwheels down the hallway. After much applause and laughter, we gathered our tote bags and headed to the Fire Pit Wood Fired Grill to toast another good school year. A week later, I packed up what was left of my classroom, and Thom and his dad helped me carry my boxes to my car. I thanked them, hugged them goodbye, and drove home wondering how it went so fast. My teaching career was ending, but I will always be a teacher. Once a teacher, always a teacher, and that would never change. I'd made many dear friends and beautiful memories over the years that I would carry in my heart as I continued on my journey of a lifetime.

But there would be lots of change, and it really didn't hit me until the end of August when everyone was going back to school, except me. I'd heard a guest on a talk show liken his recent retirement to traveling along a road at 100 miles per hour, and then suddenly coming to an abrupt stop. That metaphor simply sums up the change in the level of stress. No more waking up for work with the 6:00 a.m. alarm, and swiping our IDs to get into our school building before the 7:35 a.m. bell. No more living my life by school bells . . . bells to recite the Pledge of Allegiance at 8:00 a.m., bells to switch and start classes, bells to go to lunch, bells to restart classes after lunch, bells to signal Activity Period, dismissal bells for students, and then finally dismissal bells for us teachers. This new found time in my daily life would give me much opportunity to recalculate my life. I would have much more time to spend with my family and friends. I'd be able to travel with Eddy more, visit our daughters Bridget and Kaitlin, who lived in Houston and Boston, meet Tierney for lunch or dinner, and take my elderly mother shopping and to her doctor appointments. My first order of business would be to finish writing this book. I've always thought I knew how to end it, but just haven't had the time to devote to it. So I established a new goal to finish writing and try to get this book published by the end of 2020.

In the meantime, the summer would be spent celebrating the week of our 40th wedding anniversary in Hilton Head, South Carolina, and then remainder of the summer swimming in our backyard oasis. Hilton Head has been one of our favorite vacation destinations to celebrate our June wedding anniversaries over the years. We've taken our daughters and my mother there, and have also gone there many times by ourselves. The Lowcountry is so lush and beautiful with its picturesque palm trees, those pristine white sandy beaches and warm gulfstream waters that it always lulls us back. The world class Sea Pines Resort, famous for its golf course, is known as a golfer's paradise, and home to the iconic Harbour Town Lighthouse. The island boasts plenty of shops, boutiques, and fabulous Lowcountry food in their wonderful restaurants. Some of the prettiest sunsets I've ever seen have been while dining in the Old Fort Pub Restaurant nestled on the marsh of Skull Creek overlooking the beautiful bay. Hilton Head is a family-oriented island resort town where you can relax and enjoy all the tropical amenities with only a two hour long plane ride from Pittsburgh. We had begun our 2019 summer in June on the Atlantic Ocean Island of Hilton Head celebrating our anniversary, and would end our summer in September celebrating my retirement on another Atlantic Ocean Island across the Pond, called Ireland!

CHAPTER 23

The Emerald Isle

*T*HIS trip of a lifetime had been years in the making, ever since my sister Sheila claimed that Eddy had promised to take the *Inner Circle* there, if I ever survived my fight with cancer. Eddy is not sure he remembers saying that to her. Lol! Nevertheless, Eddy had been to Ireland on business trips at least a dozen times, and had always wanted to take me there. A business friend of Eddy's owns Calnan Cottage on Sherkin Island of Roaringwater Bay, in County Cork, Ireland, and even gave Eddy a key to cottage for us to use if I recovered. After making eleven more trips around the sun in complete remission, Sheila again reminded Eddy of his supposed promise to the *Inner Circle*. Consequently, Eddy and I decided that a family trip to Ireland would be the perfect way to fulfill his *alleged* promise to Sheila. So we issued an open invitation to anyone in the extended family that might want to join us, and still kept the key to the island cottage just for us another time in the future.

Eddy has gained quite a respected reputation as an experienced world traveler, due to his countless business trips for Medrad and Bayer Corporation over the past twenty years to the most beautiful cities in America, Europe, Japan, and Australia. Eddy, now family and friend famous for putting together and planning extraordinary and exotic itineraries, decided to create a new adventure for our trip to the Emerald Isle. After everyone checked their work schedules, finances, and availability, here's the list of family members who accompanied Eddy and me on our trip to the Emerald Isle: Bridget and Craig, my mother Mary Pat, Uncle Tim and his partner Ray, Sheila and Dom, Maura, Dominic, and Denise. Eric was kind enough to encourage Denise to go without him, as he committed to stay at home with their teenagers. We would thereafter be known as the O'Grady Party of 12, even though only Timmy was lucky enough to own that Irish surname! Eddy had asked everyone to book their airplane flights from September 6 to September 13, 2019. Eddy and Bridget planned, created, and copied the whole itinerary for everyone, and made hotel and room reservations for all parties in all the places we would stay. Their objective was to provide a good taste of Ireland in just a week. And to consider everyone from age 23 to 83!

The first challenge would be keeping our large group together touring our week in Ireland. Sheila had worked with a doctor friend who forwarded her the name of an experienced Irish tour guide who had accompanied his family during their trip there. After Sheila shared this information with our family, Bridget and Craig generously gifted our group by hiring Flan Kelly Guiding Services to chauffer us the entire week in Ireland. And wow, we traveled in style. Our tour bus was a new Mercedes Turas Coach with 17 forward facing captains' seats with an additional four rear facing. It also contained two tables where my mother, sisters, and I actually played a game of double pinochle on one of the longer bus rides one afternoon. But the best perk of all was our tour guide, Flan Kelly, a charming Irish gentleman who befriended us and proudly educated us with cultural and heritage information with his storytelling wit along the *Wild Atlantic Way*. Flan became our friend that week, and went above and beyond the call of duty in his role as our tour guide on the Emerald Isle.

We arrived at Shannon Airport early Saturday morning, September 7th, and would spend the first day in Adare with a side trip to Limerick City. Eddy made reservations for eight of us to stay in the Lodges at Adare Manor Hotel & Golf Resort while the Farina family party of four would stay close by in town at Dunraven Arms. After checking into our rooms and freshening up from the flights, we all met at Adare Manor to explore the perfectly manicured grounds. In addition to the majestic manor, at the five-star resort, there were beautiful flower gardens, ancient ruins, stone arches, magical fairy gardens and cottages, and the elegant Carriage House where we'd eat breakfast overlooking the gorgeous world class golf course and luxurious landscape. Adare Manor golf course will host the 2027 Ryder Cup, the world's biggest golf tournament. The owner, beloved Limerick businessman J. P. McManus, bought Adare Manor in January 2015 for an estimated 30 million euros. Several staff members told us he would fly in on his private helicopter every morning for breakfast, land on a special spot of the golf course, and check in with his employees on how things were going. Every employee we talked with seemed to take ownership of Adare Manor, and raved about how much everyone loved Mr. McManus. I couldn't help thinking it reminded me of how Pittsburgh loves the Rooney Family. The Steelers are like our Adare Manor Hotel and Golf Resort, because we take pride in them, support them, and love them like family.

Later Saturday morning, Flan Kelly arrived to begin our tour in the Sprinter Van, so off we went to explore Limerick. In spite of its reputation, Limerick looked lovely to us. The sky was blue and the sun was shining, contrary to what we'd expected the weather to be in Ireland. In fact, we had sunny blue skies every day we were in Ireland, with just a few sprinkles here and there. We had lunch in the heart of Limerick at Dolan's Pub famous for all types of live traditional Irish music. After a delicious lunch, Flan took us to St. John's Castle where Maura ventured up to the rooftop to capture pictures of the city from that frightening high vantage point. Several of us found a souvenir shop nearby and bought gifts. I was excited to buy my mom a Christmas tree ornament that had St. John's Castle on it, metaphoric for my parents' home. But the highlight of our afternoon in Limerick had to be our visit to the O'Grady Irish monument where all 12 of us were able to squeeze into the O'Grady Clan Photo.

Saturday evening, we went to 7:00 p.m. Mass at Trinitarian Abbey in Adare Village, across the street from the historic and quaint Adare thatched cottages. Mass was beautiful and the priest gave a wonderfully meaningful and unusually short sermon. After Mass, we went across the street to eat dinner at the Blue Door Restaurant, but they never received our reservation. Luck of the Irish, the owner took us next door to his best friend's restaurant which happened to have room for our large party of 12. That pretty much sums up the warm hospitality of Ireland. After what felt like a very long day, we went back to Adare for drinks, and then back to our rooms to sleep.

Sunday morning we met for breakfast at 8:00 a.m. in the Adare Carriage House. Flan arrived shortly afterward to begin our sightseeing tour for the day heading north to the Cliffs of Moher. Our first stop was Saint Bridget's Well, which had a personal connection for us since she is the patron saint of our daughter, Bridget. St. Bridget's Well is one of the oldest wells in Ireland said to have healing powers. It is housed in an open stone grotto which serves as a gateway to an ancient cemetery of Ireland's mythical kings and clan leaders. The well's natural beauty and mysterious pull is known for its mysticism. Bridget and her sisters are known as the Triple Goddesses, which also felt like another connection to my three daughters, who sometimes think they are three princesses. St. Bridget is known as the Patroness of Ireland and she's also considered the foster mother of Jesus. We took pictures of our Bridget standing in front of the statue of her patron saint and namesake, and said some prayers asking for St. Bridget to intercede on our behalf for a blessed tour of Ireland. Then, we were back in our van on our sightseeing trip off to the world famous Cliffs of Moher.

On our way to and from the Cliffs of Moher, we would pass the Burren, another one of the unique landscapes in Ireland. The Burren is made up of limestone formed as sediments in a tropical sea which covered Ireland millions of years ago. The Burren is a region of County Clare where the landscape is miles of cracked bedrock of glacial era limestone with cliffs, caves, fossils, rock formations, and archeological sites. As we drove by in our van, the landscape looked foreign and desolate as you would imagine the surface of another planet. But, we were headed to the southwestern edge of the Burren region along the Atlantic Ocean coastline, where we would behold one of the most beautiful views on our planet.

The Cliffs of Moher are spectacular seaside cliffs located in County Clare, Ireland. My mother was a real trooper hiking up to the tops of the cliffs which seem to go on for miles. We stopped and took pictures as the view was stunning. It was a cold, cloudy, and very windy day with a few sprinkles, but we still managed to get pictures in front of castle-like O'Brien's Tower, and on the top of the cliffs. Sheila and Timmy teasingly tried to scare us by sitting precariously close to the edge of the cliffs for pictures, until I reminded them that at last count 66 people have died there since 1993. On that sobering thought, we headed back down the path to the Visitors' Center, and then as the rains became stronger, we headed to the parking lot back to the safety of our van. Flan drove us back to Adare Manor to freshen up for our visit to the Bunratty Castle Medieval Banquet Show for dinner. That show was an interesting reenactment of how people must have feasted there back in medieval times, but it wasn't my cup of tea. After a long, cold, wet, and crowded evening there, where we were packed onto benches like sardines in a can, and served an unappetizing boiled chicken dinner with no utensils to use to eat, we happily hopped back in our van and headed for the comforts of the Adare Manor.

On Monday morning, September 9th, we would depart Adare for Kinsale, our second stop in County Cork. We boarded the van and headed south along the *Wild Atlantic Way* for the most picturesque drive in Ireland, beginning our sightseeing trip through beautiful County Kerry on to County Cork. We would bypass the Tralee Wetlands travelling south down the Dingle Peninsula, one of the westernmost points of Ireland. The Dingle Peninsula is ringed by beautiful beaches, mountainous islands, and craggy cliffs. Inland the farmlands are dotted with sheep grazing on the patchwork of green rolling hills sectioned off by ancient stone walls. The spectacular scenery along the peninsula drive was breathtaking as we made our way to the town of Dingle and Dingle Bay. The *National Geographic* once called the Dingle Peninsula "the most beautiful place on earth."

Dingle is a charming and remote harbor town known for recreational and commercial fishing, along with recent accolades as the finest destination in the countryside, and one of the gourmet capitals of the country. Dingle is now considered a *foodie town*, for many tourists. The town's colorfully painted buildings are also home to woolen garment and souvenir shops, art galleries, and more than 52 traditional Irish pubs. A statue of a dolphin named Fungie resides by the waterfront and makes for a great photo op with all the boats docked behind it in the harbor. We ate lunch at John Benny's Pub and had the most delicious seafood chowder. Our final stop before boarding our van was Murphy's Ice Cream Shop, and it was worth every calorie.

Back in our van, we travelled Slea Head Drive, the circular scenic route that hugs the Atlantic Coastline, to get to the best vantage point to view breathtakingly beautiful Dingle Bay. Fortunately, Flan was an experienced driver as he navigated the narrow mountainous roads many of which were cliff side single lane, or bordered by stone walls leaving little room for two vehicles to pass each other. Along the way, we made a few tourist stops. On our first stop, we visited the prehistoric Beehive Huts, built during the Iron Age, 3,000 years ago, about 1,000 BC. There are over 400 of these stone domes scattered throughout the Dingle Peninsula. They were named Beehive Huts because of their shape, no bees were involved! We learned these stone igloos were ordinary farmers' homes housing multi-generational families. The amazing fact is how these solid structures were made and stood the test of time. They were built utilizing the corbel style system using no mortar, simply held together over the ages by gravity and friction, and the way the stones were placed on top of each other. The domes are also waterproof and airtight. We were able to climb the steep hillside and venture inside several of the Beehive Huts were we took photos. Again, even though it was a precarious climb stepping carefully on the rugged random rocky pathways, my dear mother was still able to join us.

Our next stop on Slea Head Drive, was the life size holy Slea Head Cross white stone sculpture depicting Christ's crucifixion just a few feet from the road standing in the rugged cliffs. We got out of the van, said a few prayers, and crossed the road to take pictures of the breathtaking views of Dingle Bay and the world renowned Blasket Islands in the distance. The sun was shining, and the sky and bay were the most beautiful shades of blue. The contrast of the vivid blues against the glorious emerald shades of green provided one of the most stunning views I've ever seen. From this vantage point, we were also able to see the Three Sisters Mountain Peaks and the silhouette of the Sleeping Giant on Dead Man's Island that looks like an Irishman laying on his back with a bit of a gut from drinking too much Guinness. It was difficult to get back in the van and leave that spectacular spot, but we did because we still had miles to go on our way to Kinsale.

We travelled to Killarney and stopped at a tourist rest stop along Inch Beach. The weather was changing again, becoming cloudy, windy, and cooler, but Denise insisted we walk down to the sandy beach, so she could touch the water. So we did, because we were all about trying to make everybody happy. More pictures were taken in the wet sand. Then, we hopped back in the van and drove on until we reached Killarney National Park, which is home to the world famous Lakes of Killarney. The wooded park was beautifully planted, lush, and green. Within the park, is Muckross House, a magnificent Victorian mansion, one of Ireland's stately homes known world-wide for its beautiful gardens. It was later in the day when we were there, so we didn't tour the mansion. We meandered around the pretty park awhile, before climbing up the stone steps in search of the magical Torc Waterfalls. Again, my dear mother walked up the steep cliffs to get closer to the cascade of waterfalls as they were located at the base of Torc Mountain. After taking a few more photos of the falls, we descended the mountain, walked across the park, back to our van in the parking lot. We were finally on our way to charming Kinsale Seaport Village, world famous fishing town, where we would spend the next two nights.

We all checked into the Old Bank House Hotel in Kinsale, and then we went to dinner at the Supper Club in the center of Kinsale. The *Sunday Times* listed it as one of the 100 Best Restaurants in Ireland. After a delicious dinner, some of us went to listen to Irish music at the Gray Hound Pub, and some of us were exhausted from the long day, and went back to settle in our hotel rooms.

Eddy made no specific plans for everyone the next day, but suggested several options for our entertainment. Craig had booked a fishing trip on the beautiful River Blackwater known for its history of salmon fishing tales, while villagers claim it's the *birthplace of fly fishing*. Bridget, my mother, and I went to the local beauty salon to get our hair done, and then went shopping in the vividly colorful town shops while we strolled along the cobbled stone streets. Denise and Dom went golfing on Kinsale's Old Head Golf Links, a world-class golf course. In spite of the windy day, they both enjoyed every minute on the gorgeous golf course which offers stunning views as the unique headland juts out into the Atlantic Ocean, hundreds of feet above the water splashing against towering sea cliffs. They took beautiful pictures of the lighthouse, and the gorgeous greens, showing us the ocean right behind them. Sheila, Maura, Dommy, Tim, and Ray went to tour the Kinsale Charles Fort, constructed during the reign of King Charles II in the late 1600s, to protect the town and harbor of Kinsale. They learned that the unique design of the fort was built with star-shaped fortifications, and the fort was used as a British Army barracks for about two hundred years until it was relinquished following the Anglo-Irish Treaty of 1921. Eddy stayed back in town with us running back and forth making sure everyone was having fun doing their thing. The nonstop travelling was finally taking a toll on my mom, so she decided to rest in her hotel room the remainder of the afternoon and read her book.

Later in the afternoon, most of us jumped back on the van and travelled to Cobh, a port town in Cork Harbor, about 20 kilometers away, to participate in the Titanic Experience. Cobh was the last port of call for the ill-fated Titanic. The Titanic Experience is a tourist attraction located in the same White Star Line Ticket Office departure building. Upon entering, tourists receive a boarding card with the name and details of one of the 123 passengers who boarded on that last port of call date, April 11, 1912. The tour guide took us on a virtual journey where you experience life on the Titanic and learn about the drastically different conditions that existed for the first and third class passengers. There is an exhibition area

The Emerald Isle

filled with interactive audio visual presentations and story boards exploring the events leading up to the tragic sinking. The final element of the experience is located in the story room where you find out your fate as a passenger. It was a very moving, emotional, and educational experience that I highly recommend if you ever visit Cobh, Ireland. After leaving the Titanic Experience, we stopped in a local pub for a late lunch, and visited the majestic St. Colman's Roman Catholic Cathedral which overlooks Cork Harbor. We went inside and said a few more prayers in thanksgiving for a safe and happy trip. Then, we boarded our van to return to Kinsale and freshen up for dinner.

We ate dinner in different restaurants that evening, but later we all convened at the Armada Bar in the heart of Kinsale. We drank, danced, and sang along with the traditional Irish music of The Ferrymen that night. We even lead the other patrons in a conga line after a few too many rounds of Guinness and Baileys, which Craig referred to as "Mother's Milk!" As we started leaving the pub much later that night, the other tourists were asking us to stay longer. But when the band stopped playing music, we knew it was time to call it a night. The next morning, we feasted on breakfast in the Old Bank House Gourmet Café before departing Kinsale and rallying for the three hour drive to Dublin, our third and final stop.

On our sightseeing trip to Dublin, we headed north to County Tipperary, where we would stop at the Rock of Cashel, a twelfth century historic site. The Rock of Cashel is also known as Cashel of the Kings and St. Patrick's Rock. Cashel is reputed to be the site where the King of Munster was converted to Catholicism by St. Patrick in the fifth century. Few remnants of the early structure have survived, and most buildings on site date from the twelfth and thirteenth centuries. In the grounds around the buildings, there is an extensive graveyard. Timmy was able to locate several tombstones with the O'Grady and Rochford family surnames. Rochford was the maiden name of my mother's beloved paternal grandmother, and my Great Grandmother Katie O'Grady. And located at the foot of the Rock of Cashel is an intimate theater where Bru Boru performs traditional Irish music, song, and dance during the summer show season from late June until late August. The complex is also the setting of fictional medieval mystery shows that run from mid-September through early June, although we didn't have time to catch any of the shows. The medieval architecture atop the gorgeous green hilltop made a spectacular setting overlooking the emerald green landscape against the cornflower blue sky. The Rock of Cashel is a must-see for anyone traveling through this part of Ireland.

Back in our van, we travelled to County Wicklow through the majestic Wicklow Mountains to our next stop on our way to Dublin. Nestled in the luscious greenery of the Wicklow Mountains is the spiritual and serene valley of Glendalough. Glendalough, which translates to valley of two lakes, is the site of the medieval monastery founded by Saint Kevin in the sixth century, known as one of the great centers of learning in early Christian Ireland. After getting off our van, we all meandered in different directions along the various walking trails at Glendalough. Eddy and Denise ended up stepping across the stones in the crystal clear mountain streams, Maura and Sheila ventured further to find the lakes, and the rest of us just strolled along the peaceful paths toward St. Kevin's Cross, the Gateway, and St. Kevin's Kitchen. We all took more pictures of the natural beauty which surrounded us, and eventually ended up at the Glendalough Visitor Centre to learn more of the history of the Monastic City through the audio-visual interactive display before we drove northeast toward our destination of Dublin.

We arrived in Dublin around dinner time, and bid goodbye to our trusted tour guide, driver, and new friend, Flan Kelly. No sooner had we checked into the Drury Court Hotel, located within the heart of Dublin, young Dominic realized he left his expensive headphones on the van. Flan was already out of the city, when Sheila called to ask him to check the van for them, thinking he could mail them home to her. Flan found Dom's headphones right away, turned the van around, and drove back to our hotel to return them. We took one last photo with Flan, but regret that Bridget and Craig weren't in the picture, because they were staying at a swanky five star hotel. Once again we said goodbye to Flan, and then we all met for dinner at the Elephant & Castle Restaurant in the Temple Bar area.

Thursday morning, September 12th, we were excited to explore the history and magic of Dublin. Our group split up again and spread out in different directions. Tim and Ray started out touring the Temple Bar area which is a busy riverside neighborhood of Dublin featuring lots of pubs and live music. Bridget and Craig visited the Kilmainham Gaol Museum, the former prison where many of the Irish revolutionaries and leaders of the 1916 Easter Rising were imprisoned and then executed by orders of the British Government. After the museum, Bridget and Craig probably needed a drink, so they went on a self-guided tour of the Guinness

Storehouse Brewery, and rewarded themselves with a pint of the *black stuff*. Maura later told me that her Farina Family also toured the prison museum and brewery, but at different times than Bridget and Craig. When I asked Bridget what her favorite part of Dublin was, she said that her and Craig's favorite spot in Dublin was St. Stephan's Green, which is a beautifully planted public park in Dublin's city center. The historical garden park hosts a duck pond, artificial waterfall, playground, and flower gardens, in addition to a large number of Irish sculptures, monuments, and busts of famous people such as the poet William Butler Yeats and novelist James Joyce.

My mom, Denise, Eddy, and I walked directly to Trinity College, which is widely considered the most prestigious university in Ireland, similarly revered as is Harvard University back in the States. Trinity College is surrounded by central Dublin, located on College Green, and sits opposite the Irish Houses of Parliament. We walked around the large quadrangles, and then headed toward the Trinity Library where we would wait in line to enter the Old Library to see the Book of Kells exhibition. The Book of Kells is one of the greatest treasures of medieval Europe, and is widely regarded as Ireland's finest national treasure. The Book of Kells is an illuminated manuscript, written in Latin by early Christian monks around 800 AD, containing the four gospels of the New Testament. The manuscript pages are a masterpiece of Western calligraphy, richly decorated, vibrantly colorful, and deeply enigmatic, where figures of humans, animals, mythical beasts, and Celtic knot patterns intertwine with Christian symbolism. The exhibition was extraordinary.

From there, we proceeded to the main chamber of the Old Library, called the Long Room. Over 200 feet long, it's filled with over 200,000 of the library's oldest books. On permanent display, is a rare copy of the 1916 Proclamation of the Irish Republic, and the Brian Boru harp, the national symbol of Ireland. After that, we went to the bookstore to buy Trinity t-shirts for the girls back home. Then, we headed to Grafton Street to buy more souvenirs, and ate lunch at the Merchants Arch Bar & Restaurant, next to the Ha' Penney Bridge, where we stopped to take more photos. After lunch, we all gathered back at St. Patrick's Cathedral. Bridget and Craig went back to their luxurious hotel to rest up for dinner, and Sheila, Dom, Maura, and Dommy visited them in their lobby for drinks. The rest of us continued to shop, and later met at the Molly Mallone talking statue for more pictures on our way to O'Neill's Pub for our last dinner together in Ireland. Bridget and Craig, had a very early flight home the next morning, and decided to dine alone at the restaurant in their hotel. The next morning, we departed by taxi to Dublin International Airport. As we boarded our plane, to leave the Emerald Isle, I promised myself we would return some day, not just for the spectacular scenery, gorgeous greenery, rich history, and magical castles, but because it was part of my heritage, felt like home, and love was there.

CHAPTER 24

Gratitude

*I*N the blink of an eye, it was October. My mom called me one morning to share the sad and surprising news that Father Bill Kiel was very sick and suffering with cancer. Her church friend and holy woman, Antoinette Capo, a close friend of Father Bill, had telephoned mom knowing we felt a special connection and appreciation for his intercession in the Healing Masses he celebrated. Mrs. Capo had witnessed me resting in the spirit at the St. Agnes Church Healing Mass and my subsequent and complete remission of the cancer that had spread through my body. Toni Capo, her nickname, relayed that Father Bill was not receiving any phone calls or visitors, and let it be known that he was ready to die and be with Jesus. She told my mom that there was a group of devoted parishioners who were planning to pray the Divine Mercy Chaplet for him on Monday, October 7, 2019 at 3:00 in the afternoon, so I put it on my calendar.

On the morning of October 7th, I sat down at my laptop to write him an email of appreciation for his divine intercession and my consequent healing. I figured even if he was too sick for visitors, or phone calls, maybe somebody could read him my letter of gratitude. Toni Capo had previously sent me Father Bill's email address. Here's the email that I sent Father Bill Kiel . . .

> October 7, 2019
>
> Dear Father Bill Kiel,
> This is a long overdue thank you for your divine intercession at a Healing Mass at St. Agnes Church in North Huntingdon, Pennsylvania, in March 2009.

On February 14, 2009, my husband rushed me to UPMC McKeesport Hospital, where I was soon after diagnosed with stage four non-Hodgkin's lymphoma, a blood cancer that had spread to my liver and many other places in my digestive track. My family wasn't given much hope for my survival. I was extremely sick and could barely get out of bed, but immediately started intense chemotherapy the last week in February. Shortly thereafter, I lost all my hair and so much weight that my appearance left me unrecognizable to myself when I looked in a mirror. Three weeks later, I underwent my second chemo treatment.

On March 10, 2009, my husband Eddy, took me to the Healing Mass you conducted at St. Agnes Church. When you laid your hands upon my head, I experienced the indescribable joy and ethereal love of God resting in the Spirit. Later that month, my CT scan showed no evidence of the cancer! Miraculously, this was after I'd received my second chemo treatment. My oncologist, Dr. Kevin Kane, exclaimed, "A complete remission!" and declared, "It's a miracle if I've ever seen one!" He was checking the CT scan to determine how the cancer was responding to the strong chemotherapy cocktail, and was shockingly taken by surprise when the computer screen showed no evidence of cancer. I continued to undergo four more chemotherapy treatments to kill any possible microscopic cancer cells, and to assure the doctor that I was still in complete remission. That was ten years ago, and by the grace of God, I remain cancer free.

Subsequently, I was able to attend several other Healing Masses that you conducted afterwards, another at St. Agnes in North Huntingdon, St. Edward's in Herminie, St. Robert Bellarmine in East McKeesport, and St. Jude in Wilmerding. At each of these Masses, I was blessed again with the grace-filled gift of resting in the Spirit.

Now it's my turn to pray for you as I join many of your followers who are praying the Divine Mercy Chaplet on your behalf. May God bless you with restored health for all the times you were his instrument in healing so many others. Thank you again for your healing intercession.

With love and prayers,
Susie Guarascio

Shortly thereafter, I sent the letter to the email address for Father Bill Kiel. Minutes later, the email was returned to me. Thinking the email address was case sensitive, or that it was misspelled, I sent it again. Again, it was returned to me. Then, I telephoned my mom to confirm that we had the correct email address, and we did. My mom called Toni Capo to recheck the email address. The next day, Tuesday, October 8th, Toni called my mom to tell her that beloved Father Bill Kiel had passed away two days earlier, on Sunday, October 6, 2019. This was shocking and difficult news to digest, especially since Father Bill spent the latter part of his life helping to heal others, but unfortunately couldn't help heal himself. It reminded me of when Jesus was being crucified, and wouldn't save himself from death on a cross, even though he performed many miracles in the four gospels to cure people who were crippled, blind, possessed, or had leprosy, and even raised Lazarus from the dead.

A week later, Toni Capo saw my mother at Mass, and asked mom if she could get a copy of my email letter as evidence of a *miracle* due to Father Bill Kiel's divine intercession. So I gave my mom a couple hard copies of my thank you letter, and she forwarded them to Toni Capo. As a result of the many miraculous healings attributed to Father Bill Kiel's intercession, many of his faithful followers believe that he should be a candidate for canonization. The act of canonization is reserved to the Pope at the conclusion of a long process requiring evidence that the candidate lived and died in an exemplary and holy way, so that they are worthy to be declared a saint. The Church's official recognition of sainthood implies that the person is now in heaven with God, and may be publicly honored and venerated. To be recognized as a saint, typically two miracles must have been performed through the intercession of the Blessed Person *after* their death. The dictionary defines a miracle as an extraordinary and welcome event that is not explicable by natural or scientific laws, and is therefore attributed to a divine intervention. That sounded indicative of how I'd been cured of stage four non-Hodgkin's lymphoma after only two chemotherapy treatments. However, the two miracles must occur *after* the candidate's death, not before it.

I think it's important to note that it's not the saints who work miracles, but only the grace of God that flows through them. When we pray to the Blessed Mother or our favorite saints, we are praying for their intercession in asking God to help us, since it is assumed they are closer to him in heaven. Miracles are done by God acting through a holy person on Earth or a saint in heaven.

Time will tell if additional miracles occur after Father Bill Kiel's passing. I have a strong feeling he will be declared a saint someday in the future. When I think back to those Healing Masses, Father Bill Kiel had a very holy aura around him as he stood on the altar, always wearing white, which matched his snow white hair. He had a glorious glow surrounding him. Walking up to the altar in each Healing Mass to receive his special blessing in the laying of the hands, I felt the spiritual holiness emanating from his body, as if I was in the presence of a saint. Somehow, I believe Father Bill Kiel knows how grateful I am for my healing, even though he never read my letter. More importantly, God knows, as I've thanked him for his mercy and healing every day since Doctor Kane announced my complete remission from cancer.

CHAPTER 25

Grace and True Grit

On November 11, 2019, my mother turned 84 years old. For the first time, it really hit me, my mother is old. I try not to think about her mortality. She is such a blessing, and I'm grateful to God that she is still with us. She's always been the rock of our family. It had been four years since her diagnosis with breast cancer, and thank God she is cancer free. She endured and recuperated from two lumpectomies and the trauma that breast cancer operations entail, but it has taken a toll on her. Maybe it's the anti-cancer pill, Arimidex, she takes daily, which still keeps her awake all night. Fortunately, she only has to take it one more year, which will conclude the five year doctor recommendation. She seems fragile, still strong, but she's more anxious now than she's ever been. She was always a worrier, but more so now.

Mummy had another health scare that spring when an undiagnosed UTI (urinary tract infection) had her hospitalized with sepsis where the bacterial infection entered her bloodstream. I've never seen my mother that sick where she was shaking with fever, hours before her organs started shutting down. Luckily, as soon as the doctor started her on an IV antibiotic, she rallied, but it took her longer. Then, fear reared its nasty little head making her worry that it might happen again. Even little things upset her now that never used to bother her. Maybe she's feeling the lack of control more than ever in her life. Cancer does that to people, and so does the aging process.

Mummy's most recent health scare occurred in the autumn of 2020. Since she wasn't feeling well, and was wondering if she had a sinus infection, I suggested she go to our local Med Express to get a rapid COVID test to at least rule that out. So Mom went to Med Express. After the nurse took her blood pressure and pulse rate, and then the doctor listened to her heart with his stethoscope, he informed her that she was currently in atrial fibrillation (AFib). She did not have COVID. Mom's blood pressure was high, her pulse was faster than normal, and her heart was racing again with an irregular heartbeat. One of the biggest concerns of AFib is the risk of having a stroke, so the doctor advised her to go to the nearest emergency room as soon as possible. Mom called me, and I immediately drove her to UPMC McKeesport emergency room. There the doctors took a chest x-ray, bloodwork, and did an electrocardiogram (EKG) to confirm that she was in AFib. She was given a prescription for Eliquis, and was told to make a follow up appointment with her Primary Care Physician (PCP) and/or a cardiologist. So I took her to her PCP, and he confirmed Mom was still in AFib, gave her an additional prescription, and told her to buy a home blood pressure monitor to check and record her blood pressure twice a day. The next step was to find a good cardiologist, (Dear Dr. Awan had retired.), so mom would get specialized heart care. Sheila was able to get mom an appointment with a cardiologist in Pittsburgh, and then found a woman cardiologist who works out of UPMC East which is closer to home. While Mummy continues to see her doctors, she takes her Eliquis and monitors her blood pressure daily.

When I look around at the women of her generation in their eighties, (Mom, Aunt Jeanne, Aunt Sheila, Cousin Anna Marie, my mother-in-law Beverly, and Sheila's mother-in-law Molly), in the twilight years of their life, my heart is filled with admiration and compassion. These fellow octogenarians, once strong-willed, vital, and my young role models, are still teaching me how to grow old gracefully while being at the mercy of the ruthlessness of old age and the multitude of health issues that accompany it. In addition, they deal with the emotional loneliness of being a widow, and living alone independently. In spite of all their afflictions, diseases, and disabilities, they persevere with dignity, joy, gratitude, and grace.

Despite her health issues, my mother's mind is still highly intelligent and sharp as a tack. She's an avid reader, watches her political news shows, reads her daily newspaper, and still serves on the board of UPMC McKeesport and UPMC East Hospitals. Up until March 2020, Mom and her first cousin, Anna Marie, went to Silver Sneakers exercise class twice a week, played 500 bid card games, belonged to a bowling team, and walked around the Fairhaven Heights street circles when the weather permitted.

Anna Marie had a bad fall in autumn 2019, and broke her pelvis. She was hospitalized for a week and then sent to Woodhaven Rehabilitation Center to recuperate. My mom took Anna Marie's fall pretty bad emotionally. Mom was so worried that Anna Marie wouldn't walk again, and might lose her independence. I'm happy to report that Anna Marie has healed, but her recovery was long and grueling. Her resilience amazed me. It is such a comfort to my sisters and cousins that our widowed mothers are still next door neighbors, meet for morning coffee on occasion, and enjoy each other's company for almost sixty years!

My mother's two sisters are also now elderly. Aunt Jeanne, who's a few years younger than my mom, is also a widow, and lives independently in her home in Buffalo, New York. My cousins Cathy and Christopher worry about their mother because she is painfully thin and barely has an appetite. Even though her body looks frail, her mind is sharp, as she is fun, has a great sense of humor, an avid reader, and highly intelligent. Aunt Jeanne manages to come home to Pittsburgh once a year for Timmy's annual St. Patrick's Day party where she entertains us with her gift for storytelling and in-depth knowledge about historical and current events.

Fortunately, Uncle Bob is still healthy, so my Aunt Sheila doesn't have to deal with the loneliness of being a widow. It is such solace for our family that they have each other. Unfortunately, my sweet Aunt Sheila was diagnosed with Parkinson's disease in 2016, and has to endure the debilitating symptoms and dementia that accompany it. Witnessing her physical decline evident during each of our face-time phone calls is heartbreaking. March 2020 was the first year Aunt Sheila and Uncle Bob missed coming home for Uncle Tim's St. Paddy's Day party, and they were terribly missed. A family celebration just isn't the same or as fun without them. On August 29, 2020 Aunt Sheila turned 80, and many of us were hoping to fly to Atlanta to celebrate her beautiful life. Unfortunately, we were discouraged from making the trip due to her failing health and fear of COVID. We all sent gifts and cards, and were able to facetime her on our telephones. Her daughter Diane made a memory book for her, and asked all of us in our extended family to send our special memories of her along with a few favorite photographs to include in the book. Diane was able to show us the finished book during our facetime conversation on Aunt Sheila's birthday. The memory book is a lovely keepsake. Diane did a wonderful job putting it all together. It was a gift for all of us to honor her beautiful life.

Since she turned 80, Aunt Sheila's health has declined rapidly. On Thanksgiving Eve at home, Aunt Sheila fell and broke her hip. Diane took her to the hospital where she works as a registered nurse, and Aunt Sheila was admitted there. Thankfully, Diane was able to be with her mother during her recovery from hip surgery as Aunt Sheila was disoriented due to the drugs, side effects of Parkinson's, and unfamiliar hospital surroundings. Uncle Bob and Mariane weren't even allowed to visit because of COVID. After a few days, Aunt Sheila was sent to a nursing and rehab center to get physical therapy and speech therapy, since her Parkinson's disease has affected her ability to speak clearly, swallow, and walk. On December 11, 2020, Aunt Sheila was discharged from the nursing and rehab center, and is currently back home with Uncle Bob. Aunt Sheila has been in and out of the hospital and nursing home several times since then as her physical and mental health continues to decline. Uncle Bob keeps bringing her home to lovingly take care of her. He cooks and feeds her three meals a day along with meeting many of her other nursing needs. Their love and devotion to each other has always been a testimony to a beautiful marriage, but it's even more so now. Diane and Mariane have stepped up helping with her care, and now a home health care nurse visits a few times a week to help with her continued rehabilitation. I've been praying a novena to St. Jude and the Chaplet of Divine Mercy for a miracle and/or mercy for my sweet Aunt Sheila, Uncle Bob, and my dear cousins. Aside from sending flowers and food, prayer is all I can do to help them until the pandemic is over.

My mother-in-law, Beverly, is a year older than my mother. She's had more than her share of suffering in this life. After losing her 17 year old first born son tragically in a car accident, you may think that might have exempted her from future suffering, but life doesn't work out that way. In her fifties, Beverly was diagnosed with type-II diabetes, and a few years later she became a widow. I remember her telling me that as bad as it was to lose Rick, and it was awful, it was even worse pain and heartache for her to lose Bruce. Bruce's death was a tragedy by which she measured everything, marked time, and defined her life. In 2019, Beverly told Eddy she's been ready to die for 46 years.

Beverly has had a few health scares with pneumonia, and congestive heart failure for the past several years. The residual effects of her survival have left her with breathing difficulties and needing a portable oxygen tank. Julie has been her primary care giver most of the time, and has taken her mother to live at her home in Naples, Florida, from January through spring the past few winters. Beverly enjoys her Snow Bird Visits to Julie's tropical home as she is the hit of her gated community entertaining her new friends with her jokes and storytelling skills. Julie also comes home to Pittsburgh a lot in the summer and helps Beverly at home as well. Typically, Beverly lives independently in her apartment in White Oak, Pennsylvania, June through December, while Eddy and Danny help doing her grocery shopping and driving her to weekend Mass, doctor appointments, and the hair salon. Often, Beverly will visit Terri and Tom in State College and stay at their place for a few weeks, schedules permitting, usually in autumn. Other times, Terri and Tom will stay at Beverly's place during the weekend and help out there.

In January 2020, Beverly had no sooner arrived in Naples, where she became very sick with pneumonia and was hospitalized for several days again in congestive heart failure. After a few days in the hospital, Beverly was sent home to recuperate even though she was still feeling very sick. Julie, who is a National Account Manager for Vistar a PFG Company, had to travel in February to Las Vegas for the annual National Candy Show, and then onto other cities. Consequently, Kaitlin, Cynthia Mansfield Stinger (Bruce's high school girlfriend), Eddy and I, and Danny and his dear eldest son, Michael, all made plans to travel to Naples, each of us visiting for a week, to help Beverly, so Julie could fly to Vegas and other cities for her job the month of February. Kaitlin went the first week in February, followed by Cynthia the second week, while Eddy and I arrived the third week. By the time Eddy and I arrived at Julie's, Beverly was feeling remarkably better, and that was great news!

Before leaving for Naples, I prayed to the Holy Spirit to bless our visit with Beverly, so that we would bring her loving help, kindness, and compassion. God must have heard and answered my prayers, because we had a wonderful week with Beverly. It felt like the good old days. We went out for breakfast at her favorite morning restaurant called Skillets, one day, went to a delicious fancy brunch another day, and ate dinner at a wonderful Italian restaurant with Julie when she returned Wednesday evening. The rest of the time we made and ate our meals in Julie's beautiful carriage home. I was able to make Beverly my famous chili and corn casserole, (they're Beverly's favorite foods I make), our second night there. You would have thought I gave her a million bucks, because she was so appreciative. I was happy to help cook for her.

Julie wanted to have a soiree Thursday evening, so we could meet some of her close friends and neighbors living in her neighborhood.

Dear cousins Joe and Josephine Sdao, from New York, along with their son, daughter-in-law, and grandsons, were also able to join us. Joe and Josephine have a vacation home in the same gated community as Julie. It was a lovely dinner party, and we met some very nice and interesting people. Beverly was once again the life of the party telling jokes like a seasoned comedienne, while everyone cracked up at her punchlines. One thing everyone at the party had in common was that we all loved Julie. Julie and I had prepared tasty tapas, and the soiree was declared a success as we were all eating, laughing, and sharing stories until late that night. The next morning, Julie drove us to the airport to catch our flight back to Pittsburgh. She was planning on bringing Beverly back home to Pittsburgh for Easter the second week in April, but that didn't happen, because the world was on the precipice of a change that none of us saw coming.

In the meantime, my sister Sheila's mother-in-law, Molly Farina, was scheduled to have open heart surgery on February 27th, my beloved dad's birthday. Molly turned 90 years old May 16, 2020. Molly was known for having more energy than most young adults until the past few years, when she started having heart problems on top of Type II diabetes. Molly had a stent put in her artery in mid-February, and then was scheduled for an aortic valve replacement. She's lived independently for years in apartments in White Oak, a nice residential area outside of McKeesport. She'd also held a job working for the Westmoreland County Water Authority until she was 82 years old, telling people she just wasn't ready to retire until then! She's been another amazing woman of her generation. Molly is famous for cooking delicious Italian dinners every Sunday for her four married adult children and her eight adult grandchildren. Her February surgery was postponed until March, and then postponed again due to the Coronavirus pandemic that struck the entire world hitting the United States in mid-March. Her doctor rescheduled her aortic valve replacement surgery for a third time, this time for July 2020, hoping that the COVID-19 virus might be subsiding, but it wasn't. Molly's doctor ended up cancelling her July operation, because the stent had successfully increased her heart function from 45 percent to 60 percent, and she didn't want to risk becoming more susceptible to COVID, or possibly chance unsuccessful surgery which might result in a stroke or the need for a pacemaker. After Molly's symptoms began worsening, she and her doctor agreed to reschedule her surgery. Molly finally underwent her noninvasive aortic valve replacement surgery on September 28, 2020, and it was a success. Thank God! We were all praying so hard for her and her doctor. Molly remains in my prayers for her heart to function properly, and for her smooth recovery. The future is becoming impossible to predict, because the global pandemic has turned our world upside down, changed, complicated, and cancelled almost everything.

CHAPTER 26

COVID

*T*HE coronavirus global pandemic changed the whole world as we knew it. All elective surgeries were cancelled beginning February 2020, and soon after so were doctors' appointments, schools, colleges, people's weddings, graduations, funerals, masses, sports, and cultural events. Society was shutting down, businesses were closing, and people were told to quarantine in their homes. The last time the world had experienced anything like it was during the deadly Spanish flu pandemic in 1918. Scientists, doctors, and researchers would look back to learn what that pandemic could teach us about this deadly new global virus.

It is believed the coronavirus started in a seafood and poultry market in Wuhan, China in December 2019, however the Chinese government cover-up and the delay to contain it lasted several weeks. It was during this crucial time that the virus started spreading around the world, including Europe, and then the United States. On December 31, 2019, China told the World Health Organization's (WHO) China office about cases of an unknown illness, and by January 21, 2020, the U.S. Centers for Disease Control and Prevention confirmed the first coronavirus case in the United States. Community transmission of COVID-19 was first detected in the United States in February 2020. On February 14th, France announced the first coronavirus death in Europe, which was the first coronavirus death outside Asia. Italy had a major surge in cases the end of February as infections spiked in Europe. On February 29th, the United States announced our first coronavirus death after a patient near Seattle died. As the number of global cases rose to nearly 87,000, the Trump administration issued the first *do not travel* warning, and blocked most travelers from Europe. On March 11th, the WHO declared the coronavirus a pandemic, and by mid-March, all 50 states had reported cases of COVID-19.

The last time I felt some type of normalcy was when our extended family gathered together at Uncle Tim's annual St. Patrick's Day party which was held on Friday, March 13, 2020, the same day President Trump declared a national emergency. Two days later, the CDC recommended no gatherings of 50 or more people in the U.S. Then, beginning on Monday, March 16, our Pennsylvania Governor Tom Wolf shut down all public schools K-12 along with colleges and universities in our state. New York City, Philadelphia, and Boston were worst hit with the virus, and labeled hotspots. I worried about my daughter Kaitlin in Boston with her lowered immunity system, but was comforted by how serious my son-in-law Jason took to protecting her by being militant in the extent of their quarantine. People were dying daily by the hundreds. Schools and churches shut down across our country. Businesses closed, people lost their jobs, and the stock market crashed.

By the end of March 2020, the United States led the world in confirmed cases of the coronavirus with more than 81,000 confirmed infections, and more than 1,000 deaths, more than anywhere else on earth at that time. By the beginning of April, the pandemic had put nearly 10 million Americans out of work, including more than six million people who applied for unemployment benefits the last week of March. As of April 30, 2020 most airlines required passengers to wear face masks or face coverings to prevent the spread of the virus. By the end of April, more than 97 percent of the US population was under a stay-at-home or shelter-in-place order as the coronavirus continued to terrorize our country.

As of May 11, 2020 the U.S. coronavirus death toll surpassed 80,000 according to data from Johns Hopkins University. New York was considered the epicenter of the U.S. coronavirus outbreak with more than 26,000 deaths. I prayed daily for our friends and family in New York, and for protection from the virus for my niece, Maura, her boyfriend Antionne, and my nephew, Dominic who all live in Jersey City, across the Hudson River from New York City. Watching the daily news programs for signs of hope that the upward Coronavirus curve was flattening, became our new national pastime, since baseball and all professional sports had been cancelled.

As the infection rates and hospitalization rates declined, state governors began a phased reopening of their states. President Trump indicated many states could reopen their economies by May 1st, but many of the nation's governors, who held the power to enforce closures, disagreed. Governor Andrew Cuomo stated the reopening of New York would be done intelligently following the CDC's guidelines. Southern states such as South Carolina, Georgia, Florida, and Texas had already begun relaxing restrictions. Bridget and Craig, living in Houston, Texas were able to go out to dinner at their Houstonian Country Club to celebrate their wedding anniversary on May 6th while maintaining social distancing. Julie and Beverly had already been swimming in their community pool in Naples, Florida. However, shortly after reopening their beaches, Florida's governor had to re-shut their beaches due to overcrowding concerns. Boston, Massachusetts, where Kaitlin and Jason lived, had a phase 1 target reopening date planned for May 18th, if data in their state continued on a downward trend.

According to a Pew Research Poll, nearly two-thirds of Americans said they were concerned about their state reopening too early. In contrast, thousands of unmasked people had protested for their right to return to work and restart their economies. States would need to do testing, contact tracing, and have isolation and quarantine procedures in place before they reopened. Experts were worried that we would begin seeing increased infections in two to three weeks after states reopen. Unfortunately, there was a huge surge in COVID-19 cases in some Southern states that didn't reinforce mask wearing and social distancing. In the meantime, I followed my state guidelines for social distancing, wore a face mask in public, continued to wash my hands, and persevered in prayer.

Particularly, I prayed daily for: protection and stamina for the first responders and the selfless healthcare professionals serving on the front lines fighting the coronavirus, for the suffering patients and their families affected by the coronavirus, for the scientists and researchers working to develop a vaccine or find a cure for COVID-19, for the safety of society's essential critical infrastructure workers who had to maintain their normal work schedule, leaving them vulnerable and more exposed to the virus, for good health and protection from the virus for my family and friends, that the Holy Spirit will inspire our government officials to make educated decisions regarding directives and procedures necessary to lessen the transmission and combat the coronavirus, and finally to beg

God to bestow a miracle upon us to aid us in putting an end to the global pandemic ravaging our entire planet.

Every day I would turn on the television to watch Dr. Anthony Fauci, director of the National Institute of Allergy and Infectious Diseases at the National Institutes of Health, and a member of the White House Coronavirus Task Force, (WHCTF), along with Dr. Deborah Birx, the Coronavirus Response Coordinator, speak to the press about the ongoing national response to the coronavirus pandemic. Their daily media briefings included scientific medical facts based on state and metro area metrics used to monitor, contain, and mitigate the spread of the virus. Flattening the curve of confirmed cases and deaths was the primary goal of the WHCTF. Following the news briefs, reporters could ask the members of the WHCTF questions. I appreciated the doctors' answers, and hung onto their every word, even when the news wasn't pleasant, because their responses were based upon scientific facts and were apolitical.

We received encouraging news the end of May when Moderna, a biotech company headquartered in Cambridge, Massachusetts, announced promising early results for its coronavirus vaccine. The biotech company's vaccine produces neutralizing antibodies that bind to the virus and disable it from attacking human cells. In its clinical trial, Moderna vaccinated dozens of participants and measured antibodies in eight of them. All eight individuals developed neutralizing antibodies to the virus at levels reaching or exceeding levels seen in people who had naturally recovered from COVID-19. When Dr. Fauci praised these findings as promising, I felt optimistically hopeful. Moderna said that if future studies go well, its vaccine could be available to the public as early as January 2021. That would be an answer to many prayers.

In addition to watching the daily pandemic updates from the White House Coronavirus Task Force, I tuned into our state of Pennsylvania daily news conferences regarding COVID-19, featuring Health Department Secretary Dr. Rachel Levine, and Governor Tom Wolf. Dr. Levine delivered daily pandemic updates calmly and professionally while encouraging us to use best practices of hand-washing, social distancing, and masking to mitigate the spread of the virus. She would end every update reminding us to "stay calm, stay home, and stay safe." That soon became our mantra, because that's what we were all trying to do.

Governor Wolf instituted the following three phase color-coded (red, yellow, green) economic reopening plan for Pennsylvania. Initially, the entire state started in the red phase.

Red phase restrictions included: closing all non-life sustaining businesses, all schools remained closed through the end of the academic year, most child care facilities remained closed, large gatherings were prohibited, restaurants and bars were limited to take-out and delivery only, and stay-at-home orders remained in place, with travel limited to life-sustaining purposes. In order to progress into the yellow phase, a region or county would have a coronavirus positive-test case rate of 50 per 100,000 residents or fewer over a two week stretch. The purpose of the yellow phase was to begin reopening the economy while containing the disease as much as possible. Yellow phase restrictions included: businesses with in-person operations must follow safety orders, CDC and Department of Health guidelines for social distancing and cleaning, working remotely where feasible, child care facilities could open but must follow safety orders, CDC and Department of Health guidelines for social distancing and cleaning, large gatherings of more than 25 people were prohibited, restaurants and bars remained limited to takeout and delivery only, indoor recreation, gyms, spas, and entertainment facilities, including casinos and theaters, remained closed, in-person retail was allowed, but curbside and delivery service was preferred, and stay-at-home orders were lifted. In the final phase of reopening, most mitigation efforts were lifted, but some basic restrictions remained in place. Green phase restrictions included: all businesses operating in the yellow phase at 50 percent increased to 75 percent occupancy, restaurants and bars opened for dine-in service at 50 percent occupancy, personal care services, such as hair salons and barbershops, opened at 50 percent occupancy and by appointment only, indoor recreation, including gyms, spas, and health and wellness facilities, opened at 50 percent occupancy with appointments strongly encouraged, all entertainment, including casinos, theaters, and shopping malls, opened at 50 percent occupancy, construction activity returned to full capacity, congregate care restrictions remained in place, and prison and hospital restrictions were determined by individual facilities.

It felt like forever until Pittsburgh's Allegheny County and my suburban Westmoreland County were declared by Governor Wolf to be in the Green Phase of Pennsylvania's state reopening plan. Finally on Friday, June 5, 2020, our Southwestern Pennsylvania counties entered into the Green Phase. The first thing on my agenda was a visit to the hair salon to get my hair cut and colored after a three month wait. That seemed like such a trivial first order of business amid the changes, dire circumstances, death, and devastation brought by the coronavirus pandemic.

As of May 27, 2020, more than 100,000 people in the United States had died of COVID-19, since the coronavirus hit our country, and the count steadily grew. According to data reported in the Los Angeles Times on May 27, 2020, the COVID-19 death toll surpasses the number of Americans killed in the Korean War with 36,600 deaths, and Vietnam War with 58,200 deaths combined.

As I looked back over those first three months since COVID-19 impacted the United States, I tried to focus on how fortunate my family and friends had been relatively speaking compared to the awful images shown on the news every day. Eddy was still working remotely for Bayer Corporation from home and would attend virtual zoom meetings with employees and customers around the world. I was newly retired from teaching, feeling healthy, and grateful for the comforts of our home. While Eddy was working on his computer, I was in the kitchen on my laptop writing this book. Being in quarantine also gifted me with the time to clean out our closets, organize our drawers, and donate unused clothing to the St. Vincent de Paul bin in the parking lot of our church. I also was able to weed and garden when the warm weather arrived. Eddy designated himself the grocery shopper for my mother, Tierney, and us. He would wear his personal protective mask and buy all of us food and deliver it to my mom's front porch, Tierney's townhouse driveway, and our kitchen. He made sure we all had plenty to eat along with a stash of toilet paper, medical prescriptions, and personal toiletries. I checked in with Tierney and my mother daily to make sure they were doing well and had everything they needed. I worried about them living alone during the pandemic, especially since my mom is a senior citizen, and Tierney continued to work out in the field visiting hospice and senior care facilities, which were the hardest hit targets of the coronavirus in our state.

Eddy is also a great chef, and did most of our cooking while we were quarantined. After being the primary cook for our family for 40 years, I loved every meal he made. Whenever we made something particularly tasty, we would deliver dinners to Tierney and my mom. When we advanced to the yellow phase, we did take-out dinners a couple times a week. We also exercised and enjoyed walking laps around our local Indian Lake when the weather warmed up. We also met Tierney and her future priest dear friend, David Slusarick, to power walk for exercise at Twin Lakes in Greensburg, Mammoth Park in Mount Pleasant, and along Bushy Run Battle Field trails in Penn Township, Pennsylvania. I was happy to hear when my mother and Anna Marie would walk around the blocks in Fairhaven to get their exercise when the weather permitted. They both missed their twice a week Silver Sneakers exercise classes that were cancelled in March. The summer of 2020 was beautifully sunny and warm. Eddy and I spent most days outside in our backyard or in our pool. When autumn arrived, we'd go for long drives to Ligonier and Ohio Pyle to bike ride on the trails, view the colorful fall foliage, and stop to dine at outdoor restaurants. The warm weather was perfect for me to resume my golf game and get out on the links. My sister Denise, Maggie, or Karen and I would get together to golf once a week from July through October, usually at Manor Valley Golf Course in Export, Pennsylvania, or at one of the other local public golf courses in Murrysville or Delmont. Now I finally understand why my dad loved golf, and marvel at what a good golfer he was!

While we couldn't visit people we loved, we would face time and/or zoom our daughters, extended family members, and friends just to see them, chat, and remind them that they were loved. My teacher friends were teaching on google classroom remotely since the middle of March to the end of the academic school year. That proved to be a real challenge for parents, students, and teachers as they struggled to adapt to new ways of virtually teaching and learning the curriculum. Parents seemed to gain a new appreciation and respect for the difficult task of teaching as they tried to help their children navigate the lessons and assignments. Teachers were also holding car parades through school districts' neighborhoods to remind the children they were still important and cared for. We even placed toy teddy bears in our windows for the kiddos to see as they walked outside to play around their homes just to give them a sense of comfort. Most high school graduations were cancelled, but I saw that Gateway School District, got creative and held their graduation ceremony in the Monroeville Mall parking lot as families drove up in their cars and students were socially distanced as they walked up onto a platform to receive their diplomas. People also got creative making crafts and entertained themselves old fashioned ways like doing jigsaw puzzles and playing board games to help adjust to the time quarantined at home. After binge watching a few television shows on Netflix and Hulu, I turned to Word with Friends games on my cell phone, along with checking in on Facebook friends, and looking at Instagram posts for entertainment. My favorite binge show had to be *Schitt's Creek*, because it was laugh out loud hilarious, and had unconditional love and acceptance as its theme.

My favorite Facebook source of entertainment presented itself in a newly formed group entitled *Fairhaven Heights Growing Up*. We had about 314 members by the end of spring 2020, and I can't tell you how wonderful it was to reconnect with the kids from our neighborhood who grew up together in the 1960s and 1970s. It was like taking a trip down memory lane! We reminisced, rekindled friendships, and shared funny stories, along with mostly happy memories of our childhood. We were all interconnected in many ways, and our families had so much in common. It was amazing to remember so clearly how simple and carefree our childhood was back then. It was the best of times! Fairhaven Heights was a special place to grow up, and we all knew it, because love was there. The common themes of growing up in Fairhaven were fun, friendship, and family. We didn't have much in terms of material possessions, but we didn't care, because we had each other, and that was enough. We were free range kids, who loved the independence our parents allowed us to have. We learned great socialization skills playing our outdoor games from morning until night without parental interference. We Fairhaven kids have such a beautiful bond, because we all realize it was such a blessing growing up there. The most amazing effect of our *Fairhaven Heights Growing Up* group chats was the feeling that I was experiencing my life come full circle! Looking forward to reminiscing with old friends was one of the few perks of the pandemic. The lyrics to the *Cheers* 1980s television sitcom theme song resonates how it felt reconnecting with my childhood friends and growing up in Fairhaven "where everyone knows your name."

By the time the first week in June 2020 came along, I was starting to feel like we were going to get out of this pandemic relatively unscathed. But that wouldn't be the case. Shortly after Governor Wolf proclaimed southwestern Pennsylvania to be in the green phase, my family and friends started venturing out of our homes and back into society. Eddy and I took my mother on a drive-thru Zoofari at the Pittsburgh Zoo, and we even ate outside at a restaurant in Point Breeze called Pino's for the first time in several months. My teacher friends came over to my backyard for a day of swimming and picnicking as we began to celebrate our new emergence from our COVID cocoons. And just when it was starting to feel somewhat normal again, the other shoe dropped. On Saturday morning, June 13th, Tierney called us about 9:00 a.m. to tell us she had just received a telephone call from the Department of Health that she tested positive for COVID!

Tierney had gone into her Monroeville office on Monday, June 8th, feeling fine. On Tuesday, June 9th, she called me to tell me she was feeling sicker by the minute, so I advised her to go home the remainder of the day. The next morning, I called to check on her, and she told me she was too sick to go into work, and felt like a Mac truck had run over her. After telling me her symptoms, I suggested she go to the local Med Express on Route 30 in Jeannette, which is a designated testing site, to see a doctor and get tested on the coronavirus. She was tested for the virus on Wednesday, June 10th, and got the call Saturday, June 13th, that she had COVID-19. Then the Department of Health (DoH) sent an email letter to the person who tests positive for a Confirmed Coronavirus Disease 2019 (COVID-19). In the letter, Tierney was advised to remain in her home for a minimum of 10 days, until she was fever free with the use of fever reducing meds for 72 hours, with improving respiratory systems.

In addition, Tierney was issued eight directives from the DoH while in isolation. After two weeks of isolation and following the DoH directives, Tierney started to feel better. Eddy and I, along with Bridget, Kaitlin, Sheila, Denise, and Julie all sent dinners delivered to Tierney during her isolation. A few of Tierney's friends also sent her dinners. It was sad and difficult not being able to take care of her in person while she spent all those days alone in her townhouse, but Eddy and I were both in quarantine for 14 days since we had direct contact with her two days before she felt her first symptoms. Tierney was so tenacious and brave to endure the symptoms of the coronavirus by herself. I prayed a novena to our Lady of Knock daily asking our Blessed Mother to intercede for Tierney's recovery. Eventually, all three of us got tested again and our results were all negative. Tierney had a few residual symptoms, but that is common for a while for COVID patients. Tierney's negative test results came in on June 23th. The next thing on her agenda was to talk with her new Human Resources person to determine when she could return to work, and under what capacity. Tierney was able to return to work the last week in June, and has since been working both remotely and out in the field.

Unfortunately, Tierney wasn't the only person in our extended family to contract COVID. Both of my nieces, Meghan, who works as a counselor in a rehab center, and Rachel, who attends the University of Pittsburgh School of Pharmacy, came down with the coronavirus in autumn 2020. Fortunately, they have fully recovered as well. My family and I are extremely grateful to God that Tierney, Meghan, and Rachel have recovered from the deadly coronavirus that has killed over 300,000 people in the United States as of December 2020.

As the pandemic raged killing thousands of Americans a week, two companies moved at record speed to develop highly effective COVID vaccines. After much research and results from late stage clinical trials, on November 9th, the giant pharmaceutical Pfizer and its German partner, BioNTech, announced they developed a COVID vaccine that was more than 90 percent effective in preventing the virus. Then on November 16, 2020, the biotechnology firm, Moderna, announced they developed a vaccine that was 95 percent effective. After each company sought emergency authorization to provide the vaccines to the American public, the FDA reviewed the effectiveness, safety, and manufacturing of each vaccine.

On December 11, 2020, the Pfizer and BioNTech companies were given emergency use authorization by the FDA to be America's first coronavirus vaccine. On December 14, 2020, the first COVID-19 vaccine was administered to an ICU nurse in Long Island. While locally, the UPMC Children's Hospital in Pittsburgh was the first hospital to administer the vaccine in Pennsylvania. Early CDC recommendations advised that healthcare workers and first responders should receive first vaccine priority, followed by residents and staff of long term care facilities, then workers in essential and critical industries. The next group was people at high risk because of underlying medical conditions or age. Finally, the last group to get vaccinated was the general public, by the spring of 2021. Consequently, we followed the procedures of getting COVID vaccines and booster shots when they became available in our area. In the meantime, I continued to pray daily for an end to this global pandemic, for our medical professionals, first responders, and essential workers fighting the coronavirus, and for the patients and their families suffering from COVID-19. May God protect us from the pandemic, help us find an end to the coronavirus, and have mercy on us all.

CHAPTER 27

Perseverance

THERE is so much suffering in this world, but we can all do our part to soften the blows, to help others, to make a difference, to persevere, and to model love. We can follow the Golden Rule, and treat others the way we want to be treated. We can be a light in the darkness. We can look for the good. We can look for the love in the midst of suffering, because it's always there. We can "look for the helpers" as Mr. Rogers used to tell his young audience. We can be the helpers! At the height of the coronavirus pandemic in the midst of the ICU units, love was there in the sleep-deprived compassionate eyes and healing hands of the masked doctors and nurses working 12 hour shifts attending to their dying patients. Love was in the self-sacrifice of the first responders and essential workers who put their lives on the line to help people live theirs. Love was shown in the small acts of kindness when neighbors and family members set food and toilet paper on quarantined people's porches. Love was in the cars of the teachers as they paraded through their school district neighborhoods holding signs to reassure their students that they were still important. Love was in the classrooms when teachers went back to school in September teaching both *in person* and *virtually* trying to meet the needs of their students as the coronavirus raged. Love was in homes where parents were patiently helping their children navigate a new way of learning lessons virtually on their iPads.

Love was in the UPMC Cancer Center while I was getting chemotherapy, and Eddy never left my side. Love was in our home when Eddy brought in my medicine and groceries and lovingly cooked breakfast and dinner for me when I was suffering with cancer, and never complained.

Love was in the compassionate care my mother gave my father during his three and a half year battle with terminal lung cancer. Love was in the South Side soup kitchens when Bridget volunteered Saturday mornings to help feed the hungry, or when she did pro bono work for families who couldn't afford her legal services. Love was in the Dirksen Senate Office Building while Kaitlin worked on the Affordable Care Act to help make healthcare affordable and accessible for all Americans regardless of their socioeconomic status and/or their pre-existing conditions. Love was in the rooms of the Senior Care facilities and Nursing Homes where Tierney held the hands of her lonely hospice patients, and softly sang their favorite songs as they breathed their last breaths. Love is in hearts and hands of all the caregivers who take care of their loved ones with terminal and chronic illnesses. Love is present in the patience and perseverance of parents raising and caring for their autistic or disabled children in the midst of many daily challenges. Love is always there in the midst of human suffering if you look for it.

So in closing, I will continue to persevere in prayer. I will pray giving praise to God in gratitude for all of my blessings, especially for my miracle when he cured me of cancer. I will pray for a cure and a successful vaccine for the coronavirus pandemic. I will pray for a cure for all types of Cancers, Crohn's Disease, Ulcerative Colitis, Lyme Disease, Diabetes, Parkinson's Disease, Alzheimer's Disease, and Heart Disease. I will pray for social justice and equality for all humankind. I will pray for people who suffer, and for the people taking care of those who are suffering. I will pray for all people to respect each other and to respect our planet. I will pray that all human beings learn to love unconditionally and without reservation. I will pray for all of my private intentions and trust that God in his infinite wisdom will answer my prayers in the best way he sees fit in his own perfect timing. So, I will face the future with faith, not fear. I don't know how my journey of faith will end, but I can only hope it ends with God in heaven, because love is there.

Epilogue

AFTER finishing writing this book, I felt compelled to go back and fact-check again and again. Fast forward to June 3, 2021, when I went for my yearly appointment with my oncologist, Dr. Kevin Kane. While I was waiting for my bloodwork results, I asked him again to check my medical records to make sure I remembered correctly that my CT scan showed no evidence of cancer after only my second chemotherapy treatment. He said, "Yes, that's correct, but it wasn't the chemotherapy that cured you!" We both knew that I had been the recipient of God's grace and mercy, and that I was truly a miracle!

"Perhaps you were born for such a time as this." (Esth 4:14) Maybe writing this book was the reason I was born. I was blessed with the task of giving testimony. This wasn't really my idea. I truly believe it was the Holy Spirit. He wants me to share the good news about his love for us. He wants us to know that in the midst of all our heartache, pain, and suffering, his love is always there. Maybe God cured me of cancer, so I could share my story with you, and give witness to his love and mercy. Maybe this book will give hope to someone who needs it. Maybe this book will only be read by my family and future grandchildren after I'm long gone. According to the famous American artist Andy Warhol, "The idea is not to live forever, but to create something that will." Maybe this book will be my legacy of love written with gratitude in a time of grace.

Made in the USA
Monee, IL
17 November 2022